T0329949

Regulatory Reform of Public Utilities

To Carolyn

Regulatory Reform of Public Utilities

The Japanese Experience

Fumitoshi Mizutani

Graduate School of Business Administration,
Kobe University, Japan

Edward Elgar
Cheltenham, UK · Northampton, MA, USA

Published by
Edward Elgar Publishing Limited
The Lypiatts
15 Lansdown Road
Cheltenham
Glos GL50 2JA
UK

Edward Elgar Publishing, Inc.
William Pratt House
9 Dewey Court
Northampton
Massachusetts 01060
USA

A catalogue record for this book
is available from the British Library

Library of Congress Control Number: 2012943180

ISBN 978 1 84720 330 4

Printed and bound by MPG Books Group, UK

Contents

List of Figures   vii
List of Tables   ix
Introduction   xi

PART I   THEORETICAL BACKGROUND OF PUBLIC
              UTILITIES IN JAPAN

  1   Regulation   3
  2   Public and Private Provision   25

PART II   THE ENERGY AND WATER SUPPLY INDUSTRIES

  3   Electric Power   49
  4   Gas Utility   65
  5   Water Supply   75

PART III   TRANSPORT INDUSTRIES

  6   Railway   89
  7   Local Bus   105

PART IV   COMMUNICATIONS INDUSTRIES

  8   Postal Service   121
  9   Telecommunications   137
 10   Broadcasting   151

PART V   SELECTED TOPICS ON REGULATORY REFORMS
              IN JAPAN

 11   Yardstick Regulation   167
 12   Universal Service Obligation   187
 13   Privatization and Structural Reforms   203
 14   Private Sector Involvement   221

Appendix
    1 Mathematical Explanation for the Regulation of
       Natural Monopolies   237
    2 List of Private Ground Broadcasting TV Companies   239
    3 English-Japanese Major Terms   241

References   247
Subject Index   269

Figures

1.1	Conceptual Structure of Major Regulations in Public Utility Industries in Japan	7
1.2	Regulations for Natural Monopolies	9
1.3	A Solution for Deficits	11
1.4	Characteristics of Public Goods and Examples	12
2.1	Conceptual Figure on the Relationship Between Efficiency and Ownership-Competition Factors	39
3.1	Market Structure of Electric Power Supply System in Japan	51
3.2	Conceptual Figure of the Two-Part Tariff with Gradual Increase by Block	56
3.3	Liberalization Changes in the Electric Power Market	58
3.4	Current Market Structure of the Electric Power Supply System	61
4.1	The Two-Part Tariff Rate System in the Gas Utility Industry: Conceptual Figure of the Rate with 4 Categories	70
5.1	Major Waterworks Organizations	77
5.2	The Two-Part Tariff Rate System in the Water Supply Industry	82
6.1	The Exit Procedure System in the Regional Council	95
6.2	Major Fare Systems in the Rail Industry	97
7.1	The Exit Procedure System in the Regional Council	110
7.2	Procedure for Revision of Local Bus Fare Ceiling Price	112
8.1	Relationships among Japan Post Group Companies	123
8.2	The Postal Service System in Japan	127
9.1	Major Companies of the NTT Group	140
9.2	Regulation for Inter-Connection	144
10.1	Major Kinds of Broadcasting Systems	162
12.1	Change in Providers of Universal Service	195
12.2	System for Universal Service Application	198
12.3	System of Support for Universal Service Costs	199
13.1	Structural Changes with the Privatization of the Japan National Railway	207

13.2   Organizational Change by Privatization: Four
       Highway-related Public Corporations   212
13.3   Process for the Full Privatization of Postal Businesses   217
14.1   Types of Financing for PFI Projects   225

Tables

2.1	Characteristics of the Public Corporation	29
2.2	Major Kinds of Public Corporations in Japan	31
2.3	Empirical Results of Efficiency Comparison	36
2.4	Several Forms of Service Provision	42
2.5	Examples of Industries Featuring Competitive and Non-competitive Components	44
3.1	Profile of General Electricity Companies	52
3.2	Price Regulation in the Electric Power Industry	54
4.1	Classification of Gas Utility Organizations	67
4.2	Rate Regulation in the Gas Utility Industry in Japan	69
5.1	Trends in Water Supply in Japan	76
5.2	Trends in the Number of Waterworks Organizations	78
5.3	Size Distribution of General Water Supply Organizations in 2005	80
6.1	The Transport Situation in 2005	90
6.2	Entry and Exit Regulation in the Rail Industry	93
6.3	Fare Regulation in the Rail Industry	96
7.1	The Current Situation of Local Bus Service	106
7.2	Kinds of Local Bus Operators	107
7.3	The Current Management Situation of Local Bus Service	108
7.4	Entry and Exit Regulations in the Local Bus Service Industry	109
7.5	Fare Regulation in the Local Bus Service Industry	111
7.6	National Subsidies to Support Essential Service Routes	114
7.7	Revision of the Road Transportation Law in 2002	116
8.1	Profile of Japan Post Group Companies	122
8.2	Trends in Mail Volume	124
8.3	Kinds of Post Offices and Number of Post Offices	125
8.4	Price Regulation of Postal Services	129
8.5	Trends in Light Parcel Mail Services	131
8.6	Number of Personal Correspondence Mail Service Companies	133

9.1   Market Size and Number of Telecommunications
       Companies   138
9.2   Number of Customers in the Telephone Industry   139
9.3   Price Regulation in the Telecommunications Industry   142
9.4   Classification of Telecommunications Companies and
       Major Regulations   145
9.5   Summary of the Dominant Carrier Regulations   148
10.1   Market Size as Total Sales   152
10.2   Number of Broadcasting Companies   153
10.3   Network of Private Broadcasting Companies   154
10.4   Number of Cable TV Internet Companies and Number
       of Users   156
10.5   Broadcasting Industry Regulations   158
11.1   Corrections in Costs in Electric Power Service   173
11.2   Evaluation Method for Yardstick Regulation in the
       Electric Power Industry   174
11.3   Categories for Evaluation and Goals of Management
       Effort in Yardstick Regulation: the Case of the Electric
       Power Industry   175
11.4   Evaluation Method for Yardstick Regulation in the Gas
       Utility Industry   177
11.5   Categories for Evaluation and Management Goals in
       Yardstick Regulation: the Case of the Gas Utility
       Industry   178
12.1   International Comparison of the Universal Service
       Obligation System in the Postal Service Industry   191
12.2   The Situation in Areas with Higher Costs   196
12.3   Compensation Money for Universal Service Obligation
       Costs   200
13.1   The Current Situation of Major Providers and the
       Privatization Scheme in Japan   204
14.1   The Current Situation of PFI Projects   226
14.2   The Degree of Adoption of the Designated Manager
       System   230
14.3   Organization Type with regard to Designated Manager   231
14.4   Kinds of Facilities Adopting the Designated Manager
       System   231
14.5   The Designated Manager Selection Method   232
14.6   Terms of Appointment of Designated Managers   232

Introduction

AIM AND SCOPE

This book aims to describe regulatory reforms in Japanese public utility industries. Since the early 1990s, when I began research on privatization and regulatory issues as related to Japan, it has become clear how little information about Japanese regulatory reform has been written in English. Because of the lack of information available in English, it has been difficult both to discuss Japanese public utility industries in international forums, and to explain Japanese regulatory reform to foreign students in Japan. This book results from my desire to facilitate understanding in the international community about regulation and reform in Japanese public utility industries, and to create an effective tool for the instruction of such matters to my students at Kobe University.

It is my firm belief that information about regulatory reform in Japanese public utility industries should be made more widely known outside Japan. Unlike researchers in the natural sciences, researchers in the social sciences cannot be expected to conduct experiments, and this fact makes it vitally important to observe what consequences result from regulatory reforms, wherever they are undertaken. It is useful to look at regulatory reform in Japan, as the Japanese approach differs markedly from that in other areas, particularly European countries and the U.S. The Japanese approach, characterized by its slow steadiness, has been quite moderate compared to that of Europe, especially the UK.

There are many variations in the degree of success among public utility industries, and there have also been failures in regulatory reform. A successful example of privatization is the former Japan National Railway. Regulatory progress remains slow, however, in the water supply industry, with many smaller water supply organizations suffering from faulty management. Furthermore, even though regulatory reforms have been introduced in the bus industry in Japan, little or no improvement has been seen, even in large cities. Thus, there are many cases for which Japan needs to look to other countries for lessons in making regulatory policy.

My first goal is to explain the main regulatory structure and regulatory reforms in eight Japanese public utility industries: electric power, gas utility, water supply, railway, local bus, postal service, telecommunications, and broadcasting, all for the time period between 1990 and 2010.   Regulatory reforms as referred to in this book include organizational changes such as privatization and restructuring.   For cross-industry cases, selected topics on Japanese public utility regulatory issues are included, such as yardstick regulation, privatization, and structural reforms.   An explanation of regulatory reform in each industry is included as well.   Not included are such social regulation issues as safety and environment, which are important but which will be reserved for treatment in a future work.

STRUCTURE OF THE BOOK

The book consists of five parts and fourteen chapters. Part I, *Theoretical Background of the Public Utilities Industry*, establishes the theoretical framework for subsequent explanations of regulatory reforms and practices in public utility industries in Japan. Chapter 1, 'Regulation,' explains general economic regulation and the rationale for public involvement.   This chapter deals with the definition of regulation, options for public involvement, kinds of regulation, major regulations, the rationale for regulation in public utility industries—traditional or basic—regulations in public utility industries in Japan, the recent trend toward incentive regulation, regulatory policy in general, and regulatory failures.   Chapter 2, 'Public and Private Provision,' focuses on the form of provision in public utility industries.   This chapter contains a rationale for public provision, a definition and classification of public corporations, an overview of private provision and efficiency, empirical evidence affecting efficiency, and the definition, kinds, and purpose of privatization from a Japanese perspective, with attention to the international outlook as well.   Structural reforms are also explained in this chapter.

Part II of the book, *Energy and Water Supply Industries*, describes the practices of regulation and regulatory reforms in the electric power, gas utility, and water supply industries.   Chapter 3, 'Electric Power,' describes the market structure, the rate system and major price regulations, and the process of liberalization, which occurred four times (1995, 2000, 2004, and 2005), in the electric power industry.   Chapter 4, 'Gas Utility,' is explained similarly.   In this chapter, the market structure, the rate system and major price regulations and major regulatory reforms, occurring in 1995, 1999, 2004, and 2007, are described. Chapter 5, 'Water Supply,' follows a similar pattern.   Although the water supply industry has not been subject to regulatory reforms, there is an explanation in this chapter of the characteristics of the industry's structure and regulations, followed by a discussion of how regulatory reform relates to this industry.

Part III, *Transport Industries*, describes regulation and regulatory reform in the rail and local bus industries. Of all public utility industries in Japan, the railway industry has been most extensively reformed. In Chapter 6, 'Railway,' the organizational structure of the rail industry, regulations regarding entry and exit, fare, rail track fees, and regulatory reforms are explained. In this chapter, I discuss the competitive situation in the railway industry, noting that competition policies taken in Japan differ from those favored in Europe. Chapter 7, 'Local Bus,' describes the practice of regulation and regulatory reforms in local bus industries. This chapter includes an explanation of the organizational structure of the local bus industry in Japan, entry and exit regulations, fare regulations, regulators, subsidy schemes, and the main regulatory revisions. Included also is a discussion of the effects of regulatory reform on the local bus service industry in Japan.

Part IV, *Communications Industries*, describes practices related to regulation and regulatory reforms in the postal services, telecommunications and broadcasting industries. Chapter 8, 'Postal Services,' explains characteristics of the postal service industry, its industrial structure, the current mail situation, and kinds of post offices, postal service regulations such as entry regulation, price regulation and universal service obligation, and liberalization in postal services. Chapter 9, 'Telecommunications,' describes regulatory reforms mainly focusing on the telephone industry. This chapter contains information about the market structure of the telecommunications industry, market size, the number of telephone customers, the major telecommunications companies, regulations such as entry, price, and inter-connection regulations, and liberalization in the telecommunications industry in 1985, 1999, 2001, and 2003. Chapter 10, 'Broadcasting,' describes major regulation issues, focusing on the industrial structure of the broadcasting industry, market size, the kinds and numbers of broadcasting companies, broadcasting industry regulations, and regulatory reforms in the broadcasting industry.

Part V, *Selected Topics in Regulatory Reform in Japan*, describes several important points as they relate to several Japanese industries. Chapter 11, 'Yardstick Regulation,' discusses the theory and practice of yardstick regulation as applied to public utility industries in Japan. This chapter includes an overview of yardstick regulation, a summary of how it is applied in practice to four Japanese public utility industries—electric power, gas utility, rail, and bus service—and an assessment of the effectiveness of yardstick regulation based on previous empirical research. Chapter 12, 'Universal Service Obligation,' treats a matter under serious political debate in Japan. This chapter lists the characteristics of the universal service system in Japanese public utility industries. The main items in this chapter are a definition of universal service in Japan, an explanation of universal service as related to postal services and the telecommunications industry, the structure of the universal service obligation system, the calculation method of universal service costs, and empirical results related to universal services in Japan. Chapter 13, 'Privatization and Structural Reforms,' uses the Japan National Railways, the highway public corporations and the Japan Post Public Corporation as examples of reform. These organizations were chosen because their experiences with reform embody characteristics of the Japanese approach (Highway and Japan Post), they are classic examples of the basic Japanese philosophy to restructuring (Japan National Railway), and there has been ample time to glean information and results for performance evaluation (Japan National Railway). Last, Chapter 14, 'Private Sector Involvement,' refers to including private sector participation in the provision of public services in Japan. This chapter explains and discusses the so-called 'private sector style management' in Japan, Japanese style PFI, the designated manager system, and the local independent administrative institution scheme.

ACKNOWLEDGEMENTS

This book is based on the research of others, government information, my own lecture notes, my own research, and my research work with co-authors. Without the work, help, and support of all these people, this book would never have been completed.

Although it is not possible to list all their names, I would like to thank many members of the Japanese Society of Public Utility Economics, the Japanese Association of Transport Economics, the Japanese Economic Association and Kobe University.

I would like to thank the co-authors of my previous research work: Hideo Kozumi (Kobe University), Noriaki Matsushima (Osaka University), Keizo Mizuno (Kwansei Gakuin University), Kiyoshi Nakamura (Waseda University), Noriyoshi Nakayama (Nagoya City University), Hiroshi Sasaki (Kobe University), Kenichi Shoji (Kobe University), Tomoyasu Tanaka (Kinki University), Takuya Urakami (Kinki University), and Shuji Uranishi (Fukuyama Heisei University).

PART I

Theoretical Background of Public Utilities
in Japan

1 Regulation

1 INTRODUCTION

Public utility industries in Japan, such as electric power, gas, railways and telecommunications, are operated mainly by the private sector, the only exceptions being water supply and general roads. However, these public utility industries are subject to regulations governing such issues as entry, exit, and price. Although since the late 1980s, the process has been underway to deregulate and privatize what were once public corporations, these organizations are all still governmentally regulated as public utility industries.

The main purpose of this chapter is to explain the basic theoretical regulatory concepts related to public utility industries in Japan. The theoretical aspects of regulation are commonly known throughout the world, but I focus here as much as possible on important regulations and philosophical background. Comprehensive treatment of economic rationale and theories on regulation can be found in excellent works, such as Breyer (1982), Kahn (1988), Spulber (1989), Waterson (1988), Baldwin and Cave (1999), Viscusi et al. (2005) for general regulation, Uekusa (2000) for regulation in Japan, and Gómez-Ibáñez (2003) for more recent infrastructure regulation. As background to facilitate understanding of regulatory reforms in individual industries, this chapter and the next will focus on regulations in Japan.

The structure of this chapter is as follows. After the introduction, in the second section, regulation and the rationale for public involvement are explained. In this section, the definition of regulation, options for public involvement, kinds of regulation, and major regulations are explained, with the main idea being that regulation is one way to involve government and to reveal government policies. In the third section, the rationale for regulation in public utility industries is summarized. Government involvement is deemed necessary when there is a need to address issues such as market failures, natural monopolies, distribution of public goods, externalities, and imperfect information. There are also reasons for government involvement that involve value judgments. The fourth section concerns traditional, or basic, regulations in public utility industries in Japan, with the main topic in this section being the full cost principle and the rate of return regulation.   In the fifth section, the recent trend toward incentive regulation is explained, with reference to the franchise bidding scheme, yardstick regulation, price-cap regulation and profit sharing.   Finally, regulatory policy in general is explained, with an overview of recent trends in reform in Japan, as well as regulatory failures.

2   REGULATIONS AND RATIONALE FOR PUBLIC INVOLVEMENT

2.1   What is Regulation?

There are variations on the definition of regulation.[1]   According to Uekusa (1991, 2000), regulation is defined as legally justified actions by governments to limit or control the behaviors of individuals and firms. Some regulations affecting private firms are not discussed here.   For example, the association of public utility industries in Japan has implemented self-regulatory measures, but because many such regulations are not leagally enforced, they are not included here.

2.2   The Purpose of Regulation

In modern industrial countries, economies are generally dependent on the market mechanism, or the so-called 'invisible hand' by which resources are allocated efficiently.   In fact, according to welfare economics theory, in a purely competitive market, efficient resource allocation, or the Pareto optimal, is achieved.   Even so, there are problems that cannot be solved by the market mechanism.

One of government's roles is to help solve problems due to shortcomings in the market mechanism.   Such problems can in general be classified into two groups, the first of which concerns market failure issues, for example market failure due to natural monopoly, public goods, externalities, imperfect information and so on.[2]   In these cases, where the market cannot bring about efficient resource allocation, government involvement is justified.

The second group of problems is related to value judgment regarding, for example, fairness of redistribution, economic stability, provision of merit goods, civil minimum, regional balance, and so on.   To deal with these issues, it is assumed justifiable that government be involved in the market.[3]

2.3 Options for Public Involvement

In general, there are three kinds of government involvement: taxation, subsidization, and regulation. In the case of environmental protection, for example, taxation is used first to affect firms' and individuals' behavior. In order to reduce air pollution stemming from the use of private cars, government imposes environmental taxes on auto users and a higher tax rate on purchases of cars with higher lead emissions. Another way to control a firm's behavior is through subsidization. To encourage the use of less pollution-causing cars, there have been cases of research subsidies being granted to corporations to foster the development of electric car engines, or operating subsidies to transportation entities to support and promote the use of public transportation. Regulations aim to control firms' and individuals' behavior by law. To protect the environment, for example, the government enacts legislation limiting the permissible amount of lead emissions.

Because they sometimes include prohibitions and penalties for firms breaking the law, regulations are likely to be considered a more direct method of controlling firms' behavior than taxation or subsidization. However, if a government wants strong, direct control of a firm, the most effective method is for the government itself to hold ownership of the firm. In public utility industries, while regulations serve to control private firms, public ownership facilitates more direct involvement in fulfilling public purpose.

Current liberalization trends in public utility industries in Japan have followed two patterns: deregulation in public utility industries and privatization of public corporations in public utility industries. Deregulation has occurred in most public utility industries in Japan, notably telecommunications and the electric power industry. The process of privatization was begun in the railway and telecommunications industries in the 1980s and in the highway and postal services industries in the 2000s.

2.4 Kinds of Regulation

Regulations are often classified into two types: economic regulation and social regulation. Economic regulation has three main goals: to control firms' behavior by limiting price, service quantity and the number of firms in the market; to amend inefficiency of resource allocation in the market; and to protect consumers from unfair treatment. On the other hand, social regulation has the following aims: to control firms' behavior in order to protect employees from harmful working conditions; to maintain a good environment; and to protect against natural disasters.   In summary, when we examine regulations as they relate to market failures, according to Uekusa (1991), the purpose of economic regulation is mainly to resolve problems stemming from natural monopoly and imperfect information, while the purpose of social regulation is mainly to resolve issues related to external diseconomies and demerit goods.

As for economic regulation in Japanese public utility industries, price regulation and entry and exit regulation are applied to all.   Prices for individual users remain regulated, although prices for large-scale users have been recently deregulated, for example, in the electric power industry.   Entry regulation, which can control the quantity of utility services, is applied in several forms, such as through various systems involving licensing, granting permission, registering, reporting, and so on, respectively.   As for social regulation, the quality of utility services is stipulated in each utility service law.   There are also classifications such as quantitative and qualitative regulations.[4]

2.5   Major Regulations

In this section, major regulations in public utility industries are summarized.   Figure 1.1 shows the conceptual structure of major regulations in public utility industries.   Although in pratice there are many kinds of regulations, the following are the most important: (i) entry regulation, (ii) exit regulation, (iii) price regulation, (iv) quantity regulation, (v) service quality regulation, (vi) safety regulation, (vii) environmental regulation, (viii) investment regulation, and (ix) regulation for non-utility service.   In addition to these, regulations applying to workplace environment are also important, such as the Ordinance on Industrial Safety and Hygiene.   However, as this regulation applies to all industries across the board, we do not treat it here.

In public utility industries, traditionally entry into and exit from the market have been strictly regulated because public utility industries have characteristics of natural monopolies.   The entry regulation limits the number of firms in the market in order to maintain socially desirable results or to protect against destructive competition.   Exit regulation compels existing firms continuously to provide services to users, who would be adversely affected if service providers were freely allowed to quit the market.   Although entry and exit regulations were formerly applied universally to Japanese public utility industries, since the end of the 1990s, deregulation has brought about changes.

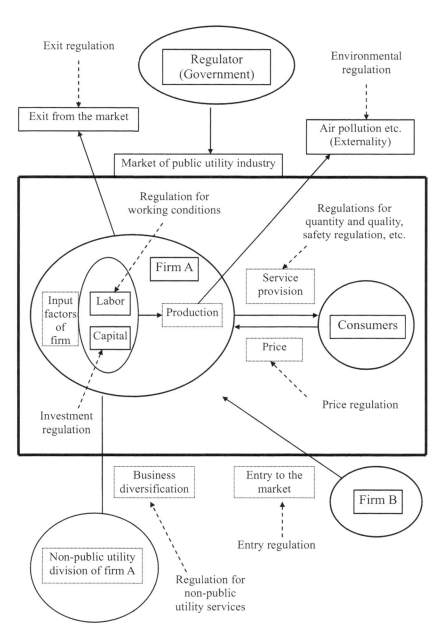

*Figure 1.1   Conceptual Structure of Major Regulations
in Public Utility Industries in Japan*

Besides entry and exit regulation, price regulation is also important in attaining efficient resource allocation, maintaining a reasonable price level, and protecting users from unfair treatment. Many public utilities in Japan are managed by the private sector and are subject to regulations controlling price, even though prices have been subject to liberalization since the end of the 90s, especially for large-scale users of electricity and gas.

As for quantity and quality regulation, it is required that services be provided on a stable basis in public utility services and that the quality of utility services be maintained. These regulations protect users from unfair treatment by a monopoly industry. In a competitive industry, these regulations protect users from a decrease in quality due to severe competition. Safety regulations are included in these categories. In addition, environmental regulations are important in controlling a society's quality of life.

In Japan, although large private rail companies have long operated non-public utility businesses such as real estate development and department stores, the former Japan National Railways was prohibited from engaging in non-rail business because it was deemed that such activities would detract from or damage private companies' business interests. In the electric power and gas industries as well, non-public utility business was strictly limited. However, as entry and price have been deregulated, restrictions on non-utility business within the rail, electric, gas, and other industries have become less severe.

3   RATIONALE FOR REGULATION IN PUBLIC UTILITY INDUSTRIES

3.1   Natural Monopoly

Traditionally, the rationale for economic regulation in public utility industries is that it is necessary for protection against natural monopoly, a situation where there exists only one firm under natural competition because of characteristics such as sub-additivity in costs or scarcity of resources (Uekusa, 1991). Such cost structure characteristics can be found in network industries such as railway, electric power, gas, water supply, and so on.

It is in general impossible to break down network facilities in such network industries. Facility costs are generally so huge that average costs decline as service output increases, so that these industries are characterized by increasing return to scale. If the government allowed free market competition in such industries, ultimately only one firm would survive because the larger firm's average costs would be lower than those of smaller firms.　However, this outcome poses a problem for society in the form of higher prices and the less than optimal services typical of monopoly firms.　Network industries are regulated to protect users from such a situation.

　　Figure 1.2 shows the concept of regulating natural monopolies.

(price), (¥)

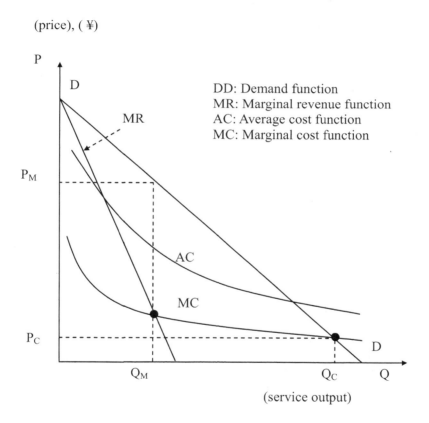

Figure 1.2　Regulations for Natural Monopolies

　　We assume that a monopoly firm in a public utility industry is a private firm seeking profits.　In a case where there is no regulation for the monopoly and the monopoly firm can provide public utility services freely, then the monopoly firm would choose a service output level of Q_M, and would charge users the price P_M for the service. In this case, marginal cost (MC) equals marginal revenue (MR), and the firm chooses this service output level because it garners the largest profits for the monopoly firm.

However, this state of affairs does not benefit society. The socially optimal case would be one where a demand for service (DD) equaled marginal cost (MC), as this case would attain the most social surplus, defined as consumer surplus minus the cost of the public utility. In this case, the service output level is Q_C and the price of public utility service is P_C.

A comparison of these two cases shows that the unregulated monopoly has a higher price level than the social optimum, as well as a smaller output. Regulation by the government can be justified, therefore, to protect utility users from the problems associated with monopoly. By applying entry regulations, the government guarantees that the monopolistic firm will provide utility services, while regulating prices relative to marginal cost. Mathematical explanations are presented in Appendix 1.

However, the socially optimal case has a problem: the firm yields deficits. In network industries such as electric power, gas, railway, water supply and so on, the average costs decrease as service output increases, as mentioned above. In this situation, marginal costs are always lower than average costs. Therefore, in the socially optimal case, the price level is fixed at the marginal cost (i.e. marginal cost pricing) but the cost for one unit of service, which is the average cost, exceeds the price.

There are three possible solutions to this problem, as shown in Figure 1.3.

First, the government can subsidize the monopoly firm. The shaded area in Figure 1.3 represents what would be the total amounts of subsidies under marginal cost pricing. A second possible solution would be direct provision by the government (i.e. governmental provision). By becoming part of the public sector, the monopoly firm would be free of bankruptcy concerns, even though in this case, it would be necessary to recoup with tax monies the difference between the lower price level and the higher cost level. As Figure 1.3 shows, a third possibility, generally deemed the second best solution, is to switch from marginal cost pricing to average cost pricing, whereby the price of the utility service becomes the average cost. As shown in the figure, this case has a price of P_{AC} and a service output of Q_{AC}. Price is higher than in the socially optimal but lower than in the monopoly. Likewise, service output is lower than

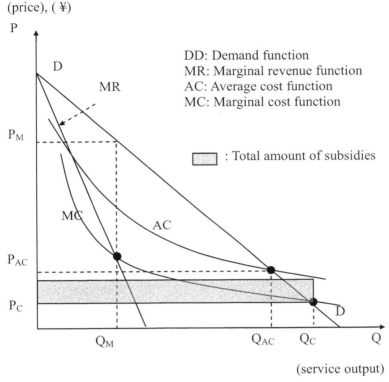

(price), (¥)

DD: Demand function
MR: Marginal revenue function
AC: Average cost function
MC: Marginal cost function

: Total amount of subsidies

(service output)

Figure 1.3   A Solution for Deficits

in the social optimal but larger than in the monopoly.   In summary, these three cases are $P_C < P_{AC} < P_M$, $Q_C > Q_{AC} > Q_M$.

In network industries in Japan, average cost pricing has been used because the full cost principle has been applied in public utility industries. As for the philosophy behind this, we will explain more fully in the section on price regulation.

3.2   Public Goods

The rationale for regulation in public utility industries is also based on the concept of public goods, which in general have two characteristics: non-rivalry in consumption and non-excludability.   Non-rivalry in consumption means that even if one person consumes public goods, the opportunity of other users to consume the same amount of public goods is undiminished.   Non-excludability refers to the impossibility, because of the prohibitive expense it would involve, of excluding non-paying individuals from consuming public goods. Public goods that simultaneously have both characteristics (i.e. non-rivalry in consumption and non-excludability) are called pure public goods. Among public utility industries, ground broadcasting and regular roads would be close to pure public goods. Figure 1.4 shows the characteristics of public goods and gives typical examples.

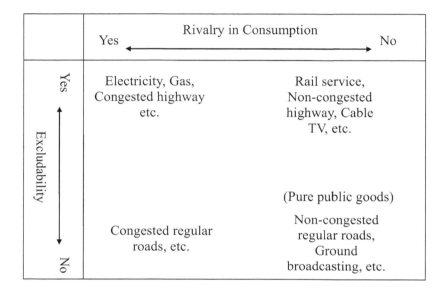

Figure 1.4   Characteristics of Public Goods and Examples

Although it is not strictly necessary for certain goods with the characteristics of public goods to be provided by the public sector, public provision by the government is in general justifiable because of the 'free rider' problem. If public services are provided by the private sector and the costs of the services are borne by users, some people may enjoy consumption of the services without paying the fee. This would be possible in cases where services have non-excludability characteristics, ultimately resulting in the service being provided at a less than socially optimal level.

Regular roads and ground broadcasting are typical examples of services with non-excludability in public utility industries. Regular roads in Japan are in general provided by the government and are funded mainly by car-related taxes such as automobile weight taxes and gasoline taxes. As for ground broadcasting in Japan, Nihon Hoso Kyokai (NHK), provides broadcasting services. Though NHK is a public organization, it supports itself financially with user fees charged to each household owning a TV. NHK has a free rider problem, however, as there are many non-paying viewers and delinquent accounts.

3.3 Externality

Another justification for regulation is externality,[5] which denotes positive or negative effects on other economic agencies without going through the market. Although externality refers to both positive and negative effects, external diseconomy as a negative effect is especially important, a typical example being environmental destruction such as air pollution, global warming, congestion and so on.

If private car usage were not subject to regulation, transportation by private auto would far exceed the social optimum. Because car users generally consider only the costs they directly incur (e.g. gasoline and ownership costs) and often fail to consider external costs such as air pollution, congestion, noise, etc., car use exceeds socially optimal levels. Regulation is therefore a justifiable option for controlling externality.

3.4 Imperfect Information

Another justification for regulation is related to imperfect information. In general, a prerequisite for efficient resource allocation is perfect information, which in the real world is extremely difficult to acquire. Users do not have access to complete information about the public utility services they consume.

As a hypothetical example, imagine what would happen if taxi services were not subject to regulation. In Japan, there is a license system for taxis, with characteristics of both economic and social regulation. In terms of the economy, the license system limits entry into the taxi market. As for social regulation, the license system ostensibly guarantees that a taxi service provider is appropriate in terms of service quality issues such as safety, taxi fare, and so on. If there were no regulation on taxi service, taxi users themselves would have to make judgments about service quality. It might be possible in such a situation to distinguish good service quality from bad because of the signals sent by high and low quality providers, but a lack of regulation would have costs: there would be search costs, and good service might be expensive.

Therefore, regulation (e.g. through a license system) is a justifiable option in light of imperfect information.

However, it is worth noting that the entry regulation might be costly because it is possible to create rent for incumbents.

3.5 Others

The reasons listed above for regulation are related mainly to market failure, or to problems with efficiency due to faulty resource allocation. But regulation is also justified for reasons related to value judgment, especially with basic public utility services affecting many economic activities. Because the services themselves are essential to daily life, regulation is generally justified as necessary to the achievement of the following goals: income redistribution, economic stability, provision of merit goods, civil minimum, promotion of regional balance, and so on.[6]

In public utility industries, price regulations are used to redistribute income, for example, by charging students and elderly passengers lower fares than higher income groups.

Related to income redistribution, the civil minimum is often made reference to in the public utility industry. Chujo (1992) criticizes the rationale for civil minimum policy in public utility industries as a tool for indirect income redistribution. He identifies three main problems with this method. First, compared with a direct income subsidy to users, any utility increase through the indirect income transfer resulting from this method is small. Second, with the civil minimum policy, users who should not receive the subsidy would nevertheless likely receive it. Last, people living in areas with no industries cannot receive the minimum services.

In order to stabilize the economy, the government is often involved in public utility industry policy making. For example, during the privatization of the Japan National Railways in the late 1990s, despite the urgent need to reduce JNR's debt, the government temporarily imposed a moratorium on selling JNR-owned land, as refraining from such sales might spur an increase in land price.

To reduce regional imbalance, the government attempts to be directly involved in public utility industries in Japan. A typical example is the national highway network, which until quite recently has been constructed almost exclusively by the national government.

Thus, while regulations and public involvement can be justified as necessary from the point of view of value judgments, in reality there are many individuals with different values. Because it is often difficult to find common ground, unfortunately policy making is often hindered by political conflict.

4   FULL COST PRINCIPLE AND RATE OF RETURN REGULATION

4.1   Regulation

This section concerns the rate of return regulation,[7] which has been applied in public utility industries to determine price level.   Traditionally, this regulation has been applied in the electric power, gas and railway industries in Japan.   As these industries are provided by privately owned companies, it was necessary to decide in advance what would be their fair return as profits.   This section explains both the full cost principle and the rate of return regulation.

First, the profits of a public utility company are added to the costs to the company for providing utility services, the sum of which becomes the full cost (*Soukatsu Genka*).   In public utility industries in Japan, the full cost principle is in general the basic principle, whereby utility charges cover all costs, including company profits.   These profits are referred to as the fair return, obtained by multiplying the fair rate of return by the rate base, as equation-(1.1) shows.   The fair rate of return is considered a reasonable profit rate for the utility company.

$$TC = OC + FR$$
$$= OC + FRoR \cdot K, \qquad (1.1)$$

Where TC: total cost for public utility services
   OC: costs for providing utility services
   FR: fair return for a utility company
   $FRoR$: fair rate of return
   K: rate base (i.e. capital stock of public utility)

In this equation, the rate base is capital stock for providing public utility services.   Furthermore, according to Ezoe (1994), in Japan the fair rate of return is in general obtained as in the following equation:

$$FRoR = r_S \cdot R_S + r_O \cdot R_O, \qquad (1.2)$$

Where r_S: cost of equity
   R_S : equity ratio
   r_O: cost of borrowed capital

R_O: borrowed capital ratio

As this equation shows, the level of the fair rate of return is calculated as the cost of capital.   According to Ezoe (1994), the average return on equity among other heavy process industries is used for the cost level of equity, as a maximum value.   As for the cost of borrowed capital, actual raised money for capital is used.

The rate of return regulation is in general applied with the following procedure.   First, when it is necessary for a public utility company to revise the price of its service, it applies to the ministry (the regulator), which requires that the company provide information about costs the company incurs for providing services, depreciation, stock of facilities, and so on.   Second, the ministry in its role as regulator evaluates whether or not the price revision is appropriate.   Third, if the costs for providing utility services are reasonable, the regulator then determines the fair rate of return based on information provided by the company. Fourth, the fair return of the company is obtained by multiplying the rate base by the fair rate of return.   Finally, fair return is added to operating costs to obtain the public utility's total costs.[8] Price is set to equal total costs.

4.2   Problems

Because it is easy to calculate, the rate of return regulation was long applied in typical public utility industries in Japan such as the railway, electric power, and gas industries.   Due to several problems, however, around the mid 1990s it was replaced by other regulations in these industries.

First, the rate of return regulation with the full cost principle does not create incentives for a public utility company to reduce costs.   As noted above, fair return as the firm's profits is decided irrespective of the magnitude of costs.   If a regulator evaluates a company's cost structure and stock of facilities, the company might have an incentive to improve efficiency, but in fact, the regulator lacks the information necessary for determining accurately whether or not the company's costs are appropriate.   The company, which is in possession of information about its own costs, therefore does not have incentive to perform at its best.

Second, the fair rate of return has the inherent problem of being hard to define.   What rate of return is 'fair'?   There is, for example, more than one method of estimating the cost of equity.   As there are several possibilities for deciding the rate of return, it seems inevitable that the application of this regulation will often be subject to regulators' discretion.

Third, the rate of return regulation tends to have excess facilities of utility services, which is known as the Averch-Johnson effect, an issue addressed by Averch and Johnson (1962). As shown in the equation for total cost of utility services, the rate base (i.e. capital stock) should be larger if the company wants to obtain larger profits. Even if the company has larger facilities, it need not reduce costs because the regulation is the cost plus type regulation. Therefore, the company tends to have excess facilities.

Fourth, use of the rate of return regulation is costly. To solve the problem of lack of incentive to reduce costs, the regulator must engage in many activities, such as strict monitoring, collecting information about costs and facilities, and so on. The necessity of performing such actions increases administrative costs.

Fifth, with this type of regulation, there is the possibility that a utility company will incur losses due to a time lag when utility service price changes. Utility prices do not change every year. Even if material costs and labor costs rise with changes in environmental conditions, the price of service and the fair rate of return do not immediately change. On average, price changes occur once every several years, during which interval the utility company must balance its budget by improving managerial efficiency. The price change time lag might even in some cases yield operational deficits. However, one study has shown evidence that the existence of this time lag serves as an incentive for cost reduction.[9]

5   INCENTIVE REGULATIONS

The rate of return regulation and other traditional regulations have several problems, the most serious of which is that they do not create incentive to reduce costs. A movement began around the 1990s toward the installation of incentive regulations, which, according to Viscusi et al. (2005), are designed to create incentives for the regulated firm to lower cost, innovate, adopt efficient pricing practices, improve quality, and the like. By introducing competition and giving rewards and penalties, incentive regulations spur a utility provider to improve performance. In this section, typical incentive regulations are overviewed.

5.1   The Franchise Bidding Scheme

Through the use of competitive tendering, the franchise bidding scheme assigns companies the right to provide monopoly utility service in a given area, for a term limited by contract. As there are neither incentives for an existing utility company to improve managerial efficiency nor threats from potential entrants under traditional regulations for natural monopolies, the franchise bidding scheme would introduce competition to the utility market.

In 1995 in the UK, for example, a franchising system was introduced when British Railways was privatized and divided into 25 franchising areas, for which railway operators were selected by competitive tendering.

In contrast to the UK experience, the franchising system has not been used in Japan. For example, when the Japan National Railways (JNR) was privatized and subdivided into six regional passenger companies (JR passenger companies) in 1987, a franchise bidding scheme was not adopted. Instead of allowing free market competition among the new JR companies, the government introduced regulatory schemes for the provision of utility services, a typical example being yardstick competition (or yardstick regulation), which will be explained in the next section.

The franchise bidding scheme has several problems. First, in order for there to be competitive tendering, it is expected that there be two or more companies which have invested in labor and capital in preparation for providing utility services. Nevertheless, there can be only one winning company per franchise area, so that from society's point of view, competitive tendering has the disadvantage of causing duplicate investment sunk costs. Some companies that would otherwise be interested in making a bid might be deterred by the potentially massive sunk costs and refrain from participating. As a result, the expected competition might not occur. If duplicate investments by both the existing and potential entrant companies are large, resources would be wasted.

Second, the franchise bidding scheme might not create effective competition, for two reasons. Because the number of companies with the ability to provide public utility services is quite limited, there may be too few participants in competitive tendering, or there might be collusion among the few companies that do participate. Also, compared with potential entrants, the incumbent company enjoys the advantage of having a great deal of information about the given franchise area, a fact which makes fair competition between the incumbent and new entrants very difficult.

Third, there remain several problems after the franchisee is selected. These include monitoring the franchise company and devising rules for changes in the contract regarding such matters as the price for utility services, investment, and resolution in the event of bankruptcy. Thus, even after the selection of the franchise company, there will be areas of uncertainty and significant coordination transaction costs.

5.2 Yardstick Regulation

Public utility industries in Japan are often subject to yardstick regulation, which I will briefly describe in this section and explain in more detail in a later chapter.

Yardstick regulation is an incentive regulation stipulating the application of common evaluation measures for plural firms operating in different markets. The regulator evaluates these firms' performance by assessing these common measures. Although firms subject to yardstick regulation are not directly competing with each other in the market, indirect competition among these firms is expected to increase their internal efficiency. Shleifer (1985) provided a theoretical foundation for yardstick regulation, details of which will appear in a later chapter.

The main purpose of yardstick regulation is to promote efficiency improvement by evaluating public utility companies' performance. For example, if the average cost of utility service is chosen as a measure of performance, each public utility company is evaluated by this measure. In the case of Japan, yardstick regulation is used in the assessment of fare revision. For example, if the average costs of utility Company A are higher than those of the average of all public utility companies, then company A will be expected to improve its efficiency, and as a penalty for its low efficiency, its proposed fare revision will not be approved. On the other hand, if the average costs of Company B are lower than that of the average of all public utility companies, Company B will receive the reward of having its fare revision proposal approved. Central to the evaluation of firms in the process of fare revision, yardstick regulation is used in the rail, bus, electric power supply and gas industries in Japan.

However, yardstick regulation poses certain problems. First, there is the possibility of collusion among public utility firms. Collusion refers to forms of coordination among firms, especially in order to raise prices or maintain a high price level for continuous profits. There are two types of collusion: explicit and tacit. Explicit collusion, which occurs when firms form a cartel entailing overt communication among them, is relatively obvious to observers because of material evidence. However, with tacit collusion, in which firms are able to achieve some mutual understanding without overt communication, it is difficult to determine whether or not the collusion is planned or intentional. Second, it is not easy to control outside conditions because in reality public utility firms operate in environments with different demand conditions.   In fact, firms to which yardstick regulation is applied are different in size and operate in different market areas.   Therefore, outside factors must be controlled for when yardstick regulation is applied.   Third, there are certain problems in evaluation, such as the selection of evaluation measures (e.g. quality consideration), the weight of the measures, and the discretion of the regulator.   Last, even if the yardstick scheme promotes managerial efficiency, it is not guaranteed to lead to efficiency in resource allocation.

5.3   Price-cap Regulation

Price-cap regulation aims to set a ceiling price.   Utility providers are free to change prices, as long as prices do not exceed the ceiling price.   The most ordinal price-cap is calculated as follows.

$$P_t = P_{t-1} \cdot (1 + (I - X)) \qquad\qquad (1.3)$$

Where P_t: the ceiling price in year t,
          I: the annual rate of change of wholesale price
          X: productivity growth rate

Price-cap regulation has been adopted in many public utility industries, notably telecommunications and gas in the UK.   The Japanese railway industry has adopted price-cap regulation with ceiling price, although it differs from the original price-cap regulation in that the targeted productivity growth rate is not included.   However, as price below the ceiling can be changed freely, the incentive mechanism is the same.

Price-cap regulation has the advantage of reducing transaction costs between regulators and public utility companies, as companies are free to act on their own within the ceiling price, without incurring regulation costs.   Second, because the price-cap formula is quite simple and clear, there is no need for the regulator to exercise discretion.

On the other hand, a potential problem with the price-cap regulation is that first the utility firm might set the price level inordinately high, without making an effort to improve managerial efficiency.   Second, there is a concern about the magnitude of the level of productivity growth rate, X, which is shown in the equation above.   The regulator determines the rate, but there is room for arbitrariness.

5.4   Profit Sharing

Profit sharing, also known as earnings sharing or sliding scale, finds middle ground by having the public utility firm and utility users share in any excess profits or earnings.   The basic idea of the profit sharing regulation is as follows.   The regulator induces public utility firms to reduce costs and engage in other efficiency-enhancing practices.   In order to do this, the regulator allows the utility firms to retain some of the profits they create, with remaining profits to be returned to consumers in the form of price reductions.

According to Viscusi et al. (2005), the general formula for profit sharing can be expressed as follows.   When *r* is the gross rate of return, which means total profits before netting out consumers' profits, the net rate of return of a public utility firm is as follows.

$$\begin{cases} r & \text{if } r \leq \underline{r} \\ \underline{r} + \theta(r - \underline{r}) & \text{if } \underline{r} < r \leq \bar{r} \\ \underline{r} + \theta(\bar{r} - \underline{r}) & \text{if } \bar{r} \leq r, \end{cases} \qquad (1.4)$$

where $\underline{r} < \bar{r}$ and $0 \leq \theta \leq 1$.

As this equation shows, when the gross rate of return, *r*, lies between $\underline{r}$ and $\bar{r}$, the regulated public utility firm keeps a fraction θ of the excess profit.   However, when the gross rate of return, *r*, exceeds $\bar{r}$, then the rate of return is capped at $\underline{r} + \theta(\bar{r} - \underline{r})$.   At the same time, if the gross rate of return, *r*, is below $\underline{r}$, then the regulator guarantees the rate of return, *r*.

The fraction θ is decided by the regulator.   As the fraction θ increases, the incentive for the public utility firm to reduce costs also increases, because the firm's profits increase.   According to Viscusi et al. (2005), the traditional rate of return regulation is when $\theta = 0$ and $\underline{r}$ is the allowed rate of return, while the case of an unregulated monopoly is $\theta = 1$ and $\bar{r} = \infty$.

6   REGULATION POLICY

6.1   Failure in Regulation

As explained previously, the purpose of regulation is to resolve problems of market failure and issues related to value judgment, such as income redistribution. Though intended to solve problems, however, regulation can cause problems itself, such as creating more costs for society, or creating unacceptable differences between people who benefit from regulation and those who bear too much of regulation's cost. There is also what is called 'failure in regulation,' when a well-meaning regulation works well at first, but over time becomes irrelevant or counterproductive. Such regulation ends up incurring more cost than benefit for society.

Failure in regulation has several causes, the first being flaws in the regulation system, a complex structure consisting of a myriad of related actors—individual consumers, regulated firms, regulators, lawmakers, and so on. Control by regulation is imperfect, involving a lengthy process of service providers seeking and securing the permission and approval of regulators.

Second, information is asymmetric. For example, regulators might choose not to report information deemed to have a negative impact on consumers or firms. The regulators might hide information and data regarding the background of regulations. Furthermore, regulators might make discretionary decisions not based on clear rules.

A third type of failure is increase in costs related to regulations, including in some cases where rent-seeking costs might occur.

Fourth, costs related to political activity might be wasteful to society. For example, before the Japan National Railway was privatized, it was necessary to get Diet approval for fare revisions and investment plans. JNR spent a lot of money on political activities related to seeking this approval. Almost none of this money produced anything or contributed to any efficiency increases in the industry, instead simply draining financial resources and wasting time.

Thus it can be seen that regulation sometimes promotes unproductive activities and creates extra costs.

6.2 Design of Regulations

In this section, I will summarize the conceptual view of regulation design in Japan. Although opinions vary about making regulation policy, the majority of researchers and policy makers seem not to agree that public utility industries should be fully subject to free market competition. That is, the prevalent view seems to be that regulations necessary for society should be retained while unnecessary regulations should be rescinded or reformed. The current view of regulations is that there may be too much government intervention and that regulation 'failures' will multiply. The general view is that regulatory design should take into consideration the expenses regulations will incur, as well as 'failure due to regulation,' such as rent-seeking costs.   In fact, one regulatory economist, Chujo (1992) has likened 'government failures' to market failure in terms of importance.   Such failures can serve as lessons to be taken into account when formulating or redesigning regulations.

Generally speaking, the Japanese government has been criticized in its role as regulator for its lack of neutrality, its apparent favoritism toward industry as opposed to consumers.   The following points are important to regulation in Japan.   First, the purpose of the regulation should be clarified.   Second, accountability should be established by requiring the publication of information and data.   Third, when deregulation is under consideration, a distinction should be made between economic and social regulations.   Fourth, a timetable should be specified for reconsidering the advisability of upholding or abolishing regulations. Fifth, a system for monitoring regulations should be set up.   Last, regulators independent of the government should be appointed.

NOTES

[1] See for example, Joskow and Noll (1981) and Spulber (1989).
[2] Other causes related to market failure are, for example, uncertainty, imperfect competition, and risk.
[3] Other reasons are to provide daily living necessities, to prevent destructive competition, to maintain standard technology, to address regional interests, to return development benefits, and so on.
[4] Qualitative regulation aims to limit economic activities of firms that cannot maintain standard criteria.   On the other hand, quantitative regulation aims to control the prices and quantities of services at what is considered the desirable level.
[5] We must classify externality.   For example, Scitovsky (1954) classifies external effects into technical and pecuniary, the latter of which is simply a transfer to a third party through the market.   An increase in land price because of highway construction would be an example of pecuniary external effect.   A technical external effect, however, is not directly the result of a market transaction.   Air pollution due to the road traffic resulting from highway construction is an example of technical externality.   The rationale for governmental intervention through regulation is to control technical external effects.
[6] Although I do not explain in detail here, there are other reasons such as to provide the essentials for daily living, to protect against destructive competition, to maintain standard rules among providers, to avoid duplicate investments, to satisfy local needs, to return profits

of development projects, and so on.

[7] In Japan, the rate of return regulation is used literally as 'the fair rate of return regulation.' I use the phrase 'rate of return regulation' here because the expression is more common.

[8] In the rate of return regulation, the return as the company's profit is always added on as costs. Therefore, this regulation is often called as 'the cost plus type regulation' in Japan.

[9] For example, Bailey and Coleman (1971) analyze the effects of time lag in regulation based on the Averch-Johnson type model. In their results, the longer the lagged regulation, the smaller the degree of excess capacity. According to their results, if the lagged regulation is long enough, the firm provides services efficiently but the redistribution of profits to consumers is delayed. On the contrary, if lagged regulation is short, redistribution to consumers can be achieved but the firm's incentive to reduce costs is decreased.

2 Public and Private Provision

1 INTRODUCTION

This chapter focuses on topics related to public corporations and private organizations in public utility industries. The public corporation is defined, and the role of public corporations and privatization policy are explained from a theoretical point of view. Although there are many kinds of public services, I will focus mainly on public utility services.

The first section provides a rationale for public provision, followed by a discussion of what factors, relative to both supply and demand, cause growth in the public sector.

In the third section, public corporations are defined and classified. Public corporations are institutional actors affecting each country's economic and social conditions, and the focus here will be on the public corporations of Japan.

The fourth section concerns private provision and efficiency, with an explanation of positive theories for private provision in the field of public services, including the public choice theory and the property rights theory. This section contains a discussion of the efficiency of private provision, with reference to related empirical evidence obtained from the results of previous economic and policy research. Factors affecting efficiency are then explored.

In the fifth section, the idea of privatization, itself an institutional subject, is summarized. The definition, the kinds, and the purpose of privatization are explained mainly from a Japanese perspective, although the international outlook is considered as well.

The last section summarizes the structural reforms often associated with privatization.

2 PUBLIC PROVISION

2.1 Rationale for Public Provision

Government's involvement in the market system is in general justified as necessary for ameliorating problems that the market itself cannot solve, such as matters related to market failures and value judgments. Among several reasons for the government to play a role in the market, the following are important: 1) to provide public goods, 2) to ameliorate the problem of natural monopolies, and 3) to protect public interests.

First, public goods are in general provided by the public sector because these goods and services are considered to be difficult for the market to provide. Traditionally, due to their 'non-rivalry in consumption' and 'non-excludability' nature, public goods have been produced and provided directly by the public sector. Public goods possess non-rivalry in consumption in that their consumption is unrelated to the number of consumers. For example, the enjoyment of a person who takes a walk in a non-congested public park is not reduced by the fact that other people use the park. Furthermore, as for non-excludability, public goods and services have the following characteristic: it is very difficult or very expensive to exclude non-paying consumers. In the case of general roads, for example, the installation of a user charge system would necessitate the construction of toll gates and barrier walls, which would be prohibitively expensive, if not impossible. Under private provision, it would not be easy to set up individual property rights, the goods and services provided might be less than optimal, and free rider problems would occur. Traditionally, public provision has been justified as a way to avoid these problems.

The second reason for government involvement in the market is related to the phenomenon of the natural monopoly. As explained in the previous chapter, to prevent problems arising from natural monopolies, regulations have been introduced. In essence, under the monopoly provision, socially optimal marginal cost pricing must be practiced. Without this regulation, the quantity of services provided is less and the price is higher than in the optimal case. However, as the public utility industry has a huge number of facilities, marginal cost pricing yields deficits,[1] a problem for which there are three possible solutions: 1) to provide subsidies, 2) to enact public provision, or 3) to use average cost pricing. Public provision has thus been justified as one option for dealing with the problem of natural monopoly.

The third reason in favor of public provision is that the public sector is presumably pursuing the public interest, according to OECD (1992). In general, private companies are considered as pursuing profits, an activity not always beneficial to the public, whose interests are broader than simply seeking profit. Because government, whose goal presumably is to attain the social optimum, cannot expect private companies to pursue public interests, the government must do so itself by establishing public corporations for this purpose.[2]

While these reasons are commonly cited to justify government involvement in the market, it remains unproven that public provision should be obligatory. First, for example, the non-rivalry in consumption, non-excludability characteristics of public goods might be rendered obsolete by technological progress. Furthermore, there is the opinion that the government does not always need to be the direct provider. Kanou (1990) contends that the role of government is not necessarily to provide services but to make and enforce rules ensuring that private companies provide services properly. Second, some doubt that the public sector truly pursues the public interest. As many empirical examples suggest, the government spends too much money on unnecessary services in the name of 'public interest.' Last, even if we accept that the public sector aims to pursue the public interest, the term 'public interest' is too ill defined to become an organization's goal. In short, while the reasons for government involvement in the market are valid, they may not signify an obligation by the government to provide goods and services.

2.2 Growth of the Public Sector

One problem with public provision is its tendency to become bloated. There are many cases where public provision is expanding. According to Savas (1987), this growth can be attributed to demand-related, supply-related, and inefficiency factors. In this section, I will summarize the factors affecting the growth of public provision, with a focus on those related to demand and supply.

First, demand-related factors include demographic changes in a society. An increasingly elderly population would mean increased engagement by the public sector, the main supplier of the medical and welfare services consumed by the elderly. Second, increased income levels resulting from economic growth also contribute to the expansion of government service, as consumers demand more expensive educational programs, libraries, or cultural events to reflect their improved status. Third, R&D in the life science and technology industries is risky and requires massive funding, which the government might deem in the public's best interest to help provide. Finally, as an economy rapidly grows, the government might find it necessary to institute new aid or welfare programs to obviate the social problems possibly arising from widening disparities in income distribution among households.

As for supply side factors affecting the growth of the public sector, first there is politics, which often works to increase the scope of public services. Second, the bureaucracy system might, despite the assumption that government behaves in order to increase the public interest, cause its own expansion simply in order to maintain itself. Third, instability in an economy could cause a conversion in ownership from private to public. A fourth factor might be that public corporations act as monopolies, with regulatory protection from market competition, leading to over-employment, inflated government salaries, and further growth of the public sector.

In this study, we focus on reforms in Japanese public utility industries, whose services are provided by both the private and public sectors. In this section, we evaluate the public sector in a regulatory environment.

3 PUBLIC CORPORATIONS

3.1 Definition of Public Corporation

This section gives an overview of public corporations in Japan. The main providers of public services, public corporations are owned by the public sector. According to Sasaki (1992, 1997), as public corporations' main role is to achieve the public interest, it is natural that such organizations be owned and managed by national and/or local governments, but it is not always necessary that they be 100% publicly owned.

Although there are various definitions of public corporations in Japan, it is commonly acknowledged that they have the characteristics of 'publicness' and 'marketability' (see for example, Oshima (1979), Toyama (1987), Uekusa (1991, 2000)). Table 2.1 is a summary of the characteristics of public in comparison with private corporations, based on previous studies in Japan.

In Japan, the broad term *publicness* encompasses the idea that the organization must contribute to citizens' welfare, in other words pursue the public interest. As Table 2.1 shows, in order to pursue the public interest, the public corporation is owned by the public sector and its behavior is restricted by regulation. The degree of publicness is measured by the degree of public ownership and regulation.

The second characteristic of the public corporation is marketability, by which concept the corporation is distinguished from non-marketable public services, such as the issue of public certificates. Certain public services such as city transport and water supply services are supplied on a market mechanism basis. Even if the services are offered in the interest of the public, efficient management should be practiced in the organizations supplying them. The public organization should be, to some degree, free of political management and profitability. Because of this feature, a public corporation is in general weaker than a private company.

In summary, a public corporation is established to achieve the public purpose of providing services under efficient management conditions. The public corporation in Japan has characteristics of both publicness and marketability.

Table 2.1   Characteristics of the Public Corporation

Main features		Public corporation	Private company
Main purpose		Public interests	Profits
Publicness	(i) Regulation	Strong	Weak
	(ii) Ownership	Public	Private
Marketability	(i) Management independency	Weak	Strong
	(ii) Profitability	Weak	Strong

[Note]: This table was written by the author and is based on Mizutani (2000).

3.2   Kinds of Public Corporations in Japan

There are various kinds of public corporations. Uekusa (1991, 2000) classifies public corporations into three categories: (i) subdivision (bureau) of government, (ii) public independent agency, and (iii) stock

company.   First, a subdivision (bureau) is one division of the
government, with the top of the division responsible for provision of the
service, which is independent from other public services.   Typical
examples of this are the former postal services provided by the Ministry
of Postal Service, the transportation bureaus, and water supply bureaus of
municipal governments.   Second, the public independent agency is an
independent public organization established by the government according
to special laws, with more autonomous management than subdivisions of
the government.   Examples of this type organization are the Japan Post
Public Corporation and the Japan Highway Public Corporation.   Third,
the stock company is a company-style corporation but with shares of the
organization partly or entirely held by the public sector.   Sasaki (1997)
classifies public corporations in Japan according to the degree of
ownership-management separation, independence of the organization,
autonomy in politics and public administration, autonomy in financing
and personnel affairs, the existence of executive directors, and so on.

Based on Uekusa (1991, 2000) and Sasaki (1997), major public
corporations are classified into four categories: (i) subdivision (bureau) of
government, (ii) public independent agency, (iii) stock company, and (iv)
third sector.   These types of public corporations are classified by (i)
ownership structure, (ii) ownership-management relationship, (iii)
relationship with regulator, (iv) range of ownership, and (v) political
interference.   Table 2.2 shows the kinds of public corporations.[3]

Classification of public corporations is almost the same as in Uekusa
(1991, 2000), with the addition of the third sector based on Sasaki (1997).
That is, the subdivision of government is one division of the government,
with the top of the division responsible for provision of service; the
public independent agency is an independent public organization; the
stock company is a company-style corporation but with shares partly or
entirely held by the public sector.   The third sector is a public
corporation jointly established by both the government and private sector.
The third sector type is often seen in cases of public corporations jointly
established by municipal governments and the private sector.

Though public corporations are established in order to achieve the
public purpose, the definition of public purpose varies according to the
kind of public corporations, and with the degree of political interference
in management.   Because the government subdivision type corporation
is part of a government body, political interference is much stronger than
with others, and financial statements require approval by the Diet.   With
the third sector type of organization—that jointly established with the
private sector—political interference becomes less cumbersome, but
monitoring of management is less vigilant, which can lead to problems of

inefficiency.

Table 2.2 Major Kinds of Public Corporations in Japan

Type of public corporation	Subdivision of government	Public independent agency	Stock company	Third sector
Ownership	Public	Public	Public	Public and private
Ownership-management relationship	Not completely separated	Separated	Separated	Separated
Relationship with regulator	Not separated	Separated	Separated	Separated
Range of ownership	Wide (citizen)	Wide (citizen)	Wide (citizen)	Narrow (share holders)
Political interference	Strong	<————————————>		Weak

[Note]: This table was written by the author and is based on Mizutani (2000).

3.3   Purpose and Service Fields of Public Corporations

Theoretically, the government establishes a public corporation for two main reasons: to resolve problems caused by market failures and to address social interests.   Broader benefits for users overrule financial concerns.

Theoretical reasons notwithstanding, there are several practical reasons why public corporations have been established, all reflecting the socio-economic conditions of individual countries.   According to Uekusa (1991), the following reasons are important for the establishment of public corporations in Japan: (i) development of infrastructure, (ii) introduction of new technology, and (iii) generation of tax revenues. To foster and support the economic activities of a modernizing Japan, infrastructure was necessary, the construction of which required huge funding. Public corporations were established to carry out this infrastructure development, to absorb the risk and expense of introducing new technology, and finally to generate tax revenues.

Public corporations have been instituted in various service fields, among which the following four are common: (i) public utility industries (i.e. electric power, gas utility, water supply, railway, postal service, telecommunications, broadcasting etc.); (ii) infrastructure (i.e. road, airport, port, bridge, etc.); (iii) education, welfare and culture (i.e. hospital, school, public housing, etc.); (iv) financial industry (i.e. bank, etc.).

3.4   Inefficiency in Public Corporations

A public corporation is in general recognized as less efficient than a private company under the same conditions, which means that a public corporation incurs higher costs than a private company when the same level of output service is produced. However, it is not necessarily true that a public corporation must always be inefficient. In fact, as I show later, there are certain cases in which a public corporation is more efficient than a private company. In this section, I will summarize reasons why a public corporation might tend to be less efficient than a private company.

First, a public corporation's inefficiency is due to its ambiguous goal. The purpose of a public corporation is not to pursue profits, but to address social interests, which are not always equivalent to social benefits. A public corporation continues providing services, even when its goals are unclear. In the name of social interest, unnecessary services are sometimes provided. On the other hand, as a private company's existence depends on the generation of profits, efficient management of the organization is required.

Second, public corporations experience almost no pressure from the capital market. Even if the management of a public corporation is not well organized, its citizen owners are so widely dispersed as to have little influence on management, a situation which exacerbates the public corporation's lack of efficiency in comparison with a private company, which is constantly under severe pressure from the capital market.

Third, regulations applying to public corporations could be a reason for their inefficiency. For example, any plans related to fare and investment at the former Japan National Railway had to be approved by the Diet, and in the name of public interest, unnecessary lines were built and unprofitable rail lines were required to provide service.

Fourth, political interference might be a reason for inefficiency. While politics is necessary to signal citizens' wishes, too much political interference in a public corporation can hinder its healthy management. In the case of the former Japan National Railway, political interference in management caused organizational dysfunction and hostile relations between management and labor unions.

Fifth, the availability of subsidies creates cost inefficiency by lowering managerial incentive to improve performance. Subsidized public corporations tend to incur higher costs than non-subsidized corporations, a fact borne out by several empirical research studies. For similar reasons, soft budget constraints also create inefficiency in organizations.

As for other reasons for inefficiency, because of their bureaucratic nature, public corporations tend to be slow at perceiving market needs, as compared with private companies. When discussing organization theory, Kamata (1985) notes that the measures of a public organization's performance are not objective and appropriate, and the salary system does not include incentives. Furthermore, too much safety-oriented behavior holds extra resources inside the organization, causing the public corporation to become inefficient.

4 PRIVATE PROVISION AND EFFICIENCY

4.1 Positive Theory for Private Provision

There are theories as to why private companies are more cost efficient than public corporations (see for example, Tittenbrun (1996), which are based on Tullock (1970), Niskanen (1971), Alchian and Demsetz (1972, 1973), Furubotn and Pejovich (1974), Alchian (1977)). In this section, I will consider the public choice theory and the property rights theory.

In the public choice theory, the public sector itself is considered as an organization that is pursuing not the public interest but the interest of each individual related to the public organization—managers, workers, politicians, union members and so on. This theory contends that these individuals behave in a way that will maximize their own interest. The managers of the public organization, for example, might be more interested in their own working conditions than in what is best for the public. In order to satisfy his own interest, a manager might spend money on a luxurious office, a private jet, and so on. Politicians are expected to supervise managers' behavior, but in order to satisfy the demands of constituents and to be reelected, they might pressure managers to provide wasteful services.   The union and workers might also put pressure on managers in order to satisfy their interests (i.e. salary increases and improved fringe benefits).   To avoid strikes, managers might meet worker and union demands.   The essence of public choice theory is that public organizations, by satisfying these myriad individual interests, incur extra costs and become less efficient than private companies.

The inefficiency of the public corporation might also be explained by the property rights theory, which would attribute its problems to ambiguous ownership.   Consider the example of a company with only one owner.   All profits belong only to him, and he would therefore use company resources as efficiently as possible to increase those profits, in particular by reducing costs.   A general private company with many shareholders would be unable to attain the level of efficiency of the one-man company because the range of ownership is wide and the identity of the owner is unclear.   While in the one-owner company, the control of management is well organized because owner and manager are one and the same, in the case of the stock company, management control might be weaker because stockholders, who each hold only a small percentage of the organization, have insufficient incentive to monitor management.   If we accept this view, the public organization tends to be less attractive for owners, whose stake in the organization is so small as to damage any incentive to seek better management.   Moreover, unlike citizen stakeholders in public corporations, private company shareholders can sell off their shares in response to bad management.   Pressure from the capital market does not work to bring about efficient management in public organizations because ownership cannot be transferred and ownership is too widely dispersed.

4.2   Concepts of Efficiency

In order to summarize the relative efficiency differences between public and private firms, it is necessary clearly to define efficiency measures. In the framework of economics, there are many expressions related to efficiency: for example, Pareto efficiency (or Pareto optimal), allocative efficiency, productive efficiency, technical efficiency, inefficiency as monopoly-induced waste, X-inefficiency, internal inefficiency, and so on.

Resource allocation in the market can be examined by comparing a monopoly situation and perfect competition.   In the market system, Pareto efficiency (the Pareto optimal) means that equilibrium cannot be replaced by an alternate state of equilibrium that would increase the welfare of some consumers without harming others. The competitive model has been regarded as satisfying the conditions of the Pareto optimum, also referred to as Pareto efficiency, or simply economic efficiency (Viscusi et al. 2005).

Allocative inefficiency is the misallocation of resources among different goods. It typically results from prices deriving from marginal cost. If the price of a good exceeds its marginal cost, we know that a suboptimal amount of that good is produced, ceteris paribus, creating allocative inefficiency. Because of its deadweight loss, a monopoly is characterized by inefficiency in terms of resource allocation, compared to organizations operating in a truly competitive environment.

Productive inefficiency occurs when inputs are not effectively used in production. Likely causes are distorted input prices that result in a suboptimal input mix and wasted inputs resulting from the lack of competitive pressure.

Similar to the concept of productive inefficiency, there is technical inefficiency, a situation where it is possible for a firm with the given know how, to produce a larger output from the same inputs, or the same output with less of one or more inputs without increasing the amount of other inputs.

Monopoly induced waste inefficiency occurs when the inefficiency created by a monopoly generates further inefficiency. For example, a monopoly firm created by the government might recognize the possibility of yielding extra profits by establishing a franchise firm by which rents may be charged. Knowing that the franchise will earn rent revenues, the firm might invest resources in lobbying the legislature or government in order to solidify the status of the franchise firm. Resources wasted in such lobbying activities become a cost to society.

X-inefficiency, proposed by Leibenstein (1966), happens when a firm operates at a point above its theoretical cost curve. Although it was assumed that both monopolists and perfect competitors combine their factors of production efficiently, thereby minimizing cost for each output level, it can be argued that the pressures of competition force perfect competitors to be cost minimizers, whereas freedom from competition makes it possible for the monopolist to be inefficient.

The phrase 'internal inefficiency'[4] is used in a way similar to X-inefficiency, to signify the concept of an organization having more wasted resources than in a situation in which there is no slack.

There are various concepts related to efficiency, and terminology must be chosen carefully.

4.3   Evidence from Relative Efficiency Comparisons

This section will summarize empirical evidence related to efficiency differences between public and private corporations.   There have been many empirical efficiency comparison studies in the US and Europe, among which are Donahue (1989), Viscusi et al. (1995) and Tittenbrun (1996).   Using results from previous studies published between the mid-60s to the mid-90s in the field of public utility industries such as electric power supply, gas, railway, air transportation, local bus, ports, telecommunications and garbage collection, Table 2.3 shows efficiency differences between the two sectors.

Table 2.3 Empirical Results of Efficiency Comparison

Industry	Private is more efficient (cases)	No difference (cases)	Public is more efficient (cases)
Electric power	10	6	5
Gas	0	2	0
Water supply	4	4	1
Railway	2	2	1
Air transportation	2	3	1
Local bus	7	0	0
Seaport	0	1	0
Telecommunications	0	0	1
Refuse collection	11	2	2
Total	36	20	11

[Source]: Mizutani (2000)

[Note]:
  This table is based on previous research results. Sources are as follows: 1) Electric power supply: Shepherd (1966), Wallace and Junk (1970), Moore (1970), Mann (1970), Peltzman (1971), Tilton (1973), DeAlessi (1974), Meyer (1975), Yunker (1975), Spann (1977), De Alessi (1977), Neuberg (1977), Pescatrice and Trapani (1980), Di Lorenzo and Robinson (1982), Färe et al. (1985), Atkinson and Halvorsen (1986), Tittenbrun (1996); 2) gas: Millward and Ward (1987), Foreman-Peck and Millward (1994); 3) water supply: Hausman (1976), Morgan (1977), Crain and Zardkoohi (1978), Bruggink (1982), Feigenbaum and Teeples (1983), Teeples et al. (1986), Byrners et al. (1986), Teeples and Glyer (1987), Donahue (1989), Viscusi et al. (1995), Tittenbrun (1996); 4) Railways: Caves and Christensen (1980), Caves et al. (1982), Miyajima and Lee (1984), Mizutani (1994) Tittenbrun (1996); 5) Air Transportation: Davies (1971), Davies (1977), Morrison (1981), Jordan (1982), Tittenbrun (1996); 6) Local bus: Perry and Babitsky (1986), Hensher (1988), Tittenbrun (1996); 7) Port: Liu (1995); 8) Telecommunications: Tittenbrun (1996); 9) Garbage collection: Hirsch (1965), Pier, Vernon and Wicks (1974), Kitchen (1976), Pommerehne (1976), Kemper and Quigley (1976), Pommerehne and Frey (1977), Stevens and Savas (1977), Collins and Downes (1977), Spann (1977), Savas (1977), Stevens (1977), Bennett and Johnson (1979), McDavid (1985), Cubbin et al. (1987), Viscusi et al. (1995).

A total of 67 cases are listed in this table.   Unfortunately, study results for some industries such as postal service and broadcasting were not found.   Although there may be studies we have overlooked, overall tendencies in private-public efficiency comparisons can be grasped.   In this section, we concentrate mainly on productive efficiency and X-inefficiency.

First, from this table it can be seen that in general, cases of private companies being more efficient than public corporations are more numerous.   As many researchers have concluded, on average the private company seems to be more efficient than its public counterpart.

Second, however, because some cases show that there is no efficiency difference between private and public corporations or that public corporations are more efficient than private companies, it is possible that ownership is not the deterministic factor.   Some previous studies are problematic in that they fail properly to control factors other than ownership, especially in studies on public utility industries, where costs vary widely according to the size and quality of output.

In the empirical studies we have done on Japanese public utility industries, where factors other than ownership can be controlled, (e.g. Mizutani and Urakami (2003), Mizutani (2004)), evidence suggests that private companies are indeed more efficient than public corporations.

4.4   Factors Affecting Efficiency

In the previous section, we observed that private companies are in general more efficient than public corporations.   We know also that efficiency differences between private companies and public corporations are affected by factors other than ownership.   In this section, we summarize factors affecting efficiency differences.

Vickers and Yarrow (1988) list factors affecting performance differences between private companies and public corporations in terms of allocative and internal efficiency: (i) the effectiveness of the respective monitoring systems, (ii) the degree of competition in the market, (iii) regulatory policy, and (iv) technological progressiveness.   Yamamoto (1994) argues that incentive for the efficient management of firms is related to (i) the ownership structure, (ii) the competitive situation, and (iii) the effects of regulation.   In addition to these factors, the availability of subsidies is important.   Some empirical studies report that public corporations receiving subsidies tend to experience cost escalation, which may be evidence in support of the soft-budget hypothesis.   It is clear that there are many factors affecting a firm's efficiency.

Does ownership really make a difference when it comes to efficiency?   Some researchers contend that ownership does not matter, as long as a competitive environment is maintained.   In other words, the competition factor is more important than ownership.

However, Parker (1994) shows that the ownership factor is important in achieving efficiency.   This can be seen in Figure 2.1, where the horizontal axis shows the competitive environments in the production market.   The far-left side indicates a monopoly situation and the far-right side perfect competition.   As the situation moves from a monopoly to perfect competition, the efficiency of a firm increases.   The vertical axis shows the ownership difference.   As the vertical axis is based on the property rights theory, efficiency increases as the percentage of privately held shares increases.   Therefore, conceptually, the fully private firm under perfect competition can achieve the most efficient situation.

We aim to show in our study that it is equally important to consider both ownership and competition factors when explaining efficiency differences.

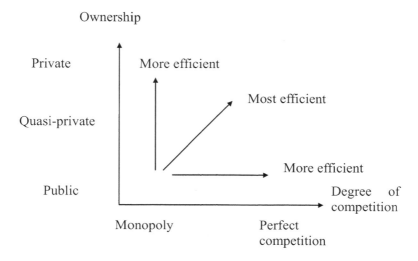

Figure 2.1   Conceptual Figure on the Relationship Between Efficiency and Ownership-Competition Factors

5   PRIVATIZATION

5.1   Definition of Privatization

Privatization was undertaken in the 1980s in the UK and has been studied both theoretically and empirically (see, for example, Vickers and Yarrow (1988), Bishop et al. (1994)).   Many countries have had various experiences with privatization over the years (see, for example, Donahue (1989), Gómez-Ibáñez and Meyer (1993), Ramamurti (1996) and Parker (1998)). In general, privatization means transferring ownership of an enterprise or public services from the public to the private sector.   This can be done either on a complete or partial basis, resulting in either full privatization, with all ownership transferred completely to the private sector, or partial privatization, with only a portion of public ownership transferred.

However, according to Thiemeyer and Quaden (1986), Adam et al. (1992) and Tamamura (1993), the term *privatization* can have several meanings. In a broad sense, privatization refers to the transfer of any government function to the private sector, reflecting the role and purpose of each country's government's role. Thiemeyer and Quaden (1986), by analyzing reforms of public services in western countries, classify fifteen types of privatization, focusing on such topics as governmental functions like revenue collection, competition policy and law enforcement. Savas (1987) defines privatization as the act of reducing the government's role while increasing the role of the private sector, in terms of activities or in terms of the ownership of assets.

In Japan, the word *privatization* has been used in many ways, according to Iwasaki (1992), Tamamura (1993) and Yamamoto (1994). For example, Iwasaki (1992) classifies privatization into four types: (i) organizational reform from a public corporation to a joint stock company type public corporation, (ii) ownership transfer from the public sector to the private sector, (iii) liberalization of management, such as a private company under public ownership, and (iv) the contracting out of public services to the private sector.

Although there are many variations in Japan, the mostly widely recognized definition of privatization in Japan encompasses the ideas of (i) the transfer of ownership from the public to the private sector, and/or (ii) private sector style management under public ownership. In the late 80s, three huge public corporations were privatized: Nippon Telegraph and Telephone (NTT) in 1985; the Japan Monopoly Public Corporation (Tobacco and Salt) in 1985; and the Japan National Railway (JNR) in 1987. In the process of privatizing these public corporations, ownership was not transferred to the private sector from the beginning, although the management style was dramatically changed from what it had been under full public ownership. Therefore, private sector style management under public ownership is included in the overall idea of privatization in Japan, even though this form might simply be a transitional stage of a firm on the road toward full privatization.

5.2   Purpose of Privatization

Privatization has been carried out in many countries, starting in the UK in the 1980s. Although there are various reasons why privatization was adopted, the major reasons are summarized as follows.

First, public corporations were the target of a great deal of criticism because of their inefficient management, which led to enormous deficits. The former JNR is a typical example of the deficit-creating public corporations slated for privatization due to its inefficient management.

Second,   the   government's   financial   difficulties   led   to   the privatization of public corporations. By privatizing public corporations, government was relieved of the financial burden of providing all the subsidies on which those public corporations had grown dependent. Furthermore, by selling the shares of the privatized corporation, the national government was able to supplement its budget revenues.

Third, privatization was adopted as a means of achieving fair competition with other private companies. One reason why public corporations had been inefficient was that they had experienced little competition. Mizutani and Uranishi (2003) found that the public sector is in general less sensitive to competition than private sector corporations. Public corporations were made private in order to create competition with other private companies.

A fourth reason for privatization was to reduce political interference. In the case of JNR, there was heavy political interference whenever rail fares were revised or new rail lines were constructed. Because decisions were made not according to economic rationale but for political reasons, confusion and inefficiency were rampant. Privatization was seen as a way to correct the problem of political interference.

Fifth, also related to political reasons, the privatization of public corporations was seen as a way to mend the management-union relationship. There were other reasons for privatization as well, among them the private sector's willingness and desire to use new technology.

Ihori's (1990) results show several advantages of privatization: (i) the reduction of vested interests, (ii) the creation of more free economic activity, (iii) the reduction of deficits by the beneficiary-pays principle, and (iv) more efficient management.

5.3 Kinds of Privatization

As mentioned above, privatization can assume any of several forms. In Japan, *privatization* is used to signify the change from public to private ownership or from public management to private company style management. In order to explain the several forms of privatization in Japan, I distinguish organization forms in Japan according to two features: ownership and management style. We consider only two sectors—the public and the private—although there is one more sector, jointly established by both public and private sectors, and known as the third sector.

First, *ownership* denotes who holds the rights to assets for services. Public ownership means that the government holds assets and facilities for providing services. Second, *management style* means how the service provision is handled. Public management style assumes that the pursuit of the public interest is the main goal of the organization. Although the public corporation must maintain marketability in addition to promoting the public interest, I define two types of management style: public management style in the name of public interest and private management style based on commercial goals. Under these conditions, there are in fact three kinds of organization forms, as Table 2.4 shows.

Table 2.4 Several Forms of Service Provision

Ownership	Management Style	Examples of organization
Public	Public	Public corporation
Public	Private	Stock-company-style special corporation
Private	Private	Private company

[Note]:
(1) *Ownership refers to the main responsible actor with regard to assets and facilities.*
(2) *Management refers to the main management style of delivering service to the consumer: public style management focuses on public interest, private style on commercial gain.*

The first type of organization is the general public corporation, which is owned by the government and provides services to users. Although utility services could be considered marketable, the main purpose of the general public organization is to serve the public interest. Thus the general corporation's management style is not commercially oriented, in contrast to that of the general private company, whose interests are commercial. A third type of organization is still partly owned by the government but is managed as if it were a private company, an example of this type being the special public corporation set up after the privatization of JNR. In the long process toward full privatization, all shares of the corporation are still held by the government, but the corporation provides services in the manner of a private company. This organization is what might be called a commercialized public corporation.

In Japan, the concept of privatization includes the practice of converting publicly owned and managed organizations into publicly owned organizations that are managed as if they were private corporations. While full privatization is the ultimate goal—with full private ownership and private management—the creation of interim organizations whereby shares remain partially government-owned is also considered as privatization in Japan.

6   STRUCTURAL REFORMS

In this section, the structural reforms of public utility corporations and infrastructure are explained. More detailed explanations of reforms can be found in, for example, OECD (2001), Kessides (2004) and Gómez-Ibáñez (2003).

As noted in the previous chapter, traditionally public utility industries, which have characteristics of natural monopolies, are highly regulated by the government. However, new ideas have recently emerged, such as the trend in dividing public utilities into components in order to introduce competition. Components are distinguished as competitive or non-competitive. Table 2.5 shows examples of industries featuring competitive and non-competitive components. The main method of restructuring organizations and networks is through unbundling, whereby components are classified according to their activities. Among unbundling methods, horizontal separation, vertical separation, and functional separation are important in Japan. In addition to these methods, there are several approaches to structural reform, such as accounting separation, ownership-control separation, and reform of ownership structure.

First, horizontal separation divides similar services into several organizations. For example, in Japan, when the Japan National Railways (JNR) was privatized in 1987, the JNR was separated into six passenger JR companies. As horizontal separation was carried out according to geographical area, horizontal separation is here called regional subdivision.

Second, vertical separation is a method to dividing different activities according to the process of service production. In the rail industry, vertical separation is divided into train operation and maintenance of infrastructure. Although vertical separation is a common policy in the rail industry in Europe, this is not the case in Japan.

Table 2.5   Examples of Industries Featuring Competitive and Non-competitive Components

Industry	Activities which are usually non-competitive	Activities which are potentially competitive
Electric Power	(i) High-voltage transmission of electricity, (ii) Local electricity distribution	(i) Electricity generation, (ii) Electricity 'retailing' or 'marketing' activities, (iii) Electricity market trading activities
Gas Utility	(i) High-pressure transmission of gas, (ii) Local gas distribution	(i) Gas production, (ii) Gas storage, (iii) Gas 'retailing' and 'marketing' activities
Railway	(i) Track and signaling infrastructure	(i) Operation of trains, (ii) Maintenance facilities
Postal Services	(i) Door-to-door delivery of non-urgent mail in residential areas	(i) Transportation of mail, (ii) Delivery of urgent mail or packages, (iii) Delivery of mail to high-volume business customers, especially in high-density areas
Tele-communications	(i) Provision of a ubiquitous network, (ii) Local residential telephones in rural areas	(i) Long-distance services, (ii) Mobile services, (iii) Value-added services, (iv) Local loop services to high-volume business customers, especially in high-density areas, (v) Local loop services in areas served by broadband (e.g. cable TV) networks

[Note]: This table was written by the author based on OECD (2001, p.9).

Third, functional separation used here refers to dividing different services into disparate organizations. This is similar to horizontal separation but with more focus on the scope of service activities. In the rail industry in Japan, for example, passenger and freight services have been separated into different organizations since the privatization of the JNR, while in the postal services industry, postal services, banking services and insurance services have been separated since the privatization of the Japan Post.

Public corporations in Japan encompass these restructuring methods into the privatization process, further details of which will appear in later chapters. Unlike the more drastic competition policies often being introduced in these industries elsewhere, a milder version of structural reform characterized by indirect competition, such as through yardstick competition, is the preferred method of privatization in Japan.

NOTES

[1] In public utility industries such as electric power, gas, railway, water supply and so on, average costs decrease as service output increases, as mentioned earlier. In this situation, marginal costs are always lower than average costs. Therefore, in the socially optimal case, the price level is set at marginal cost (i.e. marginal cost pricing) but the cost for one unit of service, or the average cost, becomes higher than the price.

[2] Other reasons for government direct involvement in provision are to distribute merit goods, to ensure the civil and national minimum service, or that the market itself is nonexistent because the industry is in its infancy, and so on.

[3] As for details regarding public corportations and private companies in Japanese public utility industries, please see Sasaki and Mizutani (2000).

[4] For example, Vickers and Yarrow (1988, p.39) use the phrase 'internal efficiency.'

PART II

The Energy and Water Supply Industries

3   Electric Power

1   INTRODUCTION

Liberalization[1] in the electric power industry is taking place in industrial countries, as Sioshansi (2006) points out in his summary of recent electricity market reforms.   Hattori and Tsutsui (2004) classify types of liberalization in the electricity supply industry in OECD countries and examine the economic impact of regulatory reforms.   According to Satake (2002), liberalization of markets of users with more than 1000kw began in 1990 in the UK, with all UK electricity retail services liberalized by 1995, while in Germany liberalization was accomplished in 1998. Jamasb and Pollitt (2007) summarize the lessons of Britain's liberalization experience.   In the US, full liberalization of the electricity market was completed in the state of California in 1998.   Japan's progress toward full liberalization has in comparison been slow.

The main purpose of this chapter is to overview the structure of the Japanese electric power industry and its regulatory scheme.   Electric power has traditionally been supplied by 10 regional private company monopolies.   Ida and Kuwabara (2000) show in an empirical analysis using data between 1978 and 1998 that there exist both economies of scale and scope in the electric power industry in Japan.   Although the market of consumers with lower demand for electricity, such as general households, is still served by these 10 general electric companies, other market sectors have since 1995 been undergoing gradual liberalization. This chapter explains the characteristics of the Japanese electric power industry and ongoing regulatory reforms.

After the introduction, Section 2 describes the market structure of the electric power industry in Japan, outlining the main suppliers, consumers, regulators and neutral institutions.   The third section summarizes the rate system, explaining major price regulations.   The fourth section focuses on the process of liberalization in the electric power industry, which has been underway since 1995, after which year major changes have occurred four times: in 1995, 2000, 2004, and 2005.

Liberalization in the electric power industry gives users freedom to choose from among suppliers, not only according to price but according to other factors as well. Ariu (2001) explores the question of what causes consumers to choose one company over another in an environment of liberalization. With a survey of Japanese companies operating in the U.S. in 2000, Ariu finds that important factors determining the choice of an electric company are the quality and reliability of electricity service, price, the financial stability of a supply company, and customer service. And more recently, based on a research survey by Ariu (2003) of the manufacturing industry in Japan in 2002, the most important factor determining the choice of an electricity company is found to be the quality and reliability of electricity supply. Price is second in importance. Furthermore, Goto and Ariu (2006) find that price and customer service quality are important factors affecting customer loyalty to electric suppliers.

2 INDUSTRIAL STRUCTURE OF THE ELECTRIC POWER INDUSTRY

2.1 Major Supplier

The market structure of the electric power industry as of August 1, 2007, is shown in Figure 3.1. Liberalization of the electricity market has progressed gradually since December 1, 1995, details of which are explained later in Section 4.

As of March 31, 1995, electric power supply companies in Japan were classified into 4 categories: (i) general electricity companies (*Ippan Denki Jigyosha*), (ii) wholesale electricity companies (*Oroshi Denki Jigyosha*), (iii) special electricity companies (*Tokutei Denki Jigyosha*), (iv) power producer and supplier companies (*Tokutei Kibo Denki Jigyosha*) (Federation of Electric Power Companies Statistics Committee (2005)).

General electricity companies are all stock holding private regional companies providing electricity to regional users. These companies perform power generation, power transmission and distribution, and retail services to end-users of electricity. As Table 3.1 shows, there are ten general electricity companies, each serving one of the 10 regions into which electrical service provision is subdivided in Japan. Although they vary in size, these ten general electricity companies are all private stock companies.

According to Yajima (2005), these general electricity companies were created when the electric power industry was reorganized on May 1, 1951, and have since been providing electricity exclusively to their

Current situation since April 1, 2005

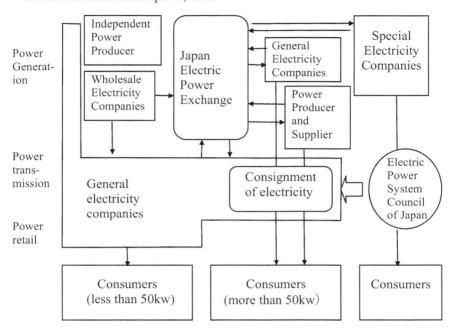

Figure 3.1 Market Structure of Electric Power Supply System in Japan

respective regional users.   However, since 2000, this monopolistic provision system has been subject to gradual change.   First of all, in 2000, the market for large scale users was opened to other electricity companies.

The second category of electricity suppliers is wholesale electricity companies, which do not have distribution areas for individual households or end-use companies but provide electricity to the general electricity companies.   According to Yajima (2005), the Electricity Enterprise Law (*Denki Jigyo-ho*) before 1995, prior to revision, lists four categories of wholesale electricity companies: (i) the Electric Power Development Company, (ii) the Japan Atomic Power Company, (iii) publicly owned electricity organizations, (iv) and jointly owned thermal power generation companies.   The revised Electricity Enterprise Law of 1995 stipulates that wholesale electricity companies be those which have power generation of more than 2 million kw and which provide electricity to the general electricity companies.   The only wholesale electricity companies fitting this definition are the Electric Power Development

Company and Japan Atomic Power Company. Other electricity companies formerly classified as wholesale are called Independent Power Producers (IPP) (*Oroshi Kyokyu Jigyousha*) and are excluded from the definition of wholesale electricity companies stated in the Electricity Enterprise Law. At the end of March 2005, there were 48 such small wholesale electricity companies.

The purpose of the special electricity company, categorized in the revision of the Electricity Enterprises Law in 1995, is to provide electricity in a specific place. The Electricity Enterprise Law was revised in 1999 and the partial liberalization of the retail sale of electricity began in 2000. A power producer and supplier company is an organization providing electricity to individual consumers by using power-transmission wires owned by the general electricity companies. There were 6 special electricity companies and 22 special size electricity companies at the end of March 2005.

Table 3.1   Profile of General Electricity Companies

Company name	Capital (million yen)	Power generation (million kwh)	Sales of electricity (million kwh)	Sales (million yen)	Employees (person)
Hokkaido	114,291	33,989	30,192	509,707	5,924
Tohoku	251,441	85,253	77,329	1,446,648	12,523
Tokyo	676,434	311,797	286,741	4,798,641	38,360
Chubu	374,519	137,995	126,663	2,044,640	16,771
Hokuriku	117,641	29,765	26,874	458,043	4,752
Kansai	489,320	157,991	144,886	2,422,583	22,478
Chugoku	185,527	63,984	58,140	951,809	10,821
Shikoku	145,551	30,688	27,211	523,537	6,016
Kyushu	237,304	88,055	80,199	1,322,995	13,493
Okinawa	7,586	8,163	7,193	136,984	1,555

[Source]: Federation of Electric Power Companies Statistics Committee (2005, pp.4-5)
[Note]: These numbers are as of March 31, 2005.

2.2   Consumers

In principle, the market has been liberalized for consumers demanding more than 50kw, so that these consumers can freely choose their suppliers. On the other hand, the market for consumers with a demand of less than 50kw has not been liberalized, and such consumers are served by the general electricity companies.

Liberalization in the electricity market has been enacted on a step-by-step basis. The market for consumers demanding more than 2000kw was liberalized in 2000, in April 2004 for consumers demanding more than 500kw, and in April 2005 for consumers demanding more than 50kw. According to Anayama (2005) and Yajima (2005), the market for general households was to have been liberalized by April 2007, but this goal has not yet been realized.

2.3   Regulators and Neutral Institutions

The main regulator for the electricity market is the Agency for Natural Resources and Energy, an external organization of the Ministry of Economy, Trade and Industry (METI), which approves electricity rates and regulates matters related to rate revision.

As for other regulating bodies, there is the Electric Power System Council of Japan (*Denryoku Keito Riyo Kyougikai*).[2]   New entrants such as electric power generation companies and wholesale electricity companies are expected to access transmission wires fairly.   In order to guarantee fair treatment to entrant companies, a new law requires that general electricity companies report the costs of power transmission and distribution separately from other items.   The Electric Power System Council of Japan was established in April 2005 as a neutral body which, according to Anayama (2005), is an aggregation of several types of organizations: general electricity companies, special electricity companies, wholesale electricity companies, other independent self-power generation organizations, and neutral academics. The role of this council is to make rules for fair access to power transmission, to monitor the performance of electricity companies, and to facilitate mediation and conciliation among companies.

Finally, the Japan Electric Power Exchange (*Nihon Oroshi Denryoku Torihikisyo*), not a government but a privately owned organization, was established and began operating in April 2000, in order to promote the efficient operation of wholesale electric power exchange.   Participation in this organization is voluntary.

3　RATE SYSTEMS AND PRICE REGULATION OF ELECTRICITY

3.1　Price Regulation

Since the process of electricity market liberalization began in March 2000, regulations regarding electricity rates have been classified into three categories.　The essence of electricity price regulation is summarized in Table 3.2.

Table 3.2　Price Regulation in the Electric Power Industry

Category	Rate in partially liberalized markets (More than 50kw)	Rate in non-liberalized markets (Less than 50kw)	
		Decrease the rate	Increase the rate
Type of regulation	Free	Report	Approval
Other regulations	None	(1) Order to change the rate, if necessary (2) Automatic adjustment scheme due to a change in fuel price	(1) Yardstick regulation scheme (2) Automatic adjustment scheme due to a change in fuel price
Examples of consumers	Large & medium scale factory, department stores, medium & small scale buildings	Households, convenience stores, small shops	

　　The liberalization of the retail market is proceeding on a step-by-step basis.　With the liberalization in March 2000 of the market for large-scale consumers of more than 2000kw, big-scale customers like factories began to purchase electricity from providers other than the 10 general electricity companies. In April 2004, liberalization of the market was expanded to include consumers of 500kw, and then in April 2005 to consumers of 50kw, making it possible for large- and medium-scale factories, department stores, and medium-sized office buildings to purchase electricity from a number of electric companies, which are in turn free to determine their own rates.

The market for consumers demanding less than 50kw has not been liberalized and is still dominated by the 10 general electricity companies, which are considered regional monopolies. This market consists of general households and small shops, and because such customers cannot choose their own electricity supplier, the ministry regulates electricity rates. If an electricity company chooses to decrease its rate to a level already approved by the government, the company can make the change simply by reporting the new rate to the government. The lower rate will be approved as long as it is deemed unlikely to dampen prices so severely as to have a negative effect on other electricity companies.

The rate for electricity of more than 50kw is called the 'liberalized rate' in Japan, while the rate for less than 50kw is called the 'regulated rate.'

When a general electricity company (*Ippan Denki Jigyoha*) wishes to increase the rate for consumers with a less than 50kw demand, the new rate must be approved by the Ministry of Economy, Trade and Industry, which assesses the reasonability of the proposed rate as compared to the rate of other electricity companies, in general by using the yardstick scheme. Details of this scheme will be explained in a later chapter, but the general idea is that yardstick regulation increases efficiency.

In the electric power industry, as in other public utility industries in Japan, the full cost principle is used to calculate price level. In essence, rate revenues cover all the costs of providing electricity services and creating an appropriate level of profit for a company.

Another important regulation related to price is the automatic adjustment scheme whenever there is a change in fuel price. This scheme was established in January 1996. In Japan, most electricity generation depends on oil, and frequent fluctuation in oil prices must necessarily cause fluctuations in the price of electricity. To handle uncontrollable conditions in the external economy, the government formulated the automatic adjustment scheme, whereby a change in energy costs is quickly reflected in the price of electricity.

3.2   The Basic Rate System and Variety of Rates

Contractor-basis electricity rates are applicable to these three groups: (i) low-voltage users (e.g. households); (ii) high-voltage users (e.g. office buildings, shops and small size factories); and (iii) special high-voltage users (e.g. large-scale factories).

The rate system for households in Japan is in general a two-part tariff system, consisting of a fixed and a variable rate.   From Figure 3.2, which shows the conceptual rate system in Japan, it can be seen that the two-part tariff with a gradual increase by block is adopted as a rate system for households.   For example, the variable rate is divided into three blocks: (i) 0 to 120 kwh; (ii) 120 to 300 kwh; (iii) more than 300 kwh, per month.   The first block is considered the minimum necessary consumption for a household.

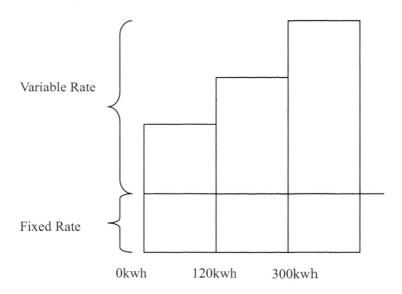

*Figure 3.2   Conceptual Figure of the Two-Part Tariff
with Gradual Increase by Block*

This figure shows that one characteristic of Japan's rate system is that the non-liberalized electricity rate becomes relatively higher as consumed electricity increases. This kind of rate system was chosen to reflect the government's energy saving policy (Yajima (2005)).

General electricity companies provide a varying menu of electricity rates. For example, there is a time zone rate system that discounts nighttime electricity consumption, a season and time of use rate that discounts non-summer and nighttime electricity consumption, and a special rate for households that use electricity to the exclusion of all other energy sources such as gas.

4 LIBERALIZATION IN THE ELECTRIC POWER INDUSTRY

4.1 The Process of Liberalization

The full-scale review of the electric power industry, which began around the mid-1990s, has been necessary for several reasons, according to Yajima (2005). First, decentralized electricity generation systems such as cogeneration systems for general households and industrial private power stations have become widespread. Second, in large metropolitan areas such as Tokyo and Osaka, electricity has become increasingly hard to supply in the medium and long term because of steadily increasing demand. Third, compared with electric rates in foreign countries, those in Japan are relatively high.

Under these circumstances, the electric power industry has been gradually liberalized, a process divided into three main stages since the major revision of the Electric Power Enterprise Law enacted in 1990: (i) 1995, (ii) 1999 and (iii) 2003. Figure 3.3 shows the changes in the electricity supply market since 1990.

(1) Before December 1995

First, before December 1995, 10 regional private companies supplied electricity services. While there were some companies such as the Electric Power Development Company providing supplemental wholesale electricity, almost all electricity services were provided by these ten general electricity companies, which are vertically integrated from electric power generation, to network transmission, to distribution, and finally to retail.

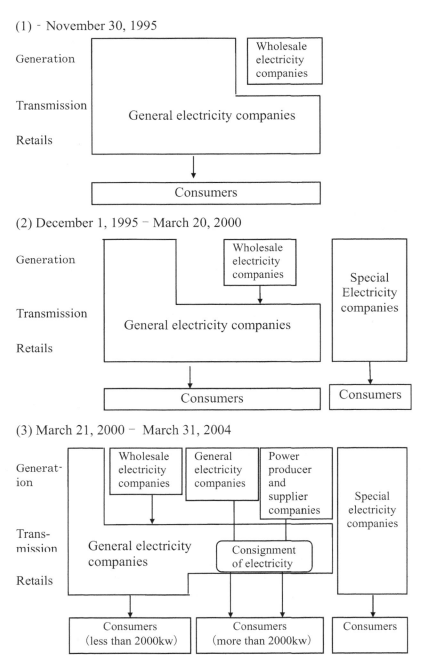

Figure 3.3   Liberalization Changes in the Electric Power Market

(2) Revision of the Electric Power Enterprise Law in 1995

With the revision of the Electric Power Enterprise Law in 1995, liberalization occurred regarding two important points. First, in the wholesale electricity field, the permission regulation was removed and a competitive bidding system introduced. According to the newly established system, new power generation companies providing electricity to the general electricity companies are called IPP and are categorized as wholesale suppliers by the law, while incumbent power generation companies such as the Electric Power Development Company are categorized as wholesale electric companies.

This revision also established the category of the special electricity company, which is defined as one that provides electricity to meet the demand of a specific spot. The government grants permission for the special electricity company to provide service, even if the spot is within the supply area of a general electricity company.

According to Yajima (2005), the introduction of competitive bidding by general electricity companies between FY1996 and FY1999 has resulted in an increase in volume of about 3% (6,580 thousand kw) of electric power generation provided by newly established wholesale suppliers. As for the special electricity companies, there existed 6 companies at the end of March 2004. Typical examples of special electricity companies are railways (e.g. JR East), and steel companies (e.g. JFE Steel).

(3) Revision of the Electric Power Enterprise Law in 1999

The revision of the electric power enterprise law has three characteristics. First, there was the partial liberalization of the retail field for large-scale consumers with demand exceeding 2000 kw of high voltage (more than 20 thousand V), such as large scale factories, hotels, department stores, hospitals, and universities. Partial liberalization meant that in large-scale electricity consumer markets, no regulations were established regarding supply obligations, rate, or entry. If a situation developed such that large-scale consumers were unable to receive electricity from contracted companies, these large-scale consumers could, as a final safeguard, fall back on the general electricity companies.

The second characteristic of the revision is the establishment of the special size company, termed the PPS (Power Producer and Supplier), which provides electricity to the liberalized market's consumers (more than 2000 kw) by using the network of the general electricity companies. According to Yajima (2005), at the end of January 2005, there were 17 companies in this category.   Trading companies, gas providing companies, and manufacturers holding their own power generators have entered the market as special size companies.

The third characteristic of the revision is the systemization of rules for using networks of transmission and distribution, which are owned by the general electricity companies.   The systemization was deemed necessary for facilitating access to networks and ensuring fairness toward entrant companies.   As for the conditions for transferring electricity, according to Yajima (2005), a contract between two organizations is a priority and the regulation is used ex post facto.   Stipulations for transferring electricity must be reported to METI, which has the option of ordering changes in stipulations so as to prevent unfair treatment.

As explained above, although the market for large-scale electricity consumers (more than 2000 kw) was liberalized, the market for other retail organizations (less than 2000 kw) was not liberalized but partially deregulated.   For example, although only applicable to cases where rate is decreased, the regulation for rate adjustments changed from a permission system to a reporting system, thereby expediting the rate change process in some cases.

4.2   Since the Revision of the Electric Power Enterprise Law in 2003

The current situation in the electric power industry took shape when the Electric Power Enterprise Law was revised in June 2003.   Major reform activities since then fall into three categories: (i) publicizing the agenda for liberalization of the retail electricity market, (ii) establishing a nationwide wholesale electric power trading market, and (iii) maintaining fairness and transparency in the field of transmission and distribution.

First, the liberalization of retail electricity sales was expanded to consumers with a demand of 50kw.   This liberalization in retail has progressed step by step, to include consumers demanding more than 2000kw in 2000, those of more than 500kw in 2004, and finally to those of more than 50kw.   According to Yajima (2005), even though full liberalization in retail was due to be completed by April 2007, this has not yet been realized.

Second, the Japan Electric Power Exchange, the wholesale electric power trading market, was established in order to acquire electricity efficiently.   As mentioned above, this organization is not a governmental body but belongs to the private sector.   Participation in the Japan Electric Power Exchange is free for companies who want to trade electric power.   The Japan Electric Power Exchange began operations in April 2005 to alleviate problems stemming from mismatches between supply and demand. When special size companies provide electricity services to consumers, the companies are obligated to supply electricity for demand at a given time, and the exchange market was established to help companies avoid shortfalls in supply and to meet demand smoothly.

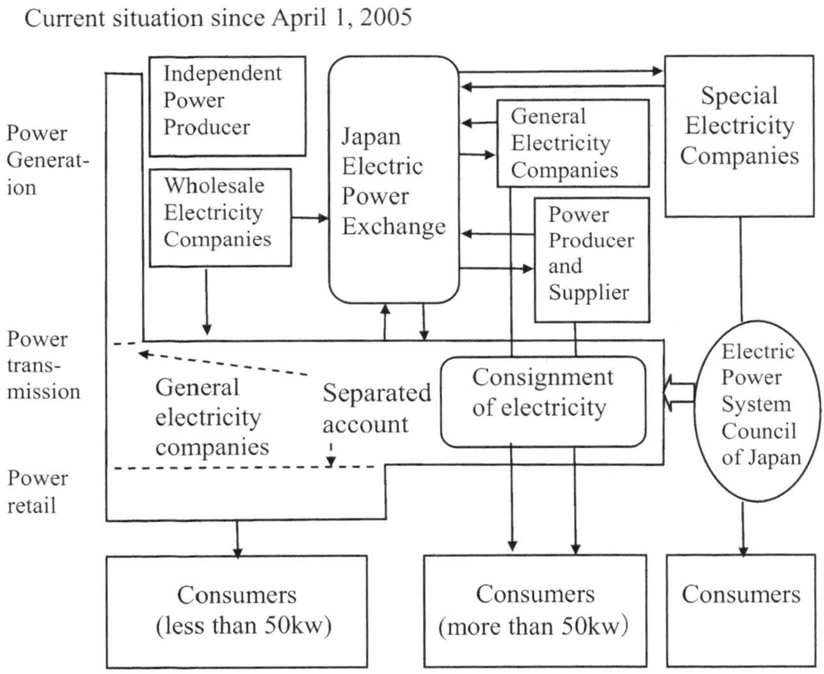

Current situation since April 1, 2005

Figure 3.4   Current Market Structure of the Electric Power Supply System

The third important point is that improvement has occurred in fairness and transparency in the field of transmission and distribution for new entrant companies as they access networks owned by the general electricity companies. In order to guarantee fair treatment, it was deemed that the field of transmission and distribution should be separated from other factors in the competition field, by such methods as (i) accounting separation, (ii) division separation, and (iii) legal separation (separation of company). After discussion, a committee of electric power enterprises chose accounting separation. In order for this system to work well, the Electric Power System Council of Japan, a neutral institution, was established.   As explained above, the role of this council is to make rules to ensure fair access to power transmission, to monitor the performance of electricity companies, and to facilitate mediation and conciliation among companies.

The government plans further liberalization in the electricity supply market, but the path to full liberalization is not easy.   According to Hattori (2004), there was considerable political debate for liberalization in the US.   Using US data, Hattori (2004) analyzes the determinants of liberalization decisions, and points out that the price level of electricity, the market share of private electricity companies, and the percentage of nuclear power plants have an impact on decisions regarding liberalization. Therefore, the road to full liberalization for customers with a demand of less than 50kw is still unclear.

5   EFFECTS OF REGULATORY REFORMS AND REMAINING ISSUES

5.1   Effects of Regulatory Reforms

Although Ezoe (2002) analyzes theoretical results related to the liberalization of the electricity market in Japan, in this section, I would like to focus on empirical results and remaining issues.

By estimating translog cost function, Ito et al. (2004) analyze the effects of regulatory reforms in the electric power industry.   Their conclusion is that the regulatory reforms in 1995 and in 2000 lowered costs in the electric power industry.   Compared to cases without regulatory reforms, the cost level between 1996 and 1999 was 7.5% lower and that between 2000 and 2002 was 11.8% lower.

Nakano and Managi (2008) evaluate the effect of deregulation over the period 1978 to 2003.   Although their analysis is limited to the steam power-generation sector, they conclude that regulatory reforms have contributed to productivity growth.

Goto and Sueyoshi (2009) evaluate productivity growth effects due to deregulation in the electricity supply industry.   They estimate the cost function of the electricity supply industry by using a data set from 1983 to 2003.   They also calculate the TFP (total factor productivity) growth rate and conclude that the empirical results indicate an improvement in productivity growth after deregulation.

Asano (2006) evaluates electricity rate as affected by regulatory reforms in the electricity supply industry, noting that this phase of deregulation contributed to an overall decline in electricity rates.   He reports that the integrated electricity supply companies reduced their rates in the regulated sector by 5.2 to 7.1 % in 2002.

Hattori (2007) analyzes the number of bidders in competitive procurement for electricity supply contracts in the electric power industry in Japan after 2000. He finds that contracts with higher load factors and multiple-year contracts tend to have fewer bidders but large-scale contracts and those for higher voltage tend to have more bidders.

Hattori (2006) analyzes whether or not patenting behavior of general electricity companies will have changed after liberalization of the electricity supply market in Japan. His statistical results show no clear effect, but Hattori notes that the amount of patenting by single electric power companies seems to increase. As for the amount of joint patenting with other general electricity companies, it is not clear whether it decreases.

Although Hosoe and Akiyama's (2009) study does not focus on regulatory impact, the authors obtained price elasticities during the regulatory change period. According to the estimation results of the demand function for nine regions in Japan from 1976 to 2006, the short-run price elasticity was 0.09 to 0.30, and the long-run price elasticity was 0.12 to 0.56.

5.2 Remaining Issues

Distributed electricity power generation might cause external diseconomies like air pollution, as Nishimura (2001) points out. Nishimura (2001) notes that newly developed power generation plants produced user benefits of about 40 billion yen annually attributable to liberalization policies but that possibly lower quality power distribution incurs potential risks to society.

Liberalization might hurt the stable supply of electricity by the nuclear power plant. In fact, Yajima (2001, 2002) notes a security problem in electricity supply. If we introduce pure and complete competition in the electric power supply market, the development of nuclear power plants would be very difficult, as Yajima (2001) maintains.

NOTES

[1] Terminology used to describe various approaches to changing the regulatory paradigm or organization and structure of the market is summarized in Sioshansi (2006, p.71). There are five kinds of regulatory reforms: (i) restructuring, (ii) liberalization, (iii)

privatization, (iv) corporatization, and (v) deregulation.

[2] Details regarding the Electric Power System Council of Japan are explained in Watanabe (2005).

4 Gas Utility

1 INTRODUCTION

The main purpose of this chapter is to overview the industrial structure and regulatory scheme of the gas utility industry. In terms of its general regulatory frame, the gas utility industry is similar to the electric power industry but is comprised of many more organizations than the electric power industry's 10 regional monopolistic privately owned companies. Furthermore, there co-exist both private and public gas providers, although most organizations in the gas utility industry are privately owned companies. Markets for large-scale consumers have been liberalized step by step since 1995. Liberalized markets represented only 36% of the market in 1995 but had expanded to 59% by 2007.

Competition has become severe in the gas supply market. For example, the gas utility industry must compete with the electric power industry for LNG, which is used in thermal power generation. In fact, according to Ide and Okamoto (2004), about 75% of LNG is used by the electric power industry as opposed to 25% by the gas utility industry, making it seem likely that electric power supply companies will enter the gas supply market as liberalization progresses.

In this chapter, I will explain the characteristics of the Japanese gas utility industry and its regulatory reforms. After an introduction, in the second section, the market structure of the gas utility industry in Japan is explained, with an overview of main suppliers and regulators. The third section summarizes the rate system and major price regulations. The fourth section concentrates on regulatory reforms and revisions in the gas utility industry since 1995, major changes having occurred in 1995, 1999, 2004, and 2007. The last section focuses on the effects of liberalization in the gas utility industry, although empirical investigation and evidence regarding this industry are less comprehensive than for other liberalized Japanese industries, such as rail and electricity.

2   CURRENT INDUSTRIAL STRUCTURE

2.1   The Market and Major Suppliers

The gas supply market in Japan can be divided into the regulated service market and the large-scale service market. The regulated service market consists of general gas users with an annual gas consumption of less than 100 thousand m^3. Entry into this market and the determination of rate are subject to the Gas Utility Enterprise Law (*Gasu Jigyo-ho*). The large-scale service market is for users of annual gas consumption of more than 0.1 million m^3. This market is characterized by free competition, gas rates being decided by the gas users themselves.

Based on the Gas Utility Enterprise Law, there are four kinds of suppliers in the gas supply industry in Japan: (i) general gas supply companies (*Ippan Gasu Jigyosha*), (ii) community gas supply companies (*Kani Gasu Jigyosha*), (iii) gas transmission and distribution companies (*Gasu Dokan Jigyosha*), and (iv) large-scale gas supply companies (*Oguchi Gasu Jigyosha*).

Using their own gas transmission and distribution networks, general gas supply companies provide gas service to general gas users such as households. In order to avoid duplicated investment in areas, general gas supply companies have been allowed to provide gas services monopolistically. At the same time, however, in order to protect regional users from the problems of monopoly, general gas supply companies are regulated by the government with regard to such matters as price and supply obligation.

Community gas supply companies provide gas service for specific small communities of more than 70 households in a housing complex. This category of organizations generates gas, mainly LP, using simplified gas generation facilities and transmitting and distributing it to the housing complex through the companies' own pipes. While regulations applied to this category of organization are not as strict as for general gas companies, the supply obligation is applied to this category and gas rates cannot be changed without government permission.

Gas transmission and distribution companies provide gas services by using their own networks. In general, this category provides gas services wholesale to either large-scale or general gas supply companies.

With the revision of the Gas Utility Enterprise Law in April of 1994, large-scale gas supply companies emerged as a category to signify those serving consumers with gas demands of more than 0.5 million m^3. But when the Gas Utility Enterprise Law was liberalized in 2007, this category came to designate companies providing gas services to consumers with demands of more than 0.1 million m^3 and became known for 'liberalized services,' whereby rate is decided on the basis of negotiation between demanders and suppliers. General gas supply companies are free to provide services to large-scale gas consumers located in different gas provision areas.

Table 4.1   Classification of Gas Utility Organizations

	General gas supply companies	Community gas supply companies	Gas transmission and distribution companies	Large-scale gas supply companies
Number of companies	212	1,601	18	28
Number of consumers (thousand)	28,380	1,500	n.a.	n.a.
Total sales (billion m^3)	32.6	0.2	n.a.	n.a.
Regulated services	○	○	—	—
Large-scale services (Free competition)	○	○	○	○

[Note]: These numbers are as of the end of March 2008.   This table was written by the author and is based on information obtained from the Agency of Natural Resources and Energy.

2.2 Regulator

The gas supply market's main regulator is the Agency of Natural Resources and Energy, an auxiliary of the Ministry of Economy, Trade and Industry (METI), which is ultimately responsible for the assessment of new entrants into the market, the approval of rates in the non-liberalized gas market, and the review of rate revision reports.

3 THE RATE SYSTEM AND PRICE REGULATION OF GAS UTILITY

3.1 Price Regulation

Gas utility rates in Japan have been regulated through an approval system, whereby the gas supply company submits a report of its rates to the government for assessment.   The deregulation of rates for large-scale gas consumers in March 1995 has led to gradual liberalization, details of which will be explained later.

In the gas utility industry in Japan, there are three kinds of rate regulation, a summary of which can be seen in Table 4.2.   First, suppliers in the market for large-scale gas consumers can set rates freely, with consumers free to purchase gas service from gas supply companies located in different areas, an option which presumably stimulates competition among gas supply companies for large-scale consumers and leads to rates being set on the basis of negotiation between suppliers and large-scale demanders.

Large-scale gas consumers are defined as consumers with a demand of more than 100 thousand m^3 of gas.   Examples of large-scale gas consumers are large factories, department stores and medium size office buildings.

The rate for smaller-scale gas consumers, on the other hand, is still regulated by the government.   As explained earlier, gas supply companies in this category are allowed to act as regional monopolies in providing gas services, with the government providing protection for consumers against unreasonably high rates and/or unfair treatment.   The government must approve rates affecting smaller-scale consumers in this category, such as general households, small shops, small office buildings, and so on.

While approval is not necessary when the rate for smaller-scale gas users is decreased, it is still necessary to report the rate change to the Minister of the METI.   This particular price deregulation went into effect in November 1999.

Table 4.2   Rate Regulation in the Gas Utility Industry in Japan

Category	Rate in partially liberalized markets (Large-scale gas users: more than 100 thousand m^3)	Rate in non-liberalized markets (Smaller-scale gas users: less than 100 thousand m^3)	
		Decrease the rate	Increase the rate
Type of regulation	Free	Report	Approval
Other regulations	None	(1) Order to change the rate, if necessary (2) Automatic adjustment scheme due to changes in fuel price	(1) Yardstick regulation scheme (2) Automatic adjustment scheme due to changes in fuel price
Examples of consumers	Medium scale factories, department stores, medium office buildings	Households, convenience stores, small shops, hospitals, small office buildings	

In the gas utility industry, there are three important schemes related to rate regulation. First, yardstick regulation is generally used when rates are to be set. Yardstick regulation, the details of which will be given in a later chapter, compares companies' performance in order to determine appropriate levels and changes in fare.

Second, the full cost principle is adopted to calculate price level. In essence, the rate revenues of gas suppliers pay all costs of providing gas services and generating an appropriate level of profit, a system very similar to that of the electric power industry in Japan.

Third, there is the automatic adjustment scheme, established in January 1996 so that changes in fuel price can be reflected quickly in gas rates.   When the price of the original sources for gas changes ±5% from the standard level, gas rates are adjusted automatically, with the rate being assessed every three months.

3.2   Basic Rate System and Variety of Rate

The gas rate system for households in Japan is in general based on a two-part tariff system consisting of a fixed (basic) rate and a variable rate. Figure 4.1 shows the two-part tariff with gradual increase by block (category), with both fixed and variable rates divided into several blocks (categories).   The number of blocks (categories) varies among gas companies.   Tokyo Gas, for example, divides rate into 6 blocks while Osaka Gas has 4 blocks.

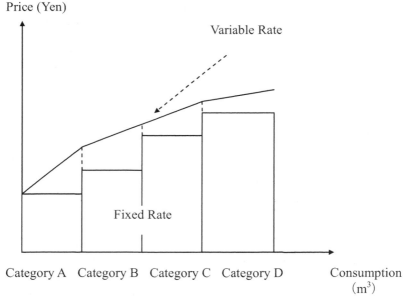

Figure 4.1   The Two-Part Tariff Rate System in the Gas Utility Industry: Conceptual Figure of the Rate with 4 Categories

In practice, there is much variety in the gas service pricing system, one example being the gas companies' strategy to increase demand for gas in the warmer seasons.   To address chronically low demand in the summer months, gas companies offer cheaper rates in this season, stimulating consumers to choose gas-based air conditioning systems, which helps sustain demand for gas during these months.

4 LIBERALIZATION IN THE GAS UTILITY INDUSTRY

4.1 Background of Liberalization

Like the electric power industry, the gas utility industry in Japan has traditionally been comprised of regional monopolies. However, as electric power and gas are the basic input materials in the Japanese manufacturing industry, manufacturers began to request that utility industries supply energy as efficiently and cheaply as possible.

To promote progress in manufacturing, the government began to mull reform of the energy industry. According to Fujiwara (2005), this policy change can be traced back to a report issued by the Ministry of Economy, Industry and Trade in May 1992, after which three important policies have been advanced by the government: (i) the development of facilities supplying natural gas; (ii) advances in the freedom of consumers to choose their energy suppliers; and (iii) a review of regulations for large-scale gas users. Regulatory reforms in the gas utility industry since 1992 have been carried out four times, with the revision of the Gas Utility Enterprise Law in 1995, 1999, 2004, and 2007.[1]

4.2 The Revision of the Gas Utility Enterprise Law in 1995

The Gas Utility Enterprise Law was revised in 1994 and enacted in March 1995. This revision is characterized by three important points of reform. First, the gas retail field was partially liberalized. Second, the systematic yardstick regulation scheme was applied in the assessment of gas rates in the smaller-scale gas user market. Third, the automatic adjustment scheme due to fuel price changes was installed.

First, as for liberalization in the retail field, a new category was established called the 'large-scale gas supply company,' defined as a supplier providing gas consumers with a demand of more than 2 million m³ annually. Entry regulations in this category were liberalized. A general gas supply company can simultaneously be a large-scale gas supply company, but in such a case, there are strict requirements that accounting for the general gas supply service be separated from accounting for the large-scale service.

Second, the yardstick regulation scheme was established to promote managerial efficiency at general gas supply companies. When the rate of the general gas supply companies is to be revised, the government evaluates a company's performance by comparing it with other companies. If a gas supply company's performance is inferior to others, then the rate revision is not approved and the company is required to make an effort to improve its performance before seeking further rate increases.

Last, in January 1996, the automatic adjustment scheme due to fuel price changes was installed in order to maintain efficient management.

The effects of liberalization in the gas retail field seem to be mild. According to Fujiwara (2005), the number of supply cases for large-scale users was not small: 726 cases in September 1998. However, there were only 8 cases of new entrants.

4.3   The Revision of the Gas Utility Enterprise Law in 1999

The revision of the Gas Utility Enterprise Law in 1999 has three important characteristics. First, the liberalization of the gas retail field was expanded. Second, the forwarding system of gas supply was developed. Third, price was essentially deregulated.

First, the definition of large-scale users as those with a demand of more than 2 million m^3 changed to consumers with a demand of more than 1 million m^3. As a result, the 36% of shares liberalized in March 1995 had increased to 40% in November 1999.

Second, as for the forwarding system of gas supply, four large private gas supply companies—Tokyo Gas, Osaka Gas, Toho Gas and Saibu Gas—were required to make stipulations for a forwarding system of gas supply, based on which smaller providers can furnish gas services by using the networks of the general gas companies. If the government deems the large gas companies' reported terms unfair to the smaller providers of gas, the government can order the four large private gas companies to change their stipulations.

Last, price regulation was changed from 'approval' to 'report' when the rate was decreased. When no increase occurs or is sought, no approval from the government is necessary. This reporting as opposed to petitioning represents partial liberalization.

4.4   The Revision of the Gas Utility Enterprise Law in 2004

The revision of the Gas Utility Enterprise Law was passed in the Diet in 2003 and enacted in April 2004. The revision contains three important points.

First, the liberalization of the gas retail field was expanded. The liberalized consumers were those with a demand of more than 0.5 million m³. These large-scale gas users could purchase gas from any provider, the result being that the liberalized market share increased to about 44% in April 2004.

Second, a new field of service, the category of 'gas transmission and distribution companies,' was established.

Last, the forwarding system of gas supply was expanded. The previous law included in this system only the four large private gas supply companies—Tokyo Gas, Osaka Gas, Toho Gas and Saibu Gas—but the revised law encompassed all general gas companies and the newly established gas transmission and distribution companies, which were thereby required to write their own stipulations, again with the government having the prerogative to order companies to change stipulations deemed unfair to gas providers.

4.5   The Revision of the Gas Utility Enterprise Law in 2007

The fourth major revision of the Gas Utility Enterprise Law was passed in the Diet in 2006 and enacted in April 2007. This revision further expanded liberalization to consumers with a gas demand of more than 0.1 million m³, increasing the liberalized market share to about 59% in April 2007. Also, rules regarding the gas supply forwarding system were changed.

5   EFFECT OF LIBERALIZATION IN THE GAS UTILITY INDUSTRY

Although there have been few empirical investigations of the effects of liberalization in the gas utility industry, some studies have reported effects. In this section, we will summarize the results of those studies.

Sumitomo Seimei Sogo Kenkyusho (1999) reports the economic effects of deregulation policies applied in the 90s to various industries such as public utilities, transportation, retail, and so on. Among these, the gas utility industry, the large-scale sector of which was liberalized during this period, was selected in order to assess deregulation policy. Based on statistical data, this study calculated users' benefits due to gas utility industry liberalization in both 1996 and 1997. Users' benefits are calculated as the total price reduction due to liberalization in the gas utility industry, which this study reports to have been about 53 billion yen on average between 1996 and 1997.

Ide (2004a) and Ide and Okamoto (2004) make an overall assessment and summarize the major effects of the liberalization of the gas utility industry since 1995.   First, they find that the number of new entrants into the large-scale gas service market increases steadily. Second, because of liberalization, costs have been reduced.   Last, many gas utility companies have reduced rates.   According to Ide (2004a), 34 gas companies reported gas utility rate decreases as of July 2002.   Thus, gas utility industry liberalization reduced costs and led to reduced gas rates.

Using quantitative methods, Kaino (2007) analyzes regulatory effects.   According to his results, average costs decreased over the past 15 years by about 15 to 20%, of which about 4 to 5% can be attributed to liberalization.   However, Kaino points out some problems.   Cost reductions due to gas utility industry liberalization certainly caused reductions in gas rates for the industrial sector.   However, gas rates for households did not change.   Noting that consumer surplus increased for the industrial but decreased for the household sector, Kaino identifies problems remaining despite the progress in the liberalization of the gas utility industry.

NOTE

[1] As for gas utility liberalization in 1995 and 1999, see, for example, Kusano (2002).

5   Water Supply

1   INTRODUCTION

While private companies provide electric power, gas utility, and railway transportation in Japan, water is supplied by the public sector, in contrast to the situation in countries such as France and the UK, where the water supply, according to Ishii (2005a), is handled by the private sector.   In France, for example, although the government is ultimately responsible for ensuring that users have access to water, about 78% of the water supply industry is comprised of private companies holding contracts with the government.   In the UK, the water supply industry has been privatized.   Although the market size of the water supply industry in Japan is 2.9 trillion yen per year, the industry remains in the public domain.

The basic principles of the Japanese water supply industry have traditionally been that water is managed with a self-supporting system and is in general supplied by municipal governments.   This system remained essentially unchanged until 2002, when the private sector began to be allowed to participate partially, under government contract, in the management of water supply facilities.   Compared with other utility industries in Japan, however, the role of the private sector in the water supply industry is minimal.

In this chapter, we will explain characteristics of the industrial structure, regulation, and regulatory reforms of the water supply industry in Japan.

2   THE CURRENT SITUATION OF WATER SUPPLY IN JAPAN

As Table 5.1 shows, in Japan the diffusion rate of water by pipe is near

100%.   While the rate hovered around 91.5% in 1980, by 2005, 97.2% of the nation was supplied by piped water.   The quality of the water is high and continues to improve.   While city dwellers formerly complained of a chemical smell resulting from agents used to protect against mold, in recent years, as water purification systems have improved and become more effective, the number of complaints has decreased.

Table 5.1   Trends in Water Supply in Japan

Fiscal Year	1980	1985	1990	1995	2000	2005
Total population	116,680	121,005	123,557	125,424	126,901	127,709
Water supply population	106,914	112,811	116,692	120,096	122,560	124,122
Diffusion rate (%)	91.5	93.3	94.7	95.8	96.6	97.2

[Note]:
(1)   This table was written by the author and is based on information from the Japan Waterworks Association (2007, p.32).
(2)   Unit: thousand persons.

One important characteristic of Japan's water supply industry is that water supply organizations are managed with a self-supporting accounting system whereby all costs related to water supply, including capital, are covered by water user charges.   Another distinguishing characteristic is that the water supply has been under the management of municipal governments.

Facilities for water supply have been constructed in almost every city.   However, according to Ishii (2005a), about 60% of current water supply facilities, most of which were built in the 1950s and 60s, are nearing their estimated limits for use and are due for overhaul.

Besides the refurbishment of aging facilities, another urgent task faced by the water supply industry is to level out water supply organizations' prices, which have grown unacceptably disparate.   Ishii (2005a) notes that the highest priced water is about 10 times more expensive than the cheapest.   Even in comparison to the national average price of water in Japan, the most expensive water costs twice as much, one reason being the huge variation in the size of organizations supplying water.

3   INDUSTRIAL STRUCTURE OF THE WATER SUPPLY INDUSTRY

3.1   Kinds of Water Supply Organizations

The Waterworks Law (*Suido-ho*) defines a 'water supply organization' as one providing water for 100 people or more, and excludes organizations supplying water to less than 100 people.

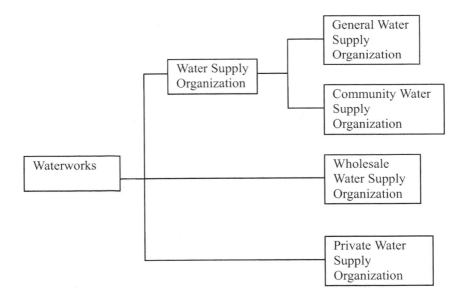

Figure 5.1   Major Waterworks Organizations

Water supply organizations include general water supply organizations (*Josuido Jigyosha*), those providing water for more than 5,000 people, and community water supply organizations (*Kani Suido Jigyosha*), which serve less than 5,000 people.   These organizations are considered general water retailers.

The most typical among waterworks entities is the general water

Regulatory Reform of Public Utilities

supply organization, which takes water from the source, mainly rivers and lakes, and after purification distributes it to final users such as households. Some general water supply organizations purchase purified water from wholesale water supply organizations.

Community water supply organizations, which in general provide water to small communities in rural areas, use relatively simple water supply facilities. Most of these organizations are held by the public sector.

Wholesale water supply organizations (*Suido Yosui Kyokyu Jigyosha*), mostly public entities owned by prefectural governments, provide water to supply organizations, not directly to consumers.

Private water supply organizations (*Senyo Suido Jigyosha*) provide water to small communities with more than 100 people, such as housing complexes and/or company housing.

At the end of FY2005, there were 17,109 organizations in Japan, 1,602 of which were general water supply organizations, 7,794 community water supply organizations, 102 wholesale water supply organizations and 7,611 private water supply organizations.

Table 5.2 shows trends in the number of waterworks organizations.

Table 5.2 Trends in the Number of Waterworks Organizations

Organization	Type of provider	1985	1990	Year 1995	2000	2005
General water supply organization	Prefecture	6	6	6	5	5
	City, town	1,837	1,872	1,859	1,865	1,541
	Cooperation	78	76	76	78	47
	Private company	13	13	11	10	9
	Subtotal	1,934	1,964	1,952	1,958	1,602
Community water supply organization	Public organization	8,513	8,221	8,022	7,576	6,802
	Others	2,790	2,325	1,806	1,403	992
	Subtotal	11,303	10,546	9,828	8,979	7,794
Wholesale water supply organization	Prefecture	48	48	46	46	45
	City, town	1	2	2	3	2
	Cooperation	49	52	62	62	55
	Subtotal	98	105	110	111	102
Private water supply organization		4,177	4,277	4,090	3,754	7,611
Total		17,512	16,892	15,980	14,802	17,109

[Note]:
(1) This table was written by the author and is based on information from the Japan Waterworks Association.
(2) Values in this table are for the number of organizations in each category.

As mentioned earlier, it is municipal governments (cities, towns, and villages) that in general manage Japan's water supply through bureaus that supply general households. Though private water supply companies exist, they are rare.

In 2005, 1,541 of 1,602 general water supply organizations, or about 96%, belonged to municipal governments. This represented a rather dramatic 20% decrease compared with the number in 2000. The decrease can be attributed to the enactment of a government policy, the Special Law on the Merger of Municipalities (*Shichoson no Gappei no Tokurei ni Kansuru Horitsu*), which resulted in many municipalities' merging and consolidating their services.

3.2   Size Distribution of General Water Supply Organizations

A striking feature of the Japanese water supply industry is that there is such variation in the size of organizations comprising it. Table 5.3 shows that in 2005, of 1,602 general water supply organizations, about 73% were small-sized organizations providing water to municipalities with populations of less than 50 thousand.

Because the smaller municipalities have no scale merit, it is clear that the policy encouraging mergers is sensible, as shown by empirical studies on economies of scale and density and/or scope in the water supply industry in Japan (e.g. Kuwahara (1998), Takada and Shigeno (1998), Mizutani and Urakami (2001), Nakayama (2002)). According to Mizutani and Urakami (2001), the organization size attaining the minimum average costs is one serving about 800 thousand people. Furthermore, Urakami and Parker (2009) show in an empirical study of Japanese water supply organizations that consolidation clearly reduced costs. However, consolidating water supply organizations is not easy, as evidenced by Urakami's (2008) study, which reports that even after municipal governments are consolidated, about half of related water supply organizations remain separate organizations.

Last, vertical integration (of water distribution and wholesale water organizations) might be an issue of concern to policy makers, an example of which would be Osaka city's water supply organization (water distribution organization), which is integrated with Osaka prefecture's organization (wholesale water organization). According to Urakami (2007), the integrated system is better in terms of cost efficiency.

Table 5.3   Size Distribution of General Water Supply Organizations in
*   2005*

Water supply population	Number of organizations	
More than 1 million	14	0.9%
500 ～ 1,000 thousand	10	0.6%
250 ～ 500 thousand	57	3.6%
100 ～ 250 thousand	133	8.3%
50 ～ 100 thousand	208	13.0%
10 ～ 50 thousand	715	44.6%
Less than 10 thousand	454	28.3%
Under construction	11	0.7%
Total	1,602	100.0%

[Note]: This table was written by the author and is based on information from the
Japan Waterworks Association (2007, p.29).

4   REGULATIONS FOR THE INDUSTRY

There are two important principles in the water supply industry in Japan:
water supply is the concern of municipalities, and water supply
organizations have a self-supporting accounting system.

According to Ishii (2005a), waterworks in Japan fall into the public
sector because water is considered closely related to public health, which
depends on preventing the spread of disease, and because the control of
water is vital in the management of natural disasters such as, for example,
the widespread fires likely to follow an earthquake.

Enacted in 1957, the basic law for the water supply industry, the

Waterworks Law, rules essentially that water supply organizations be overseen by municipalities. Moreover, municipal governments' public corporations are regulated by the Local Public Corporation Law (*Chiho Koei Kigyo-ho*), established in 1952, which stipulates that public corporations be managed by self-supporting accounting systems.

4.1 Regulators

There are two important regulators in the water supply industry. Using the Waterworks Law as reference, the Ministry of Health, Labor and Welfare (MHLW) is responsible for the overall activities of the water supply industry, such as quality standards, provision criteria, price regulations, and so on.

The second important regulator is the Ministry of Internal Affairs and Communications (MIC). Water supply organizations are self-supporting and receive no subsidies from the general account, and the MIC administers these entities as local public corporations.

Although not regulatory bodies per se, municipalities' local assemblies play a vital role in water supply organizations, especially in matters related to charges and fees.

4.2 Entry and Exit Regulations

It is necessary to be granted permission by the Ministry of Health, Labor and Welfare (MHLW) to enter the water supply market, according to the Waterworks Law, which stipulates as criteria for permission that there be no overlapping water supply in the area.

Thus, each water supply organization is given the status of a regional monopoly, although water supply services are highly regulated by the government, which does not allow regional water supply organizations to discontinue services except in the event of interruption by natural disaster. However, according to the Association of Water and Sewage Works Consultants Japan (2004), if waterworks organizations change hands, they must file reports apprising the regulatory body of any such transactions.

5 PRICE REGULATION AND THE RATE SYSTEM

5.1 Price Regulation

The basic principle for determining water rates is self-support. That is, beneficiaries pay their own full costs. All costs related to water supply, including the cost of capital, must be covered by water user charges without assistance from municipalities' general accounts.[1] According to Ishii (2005a), suppliers can easily identify water users, determine their level of use, and charge accordingly.

It is municipalities that provide water to their citizens, with local assemblies approving water rates. Users are afforded some protection by the Local Public Corporation Law, which describes water charge regulations, stipulates that water rates must be non-discriminatory, requires that any change in water rates be reported to the Minister of Health, Labor and Welfare, and stipulates that water supply costs be covered by revenues, under the efficient management of the water supply organization.

5.2   The Rate System

The rate system in the water supply industry is in general a two-part tariff system consisting of a basic (fixed) rate and a variable rate. Basic rate charges are for expenses unrelated to water volume, while variable rate charges reflect how much water volume is consumed. Figure 5.2 shows a conceptual figure of the rate system for water supply.

Price (Yen)

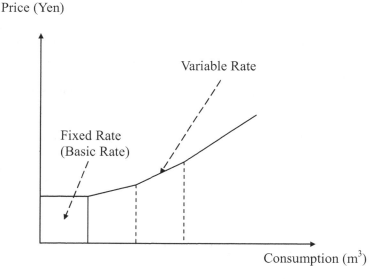

Figure 5.2   The Two-Part Tariff Rate System
in the Water Supply Industry

Different rate systems apply to two different groups. One rate system is based on the type of water consumer, whether households, commercial establishments, factories, or so on. The other rate system classifies consumers according to the width, or caliber, of water pipes by which they are served. According to the Association of Water and Sewage Works Consultants Japan (2004), about 40% of water supply organizations use the rate system classifying according to user types while about 50% use the rate system based on pipe caliber.

One important characteristic of the rate system in Japan is that the variable rate increases as more water is used. For example, in the case of Osaka city, the variable rate for households is 97 yen for the range of 0 – 20 m^3, 124 yen for 20 – 30 m^3, 168 yen for 30 – 50 m^3, and so on. Ishii (2005a) attributes the adoption of the variable rate scheme to policy makers' interest in encouraging water conservation.

The rate system is also characterized by the fact that many municipalities have adopted a 'basic water volume system (*Kihon Suiryo Sei*),' whereby variable rates do not apply to users who consume no more than the designated minimum monthly volume. For example, Tokyo's basic water volume for households is $10m^3$. Households using less than this amount are subject only to the basic rate and need pay no extra variable charge.

5.3 Major Policy Issues regarding Water Prices

There are four important policy issues related to water charges. First, there is the aforementioned huge variation in water fees among municipalities. According to Ishii (2005a), the most expensive organization is Gunma Prefecture's Naganohara town, which charges 3,255 yen per month per m^3. This is in contrast to Yamanashi Prefecture's Kawaguchiko Minami public corporation, which charges only 335 yen per month per m^3. Although there are several factors contributing to price disparity, the most obvious seems to be the wide size variation in the organizations supplying water. Beginning in the 1990s, the government has encouraged mergers among smaller water supply organizations. What might be the most reasonable size for a water supply organization? Based on an econometric analysis by Mizutani and Urakami (2001) of water supply organizations in Japan, an organization serving about 800 thousand was able to attain the minimum average cost.

Second, questions have arisen about the variable rate scheme policy whereby water becomes more expensive the higher the volume used. From an environmental point of view, this policy has helped limit consumption. Large-scale users especially, such as private companies, factories, and department stores, have made serious efforts to conserve water. However, there have been cases recently when private organizations, in order to avoid steeply higher charges because of their extensive water needs, have directly tapped underground water sources for their own use. Concerned by such developments, some municipalities have begun to rethink the increasing variable rate scheme.

Also under review is the 'basic water volume system,' whereby users consuming less water than a designated volume pay only a basic fee and no variable costs. This system has been likened to a social welfare scheme because revenues for the minimum monthly water volume do not cover costs. As water supply organizations steadily come under more financial strain, it is expected that the basic water volume system, perceived by users as unfair, will be abandoned or reformed.

Last, the current rate system does not provide funds for investment in the renovation of existing facilities, a shortcoming that has recently concerned many municipalities with aging facilities.

6   REGULATORY REFORMS IN THE WATER SUPPLY INDUSTRY

Compared with reform measures in other Japanese public utility industries such as the electric power and railway industries, change has been slow to come in the water supply industry. The two basic tenets of the industry—that water supply organizations must be financially self-supporting and managed by municipalities—have not changed at all. There have been, however, certain other important changes.

6.1   The Revision of the Waterworks Law in 2002

The Waterworks Law was revised on July 4, 2001, and enacted in April 2002. Before the revision of the law, which included the approval of a comprehensive contracting out scheme, it had been required that activities related to waterworks be carried out only by water supply organizations. The revision allowed water supply organizations to outsource some activities to private companies. A typical case of a waterworks company's contracting out its activities was outsourcing the operation of water purification plants.

The main reason for this revision was the stringent economic conditions facing water supply organizations, many of which have been forced to reduce the number of their employees and can no longer afford to retain specialists such as water purification engineers within their own organizations. To ameliorate these tough management conditions, outsourcing was seen as an alternative. It is expected that regulations will continue to change to reflect the changing conditions and needs of the water supply industry.

6.2 The Revision of the Local Autonomy Law in 2003

On September 2, 2003, the Local Autonomy Law (*Chiho Jichi-ho*) was revised, and a 'Designated Manager System (*Shitei Kanrisha Seido*)' was introduced to allow the private sector to take on the responsibility of the management of public facilities. According to Ishii (2005a), the introduction of this system made it possible for waterworks activities to be managed by members of the private sector, but the waterworks themselves would remain in the public domain, with private ownership of water supply facilities continuing to be prohibited.

NOTE

[1] There are some cases where water supply organizations may receive assistance from the general account, a typical example being to cover the costs of installing fire hydrants. According to Ishii (2005a), although this is related to fire protection activity, the water supply section installs the equipment and is reimbursed from the general account.

PART III

Transport Industries

6 Railway

1 INTRODUCTION

The main purpose of this chapter is to explain the industrial structure and regulatory scheme of the rail industry in Japan, which is comprised of more than 200 rail organizations. Most are privately owned entities where train operation and infrastructure are integrated, in contrast to the organizations making up the rail industry in Europe. Moreover, the privatization in 1987 of the former state railway, the Japan National Railway (JNR), has differed from the privatization process in other countries, with regulatory changes in Japan appearing rather moderate compared to the radical reforms taking place in, for example, the UK. Instead of introducing direct competition among operators, the indirect competition scheme of yardstick regulation has been adopted.

After the introduction, in the second section, the organizational structure of the rail industry in Japan is explained, with attention to analyzing the demand situation and classifying types of rail operators. The third section summarizes regulations in the rail industry, including those regarding entry and exit, fare, rail track fees, and others. The fourth section recounts regulatory reforms in the rail industry, beginning in 1987, when the JNR privatization began, and covering the various reforms that have been enacted since then. Last, I will discuss the competitive situation in the railway industry. In this section, I will explain how competition policies taken in Japan differ from those favored in Europe.

2 ORGANIZATION OF THE JAPANESE RAIL INDUSTRY

2.1 The Demand Situation in Rail Transportation

Rail, especially passenger rail, remains a very important transportation mode in Japan.   Table 6.1 shows the transportation situation as of 2005. Although auto transportation has been growing as in other countries, the share of rail transportation was 27.7% in terms of passenger-km in 2005. Especially in large metropolitan areas such as Tokyo, Osaka, and Nagoya, railways remain the dominant transportation mode for commuters.

Although Japanese passenger railways are financially healthy and performing well, as noted by Mizutani and Shoji (2007), freight transportation by rail is less prevalent, with auto and ship dominating the freight transportation market.   In 2005, the share of freight rail transportation was only 4.0% in terms of ton-km.

Table 6.1   The Transport Situation in 2005

	Rail	Auto	Ship	Airplane
Number of passenger-km (million)	391,215	933,006	4,025	83,220
Share of transport in terms of passenger-km (%)	27.7	66.1	0.3	5.9
Number of ton-km (million)	22,813	334,979	211,576	1,075
Share of transport in terms of ton-km (million)	4.0	58.7	37.1	0.2

[Note]: These statistics were taken from a data source of the Ministry of Land, Infrastructure and Transport (2008).

2.2   Kinds of Rail Operators

As of July 1, 2008, there were 201 organizations defined as rail operators (Ministry of Land, Infrastructure and Transport, 2008), of which 168 were heavy and light rail operators, while the remaining 33 were operators of monorails, automated guideway transit, cable cars, and such. Of the 168 rail organizations, an overwhelming number—155—were passenger rail operations, with freight rail organizations numbering only 13.

As noted by Mizutani (1999b), passenger rails in Japan can be classified in four ways: by their legal category, ownership status, transport type, and main service area. First, as for legal classification, there are three categories in Japan: private corporations, special corporations, and public organizations. As used here, private corporations are organizations legally considered to be private companies, but these are not always the equivalent of what is commonly known as fully private organizations. The category includes organizations which have portions of their shares held by the public sector. A public organization is usually a department of the government, most often sections of local governments, for example the bureau of transportation in the city of Kobe. A special corporation is an organization that is set up and regulated by special law (Uekusa, 1991). For example, the JR companies established at the time of the Japan National Railway privatization are considered special corporations because they remain subject to the special JR law enacted for their regulation. Thus, special corporations and public organizations fall under the broad definition of public corporation.

Second, as for ownership, there are three categories: private, public, and private-public joint ownership. Most Japanese rail operators are privately owned. Well known examples of the 15 large private railways are the Tokyo-based Tokyu and Seibu rail companies, and the Osaka-based Hankyu and Kintetsu rail companies, which are widely considered the most efficient railway organizations. Public ownership is limited to only 11 operators. Of these 11 publicly owned operators, 9 are subway systems such as Tokyo, Osaka, and Nagoya, with each system owned and operated by its respective city government (i.e. the transportation bureau of the city government). Although three major JR companies—JR East, JR Central and JR West—have been fully privatized, the smaller JRs—JR Hokkaido, JR Shikoku and JR Kyushu—have yet to be fully privatized, with most of their shares still held by the government. Private-public jointly owned organizations comprise what is often called the third sector in Japan, and such jointly owned organizations are most often found in small communities.

Last, as for the type of transportation and service area, the most common type of rail organization is the urban railway. Most railway companies operate in large metropolitan areas. The 15 large private railways, 9 public subway systems, and medium-size private railways are almost all urban operators.   However, the JR companies offer both urban and intercity rail services, with JR East, JR West and JR Central operating the famous bullet train intercity Shinkansen system, as well as providing rail services within large metropolitan areas such as Tokyo, Osaka and Nagoya.

3   REGULATION

3.1   General Regulations

Although progress has been made toward deregulation, in fact the railway industry in Japan remains highly regulated.   The Railway Business Law (*Tetsudo Jigyo-ho*), has applied to all rail companies since April 1, 1987, when the privatization of Japan National Railway (JNR) was enacted. Before the 1987 privatization, regulations applicable to JNR differed from those affecting other railways: JNR was subject to the Japan National Railway Law (*Nihon Kokuyu Tetsudo-ho*), while other railways, such as private railways and public subway systems, were subject to the Local Railway Law (*Chiho Tetsudo-ho*).   In addition to the Railway Business Law, there are more than 150 laws directed at the industry and enforced by the Ministry of Land, Infrastructure and Transport (MLIT).

3.2   Entry and Exit Regulations

Table 6.2 shows entry and exit regulations in the railway industry.   In order to enter the market, it is necessary for a rail organization to secure permission from the Minister of Land, Infrastructure and Transport. According to the Railway Business Law (Article 3), if an organization is deemed qualified by the Minister of Land, Infrastructure and Transport, then the organization can commence rail services.   Before 2000, entry was based on a license system but has since become based on a permission system.

As for the rail business in Japan, services are classified into three categories based on the Railway Business Law (Article 2): Class 1 to Class 3, summarized as follows.

Class 1: enterprises that provide rail passenger and/or freight services while holding their own rail infrastructure;

Class 2: enterprises that provide rail passenger and/or freight services using rail infrastructure owned by another organization;

Class 3: enterprises that build rail infrastructure for sale to a class 1 enterprise, or enterprises which own infrastructure and rent it to a class 2 enterprise.

Table 6.2   Entry and Exit Regulation in the Rail Industry

Kinds of regulation	Major points
Entry regulation	Permission system (individual operator basis) There are 3 classes. Class 1: Integrated rail organization Class 2: Rail operation organization Class 3: Infrastructure organization
Exit regulation	Report in advance (1 year prior)

The most striking feature of the Japanese rail industry is that vertical integration is the norm.   Unlike in the European Union, where vertical (operation-infrastructure) separation is a common policy, in Japan, most railway organizations are class 1 enterprises, well known examples being JR East and JR West, large private railways such as Tokyu and Kintetsu, and public subway systems such as Osaka's and Nagoya's subway networks.

On the other hand, there are few class 2 and class 3 enterprises in Japan.   A typical example of a class 2 enterprise is JR Freight, which provides freight service by using rail tracks belonging to the six JR passenger companies.

An example of a class 3 enterprise is Kobe Rapid Transit Railway (*Kobe Kosoku*), a rail track holding company connecting points in downtown Kobe.   Although further details regarding Kobe Kosoku can be found in Mizutani and Shoji (2004), the arrangement is that four private rail operating companies—Hankyu, Hanshin, Sanyo and Kobe Dentetsu—provide rail operating services by using rail tracks owned by Kobe Kosoku.   In other words, Kobe Kosoku owns the track and collects fees for its use by the four private operators.

Categories are not exclusive.   It is possible for an individual rail organization to fall into more than one category. A private railway might engage in various operations that would cause it to be classified as both class 1 and class 2. For example, in the abovementioned case of the Kobe Kosoku line, Hankyu Railway is considered a class 2 enterprise because a section of its services involves running its own trains on tracks belonging to the Kobe Kosoku company. In its relation with the Kobe Kosoku Line, then, Hankyu is a class 2 enterprise. However, most of Hankyu's extensive network is considered a class 1 enterprise because Hankyu owns the remaining rail tracks on which its trains operate.

Article 5 of the Railway Business Law describes the criteria for obtaining permission to operate a rail business. The Minister of Land, Infrastructure and Transport gives a rail operator permission to provide rail services if these four criteria are met: (i) the plan is sound from a business point of view; (ii) the plan is adequate from a safety point of view; (iii) there are adequate operational plans in addition to an overall plan; and (iv) the potential entrant takes on financial and technological liability.

In general, the duration of permission is not stated in the Railway Business Law. Therefore, once a rail operator is allowed to operate the rail service, the operator is indefinitely responsible for providing rail services, except in cases where permission is cancelled due to negligence, or where the operator voluntarily exits the market.

Figure 6.1 shows the exit procedure under the regional council system.

Exit regulations were also lightened after deregulation. The former regulation required operators to obtain permission to exit the market, but the new regulation, the Railway Business Law (Article 28.1), requires only that operators notify the Ministry of Land, Infrastructure and Transport one year prior to terminating rail services. However, in order to quell concern that rail services in rural areas might be too easily abandoned, the regional council system was also instituted.

If there are dissenting opinions with regard to the termination of rail services, the problem is discussed in the regional council, a body comprised of related organizations such as the municipal government, the prefectural government, the rail operator, and so on. The purpose of the regional council is to serve as a mediator or conduit between rail operators and rail users. For example, regional councils are likely to discuss such matters as whether or not the rail operator might be able to continue providing service if the government agrees to provide operating subsidies, or, if termination of services is unavoidable, what alternative transportation modes, such as bus services, can be guaranteed for regional users.

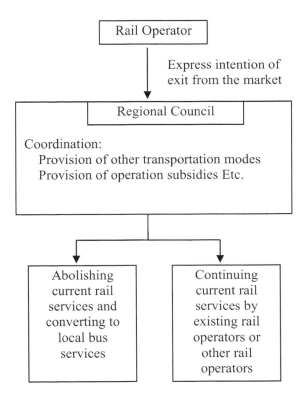

Figure 6.1   The Exit Procedure System in the Regional Council

3.3   Fare Regulation

Fare Regulation

Rail fare in Japan is regulated according to Article 16 of the Railway Business Law.   In general, the full cost principle is applied.   As for fare regulation, there are several important points, as can be seen in Table 6.3.

First, the ceiling price of rail fare is set by the government and must be approved by the Ministry of Land, Infrastructure and Transport.

Second, as mentioned above, because the Japanese railway industry is based upon the full cost principle, it is assumed that rail fare will cover rail costs plus generate profits for the operator.   Generally rail operators are expected not to receive subsidies.   Therefore, in general, the ceiling price level is set to cover rail costs.

Third, as for changes in rail fare, if the changed fare falls under the ceiling price, the rail operator does not need approval by the regulator, but needs only to report the change to the Ministry.

Fourth, in order to avoid inefficient rail operation management, the regulator applies yardstick regulation, the details of which are explained in a different chapter, but the essence of which is that the regulator evaluates the performance of a rail operator by using common measures such as average cost.   If an operator's performance is inferior to the standard level, then the regulator as a penalty orders the operator to reduce costs.   Since 1997, yardstick regulation has been applied to three railway groups: the JR passenger companies, 15 large private railways, and 10 subway systems.

Fifth, operators are required only to report to the Ministry when setting up new fares, such as for express service.   If the rail fare increase can be shown to discriminate against any group and/or if the fare causes unfair competition with other railways, the Ministry can order a revision in the fare.

Table 6.3   Fare Regulation in the Rail Industry

Kinds of regulation	Major points
Ceiling price	Approval
Price under the ceiling price	Report
Incentive system	Yardstick regulation
Fare level	Full cost principle as standard cost
Other fares	Report There is a wide variety of rail fares (express, off-peak discount tickets, etc.)

The Fare System

There are four major kinds of rail fare systems in Japan, as Figure 6.2 shows. With the first, a km-based fare system, fare level increases according to distance traveled (km). This fare system is used in the JR passenger companies.

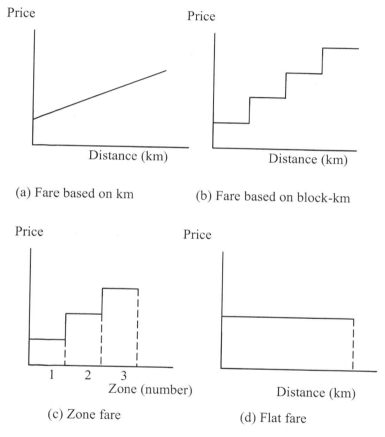

Figure 6.2 Major Fare Systems in the Rail Industry

Second is the fare system based on block-km, whereby fare accumulates with each block traveled.   For example, if a rail operator takes 3km as one block, the fare increases every 3km.   The block-km system is the most commonly adopted fare system among Japanese rail operators, including the 15 large private railway companies and 10 subway systems.

Third is the zone rail fare system, which divides the rail network into more than two zones, with the fare level increasing in the   proportion to the number of zones through which users pass.   Eizan Dentetsu in Kyoto uses the zone rail fare system.

The fourth rail fare system is the flat fare, with uniform charges regardless of distance traveled.   This fare system is used by light rail organizations such as Hiroshima Dentetsu and Toyohashi Dentetsu.

3.4   Rail Track Fee Regulations

As explained above, in Japan, there are few rail infrastructure providers categorized as class 3 organizations.   Therefore, regulations regarding rail track fees remain rather general.   For example, Article 15 of the Rail Business Law states only that class 1 or class 3 organizations must gain approval of their rail track fees from the Ministry of Land, Infrastructure and Transport.   The Ministry does not regulate the amounts paid by rail operators to track holding organization, but does require that track fees and conditions of usage be approved by the Ministry.

There are no specific criteria for the assessment of rail track fees. However, Article 30 of the Enforcement Regulation of the Railway Business Law (*Tetsudo Jigyo Seko Kisoku*) describes the requirement that the provider submit documents for evaluation by the Ministry of Land, Infrastructure and Transport.   These documents detail how rail track fees are calculated.

There is no single method for setting rail track fees in Japan.   As for JR Freight, avoidable cost principle is used.   In general, because rail track fees are set up to cover providers' cost, the Ministry of Land Infrastructure and Transport assesses whether or not the cost is reasonable.

3.5   Other Regulations

One important feature of the rail industry in Japan is that private railway companies play such a vital role. Because private railways also engage in non-rail services such as real estate development and retail sales,[1] some researchers might raise the concern that the good financial performance of these Japanese private railways can be attributed to cross-subsidization from their non-rail business. However, while Japanese private railways have long been allowed to conduct non-rail as well as rail business, with many private rail companies engaging in real estate development, retail ventures such as department stores, and other transportation businesses such as bus and taxi services, rail business and non-rail business are strictly separated according to Railway Accounting Regulations (*Tetsudo Kaikei Kisoku*). A railway company is forbidden to allocate rail and non-rail cost at its own discretion, but must follow accounting regulations describing in detail how to allocate the costs of common facilities and administration.

Therefore, it is possible to capture externality in the effects of rail-company generated housing developments along rail lines, for example, but railway organizations must avoid intentional cross-subsidy strategies like charging high rail fares or transferring costs to and from non-rail services.

3.6 Regulators

It is mainly the Ministry of Land, Infrastructure and Transportation's responsibility to make and enforce regulations as well as to formulate policy in the rail industry. As mentioned above, this regulator must approve the ceiling price for local rail service. Furthermore, in order to apply yardstick regulation to the rail service industry, the results of several performance evaluation measures are collected and the standard costs of each operator are determined by this regulator. Subsidies are extensive, but the subsidy scheme for the rail operators is administrated by the Ministry of Land, Infrastructure and Transportation.

In addition to the Ministry of Land, Infrastructure and Transportation, the Ministry of Internal Affairs and Communications (MIAC) plays a role in publicly owned subway systems. Related to this ministry is the Local Public Corporation Law (*Chiho Koei Kigyo-ho*), which details rules regarding the administrative responsibilities and the corporate bonds of public corporations.

4 REGULATORY REFORMS IN THE RAILWAY INDUSTRY

Deregulation in the rail industry has been gradual, with major regulatory reforms taking place three times. The first reform, on April 1, 1987, was the enactment of the Railway Business Law (*Tetsudo Jigyo-ho*), which brought about the privatization of the JNR.   The second reform was the introduction in 1997 of ceiling price and yardstick regulation.   The third reform was the modification of the Railway Business Law in 2000.   In this section, I will explain the changes that occurred on these three occasions.

4.1   Enactment of the Railway Business Law in 1987

In 1987, an epoch-making reform took place in the railway industry. The former state railway organization, Japan National Railway (JNR) was privatized and subdivided into 6 regional passenger JR companies and one nationwide JR freight company.   The details of the JNR privatization are explained in a different chapter.[2]

With the advent of the JR companies in 1987 came the introduction of the Railway Business Law, comprised of new regulations to replace those contained in the Japan National Railway Law (*Nihon Kokuyu Tetsudo-ho*), which had applied to the former JNR before 1987, and the Local Railway Law (*Chiho Tetsudo-ho*), which had applied to other railways such as private railways and public subway systems.

The Railway Business Law stipulated that in order for organizations to provide rail service, they must obtain a license and be classified as class 1, class 2, and/or class 3 organizations.

4.2 The Regulatory Reform of 1997

Further regulatory reform in the rail industry took place in 1997, mainly with regard to fare.   Although details of the regulatory reform can be found in Okabe (1997, 2004), two important points can be summarized as follows.

First, the ceiling price system was adopted.   The ceiling price is obtained as each individual railway company's full cost level.   The ceiling price in Japan is different from the general ceiling price under the price-cap regulation, which is obtained by the deflator of the consumer price index (CPI).   The ceiling price must be approved by the regulator. However, if the price level is below the ceiling, it is not necessary to gain approval for the fare.   The rail operator need only report the price level to the regulator.

Second, comprehensive yardstick regulation was installed, details of which are explained in a separate chapter.   Before 1997, yardstick regulation had been applied to large private railway companies, with some degree of effect, according to Mizutani (1997).   However, the new yardstick regulation scheme was different from the old scheme in the following ways.

First, the old yardstick regulation was applied to only 15 large private railways. In the newly established comprehensive yardstick regulation scheme, three kinds of railway groups are included: (i) 15 large private railway companies; (ii) 6 JR passenger companies; and (iii) 10 subway systems.

Second, with the newly established yardstick regulation system, information about such matters as the standard average cost for the assessment of each individual rail operator and the methods of evaluation are transparent and open to the public. In the old system, information about measures and methods of evaluation were unavailable to the public. The new system puts pressure on railway companies to improve their efficiency.

Third, the new yardstick regulation contains an incentive scheme for a railway company to improve its efficiency. A railway operator that demonstrates better performance (i.e. by reducing cost) is awarded half of the reduced cost for its belt-tightening efforts. While the new incentive system encourages improvement through a system of rewards, the only incentive in the old yardstick regulation system was the threat of penalties for poor performance.

4.3 The Revision of the Railway Business Law in 2000

In 2000, the Railway Business Law was extensively reformed. First, entry regulations changed from a licensing to a permission system. While on the surface these two systems would seem similar, in fact they differ, the license system having been based on the philosophy that entry to the rail market should be prohibited or limited to very few companies. On the other hand, the permission system theoretically grants potential entrance to any organization. This change in law represents considerable liberalization in the rail market.

Second, before 2000, the demand and supply situation of rail services was heavily considered when any potential new entrant appeared. Two criteria related to the supply/demand balance were written into the old Railway Business Law: (i) it must be determined that demand for railway service is sufficient; and (ii) there should be no imbalance between supply and demand for rail service when a potential entrant enters the market. However, with the revision of the Railway Business Law, stipulations controlling the balance between supply and demand were abolished.

When the old Railway Business Law was enacted in 1987, there followed criticism of the criteria, particularly of the supply-demand controlling regulation, which provided no description of the specific conditions necessary to get a rail license, such as the minimum demand level and the degree of demand-supply imbalance that would make new entry into the market unadvisable. These vague and unclear criteria often overprotected incumbent operators and were abolished in the 2000 reform because of their effect in deterring competition.

Third, exit regulations were also lightened after deregulation. The old regulation required permission to exit, but the new regulation, under the Railway Business Law, requires only notification to the Ministry of Land, Infrastructure and Transport one year prior to terminating rail service. The former law stipulated that exit of rail service providers would be allowed if such closure did not damage public interest. This vague description seemed to allow an easy exit for railway service providers, but in fact it was very difficult for railways to go out of business (Saito, 1993).

Last, fare was deregulated. Before 2000 it was required that rail fare be approved by the regulator, but after revision, approval by the regulator became necessary only when rail fare exceeded the ceiling price.

5   COMPETITION IN THE RAIL INDUSTRY

Because it is still heavily regulated, there seems to be little intense competition within the Japanese rail industry. For example, even though entry regulations changed to allow for a permission-based instead of a license system in 2000, there seems to exist almost no competition for the rail market, because the duration of the effective term for permission is not described. The basic concept for this entry regulation seems based on the monopoly status that railways traditionally enjoyed. Despite appearances, however, there is indeed a certain amount of competition in the rail market in Japan, types of which I will summarize in this section.[3]

5.1   Competition for the Market and in the Market

First, there are generally two types of competition in the rail market: competition for the market and competition among railway companies already in the market. In Japan, the rail market is generally characterized by competition among railways already in the market, with little concern about competition from potential new entrants.

According to Mizutani (2005), the system has advantages and disadvantages. One advantage is that a rail operator can concentrate on providing better service in the long run, because the system protects incumbent rail enterprises from potential entrants as long as incumbents' services are not egregiously bad. Although there is no direct competition with potential rail entrants, there is always competition with other transportation modes such as the private auto. Furthermore, as private railway companies develop areas along rail lines and stations by building housing and operating department stores, they have incentives to provide better and more varied service to capture rail passengers.

On the other hand, the efficiency of incumbent rail operators may suffer in the absence of rigorous competition. Rail operators in large metropolitan areas in particular might become complacent because commuter services to large central cities from suburbs are dominated by rail. In order to avoid inefficiency due to a monopolistic situation, the yardstick competition scheme has been introduced.

5.2 Competition in the Same Market

Because most rail operators are class 1 operators providing rail services along their own tracks, there is almost no competition of the type that would exist if several competing rail operators were operating trains along the same track. Of course, there exist cases where a rail company runs trains on a different rail company's tracks, but most such cases are the result of cooperative agreements among organizations deeming it in their best interest to provide more convenient services for rail users, such as by offering direct train services from suburb to suburb through central cities, over tracks belonging to more than one company.

However, as described by Mizutani and Nakamura (2000), there are cases of competition between lines, such as along the Kyoto-Osaka-Kobe corridor, where there are parallel lines owned by different railway companies. Between Kobe and Osaka, three different rail companies operate trains—JR West, Hankyu and Hanshin. Because users in this market choose rail operators according to personal taste, there is severe competition among these organizations to capture more rail ridership. Thus, although direct competition between rail lines is limited to a few markets in large metropolitan areas, there are indeed cases of intense competition in the rail industry in Japan.

There is also inter-modal competition. According to Mizutani and Nakamura (2000), the JR-owned Shinkansen competes with air travel in the long distance transportation market. As the Shinkansen has increased in speed and frequency, taking a Shinkansen has become a reasonable alternative to flying, even for longer-distance travel. For short-distance travel as well, within the same metropolitan area there is intermodal competition, a typical case being the off-peak period competition between rail and the private auto.   In fact, private auto use has increased steadily over the years, to the point that in small metropolitan areas the passenger transport market is now dominated by the private auto.

5.3   Yardstick Regulation as Competition Stimulus

In the yardstick regulation scheme, applied to rail operators in different markets, a regulator sets up several performance measures, such as operating cost, and evaluates rail operators' performance.   Five measures related to operating cost are used: (i) track costs, (ii) catenary costs, (iii) rolling stock costs, (iv) train operating costs, and (v) station operating costs.   The standard costs for these five measures are obtained by using each individual rail operator's data.   And, by comparing the actual cost of each rail company with its standard cost, the performance of each rail company is evaluated.

For the less efficient rail operator, whose actual costs are higher than its standard costs, reasonable costs for the fare level are equivalent to standard costs.   Therefore, in the period following evaluation, the rail operator is expected to reduce actual costs to the level of standard costs. On the other hand, for the more efficient rail operator, whose actual costs are lower than its standard costs, reasonable costs for the fare level are set at half the sum of the actual costs and the standard costs, with half the difference between the actual and standard costs remitted to the efficient rail operator as a reward.   A recent empirical study by Mizutani et al. (2009) shows that yardstick regulation works to reduce costs.

NOTES

[1] For details on business diversification and its effects, please see, for example, Mizutani (1994, 1999b, 2006a).
[2] We conducted a series of empirical studies on the privatization of Japan National Railways.   For example, please see the following references: Mizutani and Nakamura (1997, 2000, 2004) for an overview of privatization, Mizutani and Nakamura (1996) for privatization's effect on labor productivity and safety, Mizutani (1999a) for local community service quality, and Mizutani and Uranishi (2007) for productivity effects and capital adjustment.
[3] Discussions related to competition are based on our previous studies, such as Mizutani (1999b, 2005), Mizutani and Nakamura (2000, 2004).

7 Local Bus

1 INTRODUCTION

Both the public and private sectors supply local bus service in Japan.[1] In terms of the number of bus operators, private bus operators are in the majority, accounting for 97% in 2007. The public sector, by way of the transportation bureaus of local governments, provides local bus services. Large local governments, such as the Tokyo and Osaka metropolitan governments, normally own both subway and local bus systems.

Local bus services in Japan have been in continuous decline. The percentage of the national population using buses was 96.4 in 1970, 69.2 in 1980, 52.8 in 1990, 37.7 in 2000, and, according to the most recent available statistics, 33.6 in 2007. This steady decline is clearly attributable to the loss of market share to the private auto, and the downward trend is causing serious financial deficits in the bus industry.

To address this problem, regulatory reform has been undertaken. Compared to reform measures taken in other public utility industries such as the railway industry, however, those taken in the bus industry have been mild. While the local bus industry was deregulated in 2002, the main regulatory reform was that entry into the local bus service market has been made easier. In this chapter, I will explain the characteristics of the industrial structure, the regulation of the local bus industry, and the regulatory reforms in the local bus industry in Japan.

After the introduction, in the second section, the organizational structure of the local bus industry in Japan is explained, with a description of the market structure of local bus services and kinds of local bus operators. The third section contains an explanation of entry and exit regulations, fare regulations, and regulators in the bus industry. In the fourth section, subsidy schemes are explained. The fifth section deals with regulatory reforms in the local bus industry, with an explanation of the regulatory situation before 2002, followed by an account of the main regulation revisions of 2002.   Last, referring to results obtained through empirical studies, I will discuss the effects of regulatory reform on the local bus service industry in Japan.

2   INDUSTRIAL ORGANIZATION OF THE LOCAL BUS SERVICE INDUSTRY

2.1   Market Structure

According to Table 7.1, which shows the recent situation of local bus service in Japan, the total route-km of local bus service was 396,955 km, the annual vehicle-km was about 3,033 million km, and the number of transported passengers was about 4,246 million passengers in 2007.

Table 7.1   *The Current Situation of Local Bus Service*

Fiscal year	2000	2001	2003	2005	2007
Route-km (km)	304,023	314,376	340,898	357,103	396,955
Vehicle-km of local bus service (million km)	2,897	2,924	3,009	2,974	3,033
Passengers (million persons)	4,803	4,633	4,448	4,244	4,246
Passenger-km (billion)	27.0	26.8	27.7	27.7	28.6
Passengers per total population (million)	37.7	36.6	35.0	33.3	33.6

[Note]: These statistics were obtained from a data source of the Ministry of Land, Infrastructure and Transport (2009).

Just as in other industrialized countries, the number of bus users has been declining in Japan. In terms of passenger numbers, by 2007, the percentage of bus users among the population had decreased by about 12% to 33.6%, which represents average bus use of 2.8 times per month per person. The numbers in 1995 were much higher at 46.1% of the population, according to Mizutani (2006b). This represents a sharp decline in demand for local bus service.

2.2 Local Bus Operators

As Table 7.2 shows, there are mainly two kinds of local bus service operators in Japan—privately owned and publicly owned. Privately owned bus operators generally take the form of a joint-stock company, while publicly owned bus operators are generally managed by transportation bureaus of city governments.

Table 7.2   Kinds of Local Bus Operators

Fiscal year	2001	2002	2003	2004	2005	2006	2007
Operators (total)	451	485	511	516	513	1,087	1,185
Privately owned bus operators	406	440	466	477	474	1,049	1,147
Publicly owned bus operators	45	45	45	39	39	38	38

[Note]: These statistics were obtained from a data source of the Ministry of Land, Infrastructure and Transport (2009).

In 2007, in all Japan, there were a total 1,185 local bus operators, of which privately owned organizations numbered 1,147, or 96.8%, while publicly owned bus operators numbered 38, or only 3.2%.

Since the deregulation of local bus services in 2002, the number of bus operators has increased. Most of the increase has occurred in the private sector, beginning in 2006. This increase is in contrast to what has happened in the public sector, where the number of public operators decreased between the years 2001 and 2007. A more detailed explanation of these changes will appear later.

One important point regarding the local bus service industry is that both privately and publicly owned bus operators have faced financial difficulties. While publicly owned bus operators in Japan have in general been expected to manage without subsidies, total financial independence may no longer be feasible. As Table 7.3 shows, almost all publicly owned bus operators created deficits in 2007. Compared with publicly owned bus operators, privately owned organizations fared somewhat better financially, but nevertheless two thirds of privately owned bus operators created deficits and required subsidies from either public organizations or related companies.

Table 7.3   The Current Management Situation of Local Bus Service

| Kinds of operators | Average annual profitability | Number of operators | | |
		Making profits	Making deficits	Total
Private	0.950	66	162	228
Public	0.871	3	25	28
Total	0.930	69	187	256

[Note]:
(1) These statistics were obtained from a data source of the Ministry of Land, Infrastructure and Transport (2009).
(2) These statistics are for FY2007.
(3) Annual profitability is annual revenues divided by annual expenditures.
(4) This table includes only operators with more than 30 vehicles.

Financial conditions among both national and local governments have recently been stringent, and direct subsidies from the national government to local bus operators have diminished, contributing to local bus operators' financial difficulties. Private bus operators have experienced fewer financial problems than their public counterparts because, according to Mizutani and Urakami (2003), private operators are more cost efficient.

3 REGULATION OF THE LOCAL BUS SERVICE INDUSTRY

3.1 Entry and Exit Regulation

The main law applicable to local bus services is the Road Transportation Law (*Doro Unso-ho*). Entry and exit regulations of local bus service are summarized in Table 7.4.

Table 7.4 Entry and Exit Regulations in the Local Bus Service Industry

Kinds of regulation	Major points
Entry regulation	Permission system (individual operator basis)
Exit regulation	Report in advance & Regional council

As for entry regulation, a system has been adopted whereby a potential entrant to the local bus service market must obtain permission from the Minister of Land, Infrastructure and Transportation. Criteria for permission are whether or not (i) the operation plan for the new local bus services is safe, (ii) the operation plan is adequate and feasible, and (iii) the operator has the ability to carry out the service. Entry was formerly based on a license system, but this changed with deregulation in 2002.

For exit regulation, an advance-reporting system has been adopted, whereby an existing bus operator terminates local bus service by notifying the Minister of Land, Infrastructure and Transport six months prior to termination. The public is also notified, and if there are no dissenting opinions, the bus operator is allowed to exit the market.

With deregulation in 2002, exit became contingent only upon advance notification of the intention to terminate services, instead of the request for permission upon which the system had been based in the past. To allay concerns of residents of rural areas about local bus services being easily abandoned, a regional council (*Chiiki Kyogikai*) system was also instituted.   Figure 7.1 shows the exit procedure system as it relates to the regional council.

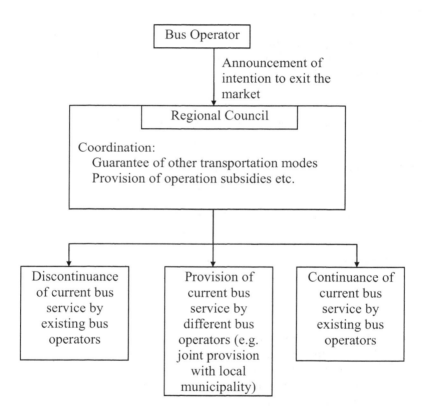

Figure 7.1   The Exit Procedure System in the Regional Council

If there are dissenting opinions about the termination of local bus services, discussions are held by the regional council, whose members consist of related organizations such as the municipal government, the prefectural government, the local bus operator, etc. With the goal of coordinating the needs of local bus operators and local bus users, the regional council discusses, for example, whether or not the local bus operator would be able to continue service if offered government subsidies, or, if the termination of bus service is unavoidable, what other transportation mode can be guaranteed for regional users.

3.2   Fare Regulation

Important points regarding fare regulation of local bus service in Japan are summarized in Table 7.5.

Table 7.5   Fare Regulation in the Local Bus Service Industry

Kinds of regulation	Major points
Ceiling price	Approval
Price under ceiling price	Report
Incentive system	Yardstick regulation
Fare level	Full cost principle as standard cost

First, approval of the ceiling price of local bus service must be obtained from the Minister of Land, Infrastructure and Transportation. In cases where fares fall below the approved ceiling price, they do not require Ministry permission but must be reported to the Ministry. While all local bus fares were formerly subject to approval, since deregulation in 2002, only the ceiling price remains subject to Ministry approval.

Fare level is in general determined according to the full cost principle. However, as this system is the cost plus system, cost reduction might not be pursued as a matter of course. Therefore yardstick regulation is also used for the standard cost, which is the base cost for the ceiling price of local bus services.

Although more details of yardstick regulation are explained in a separate chapter, in the local bus service industry, yardstick regulation is applied separately to 25 regions.   Local bus operators in each region are compared and their costs evaluated.   The average cost of each region is considered the standard cost.   If a bus operator has costs higher than the standard cost, this operator is evaluated as less efficient and is expected to reduce costs.   If a bus operator's costs are less than the standard cost, this operator is evaluated as efficient and is awarded half the difference between the standard cost and the actual cost when fare level is being set. Thus, yardstick regulation has evolved as an incentive for bus operators to reduce costs.

The procedure for revision of the ceiling price is shown in Figure 7.2. The Ministry of Land, Infrastructure and Transportation evaluates the ceiling price of local bus fare based on operators' financial and managerial conditions such as costs, wage level, operating schedules and so on.   After consulting with the Transportation Council as to whether or not a revision of the fare ceiling price would be reasonable, the Minister of Land, Infrastructure and Transportation makes a decision to grant or withhold approval of the revision.

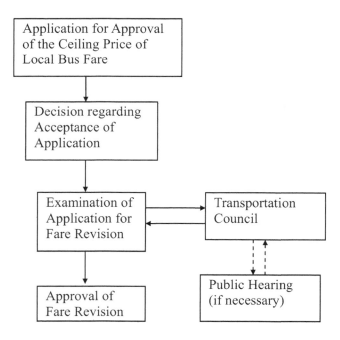

Figure 7.2   Procedure for Revision of Local Bus Fare Ceiling Price

3.3 Regulators

It is mainly the Ministry of Land, Infrastructure and Transportation (MLIT) that is responsible for regulations and policy-making in the local bus service industry. As mentioned above, this regulator must approve the ceiling price for local bus service. Furthermore, because yardstick regulation is applied to the local bus service industry, several measures for evaluating operators' performance are collected in order for the regulator to set the standard costs of each operator. Also, for the many private local bus operators creating deficits, the government provides assistance in the form of subsidies, in a scheme administrated by the Ministry of Land, Infrastructure and Transportation.

In addition to the Ministry of Land, Infrastructure and Transportation, the Ministry of Internal Affairs and Communications (MIAC) plays a role in the regulation of publicly owned local bus operators. For example, the Local Public Corporation Law (*Chiho Koei Kigyo Ho*) identifies this ministry as holding certain responsibilities related to the administration of public corporations and their corporate bonds.

4   SUBSIDY SCHEMES

To alleviate the financial difficulties of local bus operators, the national government has set up certain subsidy programs, the most important of which provide support for essential service routes. This support program consists of two kinds of subsidies: operating subsidies to help with operation costs and capital subsidies for purchasing new buses.

According to the Ministry of Land, Infrastructure and Transport (2009), this subsidy program is provided to local bus operators with the following conditions.

(i)   The bus route is approved by the regional council as worthy of being maintained and is deemed an essential service route by the governor of the prefecture.

(ii) The bus route covers multiple municipalities.

(iii) The bus route is longer than 10km.

(iv) The total passengers per day of the bus route are 15 to 150 persons.

(v)   There are more than three buses operated daily.

(vi) The bus route accesses the central city of the region.

(vii) The current revenue and expenditure ratio of the bus route is more than 11/20.

If the bus route satisfies the above conditions, then it can be subsidized.

Subsidies are given to bus operators to cover the current revenue and expenditure difference of essential bus service routes. These subsidies are borne equally by the national and the prefectural governments, with an upper limit of 9/20 of the current expenses of the essential bus service route.

Second, there are subsidies given to bus operators to support the purchase of new vehicles for essential bus service routes. These subsidies are also borne equally by the national and the prefectural governments, with an upper limit of 15 million yen for a bus equipped to accommodate handicapped passengers.

Table 7.6 shows trends in these subsidies borne by the national government.

Table 7.6   National Subsidies to Support Essential Service Routes

Fiscal year		2003	2004	2005	2006	2007
Subsidies supporting essential service routes	Amount of money	6,659	6,400	6,460	6,672	6,576
	Number of operators	206	219	217	217	213
	Number of bus routes	1,860	1,895	1,799	1,725	1,645
Subsidies supporting the purchase of new vehicles	Amount of money	630	780	690	747	1,096
	Number of operators	97	80	71	71	84
	Number of vehicles	193	131	139	128	161

[Note]:
(1)   These statistics were obtained from a data source of the Ministry of Land, Infrastructure and Transport (2009).
(2)   Unit amount of money is million yen.

In 2007, the total amount of subsidies for essential service routes was 6,576 million yen, and that for the purchase of new vehicles was 1,096 million yen. Of the 1,185 bus operators in 2007, about 18% received subsidies for essential service routes, and 7% received subsidies for purchasing new vehicles. Although bus operators in rural areas have been facing financial difficulties, the national government has been unable to increase the amount of subsidies because of its own financial constraints. The availability of subsidies, however, can cause problems, such as dependence among bus operators. Tanabe (2002) shows that the availability of subsidies causes a decrease in the productivity of bus operators. It is true, however that bus services in Japan cannot be maintained without subsidies.

5 REGULATORY REFORMS IN THE LOCAL BUS SERVICE INDUSTRY

5.1 Regulatory Reforms Before 2002

Major regulatory reforms in the local bus service industry occurred in 2002. However, several minor regulatory reforms had earlier occurred in the local bus service industry and are listed as follows.

First, according to the Ministry of Transportation (1995), fare was deregulated in 1994. Several discounted fares of local bus services were deregulated from an approval to a report system. Examples of discounted fares include one-day-long bus passes and fare for special seats. Because the number of bus users has been declining, the government loosened regulations to help bus operators increase ridership with new kinds of discounted fares. As a result, the Ministry of Transportation (1996) reported that 328 bus operators provided discounted bus fares at the end of March 1995, 5 times the number that had done so in 1990.

The second important regulatory movement occurred in 1997. Traditionally, in the local bus service industry as well as in the tax industry, a supply-demand adjustment regulation (*Jukyu Chosei Kisei*) has been applied, the purpose of which is to avoid disastrous competition by controlling the supply and demand balance. This created problems such that new entrants, with the fresh ideas they might otherwise bring to the local bus service industry, were restrained. In 1997, the Cabinet resolved to phase out the supply-demand regulation by 2001.

5.2 The Revision of the Road Transportation Law in 2002

In December 1996, the Ministry of Transportation resolved to make major changes to the traditional transportation policy and began to pave the way for change (Ministry of Transportation (2000)). The Road Transportation Law (*Doro Kotsu-ho*) was revised in 2002. A summary of the revision can be seen in Table 7.7.

Table 7.7 Revision of the Road Transportation Law in 2002

Item	Before Revision: Road Transportation Law	After Revision: New Road Transportation Law
Entry	License	Permission
Exit	Permission	Report (6 months in advance) Establish regional council
Fare	Approval	Approval for ceiling price Report for under ceiling price
Others	—	Establish qualifying examination system for the bus operation manager

According to Terada (2005), the 2002 deregulation can be summarized as follows. First, entry regulation changed from a license to a permission system. Basically, if safety conditions are satisfied, the new entry can be admitted. Bus operation plans such as route plans, formerly items of entry regulation, are separated from entry regulation and become approval items. It is necessary only to report bus schedules, but there is a built-in scheme to enforce change to avoid cream skimming.

As for exit regulation, bus operators contemplating exiting the market no longer need permission but must report to the Minister six months in advance of terminating service. If there are no objections, the bus operators can exit the market. If there are potential problems, discussions are conducted in the regional council to resolve the issues.

Last, as for fare regulation, only the ceiling price of the local bus service remains subject to approval. For bus fares under the ceiling price, bus operators can change the fare level simply by reporting to the ministry. Thus, in many ways, the local bus service industry was deregulated in 2002.

Traditional regulation treated local bus service operators as regional monopolies obligated to provide adequate bus services. New entrants to the local bus service market were thus restrained.

However, after the policy changed, more competition was introduced. That is, the new policy allows new entrants into gap areas surrounded by areas already covered by existing operators. Although the new regulation aims to prevent cream-skimming behavior, there is still concern about whether or not the regulation is effective in doing so.

6 EFFECTS OF REGULATORY REFORMS IN THE LOCAL BUS SERVICE INDUSTRY

Based on previous studies, this section summarizes the effects of the 2002 regulatory changes.

Mizutani (2006b) uses statistical data to analyze the effects of the 2002 local bus industry deregulation. He compares the results of before and after deregulation in several measures such as demand, service quality, cost structure, financial situation, and availability of subsidies from the macro (whole country) point of view. He obtains the following results. First, the number of local bus passengers transported tends to decline even after deregulation. However, at the micro (individual local bus market) level, as Terada (2005) points out, the number of passengers changes to increase.[2] There remains room to stimulate the market, as new entrants increase in number and exiting operators decrease. Second, as for service quality, the fact that bus network density in given areas increased shows that accessibility to the bus network increased after deregulation. Third, as a result of the competition introduced among bus operators by deregulation, costs of bus operators were on average reduced, especially among private operators. Last, cost reduction occurred in the expenditure for labor. On the other hand, negative effects occurred, such as the fact that the number of bus services tended to decrease. This might be a result of cutting unnecessary services in order to increase managerial efficiency. Second, in rural areas, the number of bus operators obtaining subsidies for maintaining local bus routes increased. Furthermore, the number of passengers relative to the total population continued to decline even after deregulation. From these results, it is apparent that the effects of deregulation in the local bus industry are minimal or limited.

As for the limited effects of deregulation, Ooi (2008), for example, using a data set for regional areas between 1994 and 2005, evaluates how deregulation affects the cost structure of privately owned bus operators. He estimates translog cost function of private bus operators and reaches the following conclusion. Although cost was reduced during these periods, it is not always deregulation that caused the reduction, for two reasons. First, because demand for bus service had been decreasing even in the before-deregulation period, individual private bus operators had been making efforts to reduce costs. Second, severe competition after deregulation has not occurred.

There are studies showing the effects of deregulation on service quality. For example, Maeda (2003) investigates the service quality of local bus services after deregulation. Although his case study is limited to one large private bus company, Nishitetsu, based in Fukuoka prefecture, he concludes that service quality has improved and contributed to increasing bus ridership. Furthermore, Kato (2004) points out that since deregulation, bus companies such as those associated with JR have used more strategic behavior. Whereas bus companies were formerly strongly controlled by the government, as a result of deregulation they have started to build their own business strategies.

NOTES

[1] In Japan, the bus service industry is divided into two kinds of bus services: local bus services provided by bus operators as scheduled services, and hired bus services, which are not scheduled service but provided according to individual demand. In this chapter, I focus on scheduled bus service in the given area.

[2] In fact, Terada (2005) reports an increase in the number of bus passengers after the reorganization of bus routes at Hiroshima Dentetsu and a decrease in bus fares at Asahikawa Denki and Akiden Dohoku bus companies.

PART IV

Communications Industries

8   Postal Service

1   INTRODUCTION

The postal service industry was formerly one of the most conservative public utility industries in Japan. From the advent of a modern postal system in 1871, postal service was provided by the government. In October 2007, however, under the administration of Prime Minister Koizumi, the Japan Post Public Corporation was divided into five group companies, and this began the process of fully privatizing postal service in Japan.

The privatization of postal service differs from that of other formerly state-owned entities in that reform has not been drastic and there have been few regulatory schemes introducing competition and liberalization. The Japan Post companies continue to play an important role in the postal service market.

Although there are several good summary papers regarding regulatory reform of postal services, for example, Ishii (2005b) and Ide (2004b), these are written in Japanese and do not describe the current situation. Therefore, this chapter will describe characteristics of the postal service industry and explain its industrial structure, current mail situation, and kinds of post offices. Second, I will explain postal service regulations, focusing on entry regulation, price regulation and universal service obligation. Third, liberalization in postal services will be explained. Last, remaining policy issues will be discussed.

2   THE POSTAL SYSTEM IN JAPAN

On April 1, 2003, the governmental body known as the Postal Service Bureau became a public corporation called Japan Post, which continued in existence until privatization on October 1, 2007.

2.1   Industrial Organization of the Postal System

Broadly defined, the postal business in Japan consists of three main services: (i) ordinal postal services such as letters and parcels; (ii) postal savings; and (iii) postal life insurance. Formerly provided by the public corporation called Japan Post, these services have been provided since October 1, 2007, by the five private companies which have replaced the formerly public entity but which continue to be referred to in English as Japan Post. Details of the privatization of the Japan Post will be explained in a separate chapter. Table 8.1 shows a profile of these private companies, known as the Japan Post group companies.

Table 8.1   Profile of Japan Post Group Companies

Company	Japan Post Holding Company	Japan Post Network	Japan Post Service	Japan Post Bank	Japan Post Insurance
Establishment	January 23, 2006	October 1, 2007	October 1, 2007	September 1, 2006	October 1, 2007
Capital (billion yen)	3,500	100	100	3,500	500
Shareholders	Ministry of Finance 100%	Japan Post Holding Company 100%	Japan Post Holding Company 100%	Japan Post Holding Company 100%	Japan Post Holding Company 100%
Employees	3,500	119,900	99,700	11,600	5,400
Main services	Management of group companies	Counter services of postal service, bank, insurance etc.	Postal service, international & domestic logistics	Banking	Insurance
Major branches and offices		Branch:13, Post office: about 24,000	Branch:13, Branch office: 1,093, Distribution center: 2,560	Business office:234	Directly managed store: 81

[Note]:
(1) *This table was written by the author and is based on materials provided by the Post Office group companies.*
(2) *The numbers are for May 28, 2008.*

First, the Japan Post Holding Company is a stock holding company serving the other four group companies. The Japan Post Service provides postal services such as the dispatch and distribution of letters and parcels. Japan Post Bank is a financial institution. Japan Post Insurance is a life insurance company. Japan Post Network is a counter service company providing services to customers by contracting with three business companies. Figure 8.1 shows the relationships among these five companies.

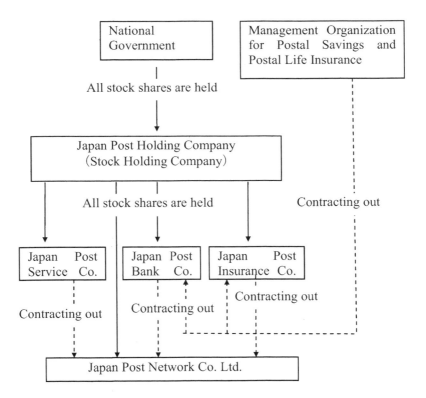

Figure 8.1   *Relationships among Japan Post Group Companies*

2.2 Current Mail Situation in Japan

Ordinal postal services can be classified into various types, including delivery of individual letters and post cards, delivery of periodicals such as newspapers and magazines, and delivery of non-commercial printed material such as academic prints.   Table 8.2 shows trends in major mail items.

Table 8.2   Trends in Mail Volume

Fiscal year	Mail service (billion items)	Parcel delivery service (million items)			International mail service (million items)	
		Post Office	Private carrier	Share of Post Office	Outgoing mail	Incoming mail
1997	25.8	163	1,617	9.2%	131	309
1998	25.9	155	1,833	7.8%	119	279
1999	26.1	154	2,357	6.1%	113	292
2000	26.9	155	2,574	5.7%	106	298
2001	26.7	162	2,654	5.8%	99	287
2002	26.2	166	2,751	5.7%	91	269
2003	25.6	182	2,834	6.0%	84	238
2004	25.0	215	2,874	7.0%	81	215
2005	24.8	247	2,928	7.8%	78	211
2006	24.7	268	2,939	8.4%	76	202
'06/'97	0.96	1.64	1.82	0.91	0.58	0.65

[Source]: Japan Post (2007, p.172)

Japan Post deals mainly with ordinal mail such as letters and cards, which have diminished in number after a peak in 2000.   Private carriers have also begun to enter this market since deregulation, making it difficult for Japan Post to monopolize the market.   As Mizutani and Uranishi (2003) note, more serious competition is threatening Japan Post in the parcel delivery market.   Since the entry into the market of Yamato parcel delivery service in 1976, the parcel delivery market has been dominated by this hugely successful private carrier. Japan Post is losing share in the international delivery market as well. The imbalance between incoming and outgoing mail pushes the cost structure upward.

2.3 Mailing System

In this section, I will briefly explain the mailing system in Japan. The classification of post offices was slightly altered with the privatization of the Japan Post in 2007. Table 8.3 shows the current number of post offices.

Table 8.3   Kinds of Post Offices and Number of Post Offices

Year	Directly managed post office					Summary post office
	Ordinal post office		Special post office			
	C&D	Non-C&D	C&D	Non-C&D	Total	
2001	1,257	51	3,627	15,307	20,242	4,531
2002	1,260	50	3,563	15,378	20,251	4,501
2003	1,262	48	3,530	15,405	20,245	4,470
2004	1,261	47	3,465	15,458	20,231	4,447
2005	1,257	47	3,438	15,479	20,221	4,410
2006	1,243	51	2,418	16,506	20,218	4,356
2007	n.a.	n.a.	n.a	n.a.	20,234	3,859

[Note]:
(1) This table was written by the author based on information from the White Paper of the Ministtry of Internal Affairs and Communications (2007d, 2008).
(2) C&D (Collection and Delivery Post Office), Non-C&D (Non-Collection and Delivery Post Office).
(3) After the privatization of the Japan Post in 2007, no distinction was made between ordinal and special post offices.

First, before the privatization of the Japan Post, post offices in the Japanese postal system were classified into three kinds according to management form and two kinds according to functional form.   As for management form, there are ordinal post offices, special post offices, and summary post offices.

The ordinal post office is directly owned and operated by the Japan Post Public Corporation.   Its buildings and facilities are owned by the Japan Post Public Corporation, and its employees are public employees. The special post office, in contrast to the ordinal post office, could be considered a kind of franchisee of the Japan Post Public Corporation, with its buildings generally owned by the postmaster of the post office or some other private citizen and rented by the Japan Post Public Corporation for the purpose of providing postal services.   Although the postmaster of the special post office is a public employee, it is customary for a family member of the postmaster to inherit his job when he retires. A more detailed description of the special post office will be presented in the next section.   Last, the summary post office is one which has been contracted out to the private sector.   The Japan Post Public Corporation engages a contractor who operates the summary post office in a rented part of an office building, for example.

However, since privatization, no distinction has been made between ordinal and special post offices.   These are counted as directly managed post offices.

Figure 8.2 shows the postal service system in Japan.

There are two kinds of post offices in terms of functional form: the collection and delivery (C&D) post office, and the non-collection and delivery (non-C&D) post office.   The C&D post office's role is the collection and delivery of letters and parcels to users and regional centers in the system, while the non-C&D post office only receives letters and parcels.

Thus, the C&D post office can be characterized as a distribution center of postal items while the non-C&D post office resembles a retail shop serving residential areas by providing postal services.   After privatization, most non-C&D post offices became part of the Japan Post Network company, and most C&D post offices were incorporated into the Japan Post Service company. Again, since the privatization of the Japan Post, there has been no statistical data on these categories, although the mailing system remains unchanged.

Table 8.3 clarifies trends related to each kind of post office.   First, most ordinal post offices are C&D type post offices.   In 2006, of 1,243 ordinal post offices, the C&D type accounted for 96%.   Second, special post offices comprise two types, the majority being non-C&D but with about 13% being the C&D type.   Another feature of the Japanese postal situation is that there are so many post offices.   In 2002, there were

24,752 post offices, making post offices the most numerous type of public facility in the nation. According to Japan Post (2003), there is on average a post office at every 1.10 km interval, while other public facilities are not as numerous (e.g. elementary schools (1.1km), police station (1.4km), national and public hospitals (4.0km), fire stations (2.3km)).

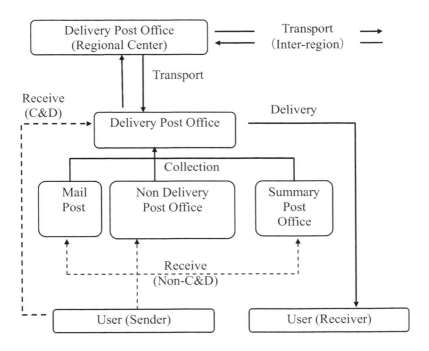

Figure 8.2 The Postal Service System in Japan

[Note]: This figure is the author's modification of an earlier version by Mizutani and Uranishi (2006).

Another puzzling feature of the postal system in Japan is that the number of summary post offices, which operate at lower cost, has decreased while the number of more expensive C&D type post offices has increased, and that since the privatization of the Japan Post this tendency has not changed at all.

3   REGULATION OF POSTAL SERVICE

3.1   Entry Regulation

Under the state monopoly organization, strict regulations virtually ensured that personal correspondence, such as through letters, would be handled by the public postal service.   Private companies were not allowed to enter the field of personal correspondence.   According to Ishii (2005b), the state monopoly was justified for the following reasons. First, it was believed that postal services should be provided broadly and fairly all over Japan.   That is, the post office was obligated to provide universal service.   Second, it was imperative to maintain privacy in communications, and there was concern that the private sector might not maintain that privacy.   Third, in delivery operations, there exist economies of scale, so that a larger organization is deemed better.   Last, a vertically organized nationwide network system (i.e. receipt, collection, classification, distribution and delivery of letters) was expected.

However, with the 2003 establishment of the Japan Post, entry was deregulated, and the Personal Correspondence Mail Service Law (*Shinshobin-ho*), enacted in April 2003, allowed the private sector to enter the market.   Since then, after obtaining permission from the Minister of Internal Affairs and Communications, private companies have been able to enter the market.

3.2   Price Regulation

Table 8.4 shows price regulations related to postal services.   There are four kinds of ordinary mail provided by the Japan Post Service company: Class 1 (letters), Class 2 (cards), Class 3 (periodicals such as newspapers and magazines) and Class 4 (mail related to education and welfare).   The prices for sending these types of mail are uniform all over Japan.

First, prices of Class 1 and Class 2 mail are less regulated than for other categories.   The Japan Post Service company reports the prices to the Minister of Internal Affairs and Communications, and as long as the Ministry considers the prices reasonably low, no changes will be ordered.

Second, the Ministry must approve prices of Class 3 and Class 4 mail because mail items in these categories are related to education and welfare and their prices are set in order to achieve policies.

Third, as mentioned above, the Personal Correspondence Mail Service Law (*Shinshobin-ho*) allowed the private sector to enter the personal correspondence mail services market in April 2003.   Personal correspondence includes letters, invoices, licenses, certificates, and so on.

This type of service is divided into two categories: the general personal correspondence mail service, which supplies nationwide demand, and the special personal correspondence mail service, which supplies specific demand. Private companies can enter the market by reporting their prices for general personal correspondence mail to the Minister of Internal Affairs and Communications.

Last, private companies are free to set their own prices for other mail services.

Table 8.4   Price Regulation of Postal Services

Provider	Kinds of mail	Price regulation
Japan Post Service	Class 1 and 2 (letters and cards)	Prior report
	Class 3 and 4 (periodicals, etc)	Approval
Private correspondence mail companies	General personal correspondence	Prior report
	Other mail	Free

[Note]: This table was written by the author and is based on information from the Ministry of Internal Affairs and Telecommunications.

3.3   Universal Service Obligation in Postal Services

Ordinary postal services in Japan are provided according to the universal service obligation, details of which are explained in a separate chapter. According to Ishii (2005b), universal services in Japan are required to have three characteristics: (i) non-discriminatory provision to people who pay for services, (ii) nationwide service provision, (iii) uniform charges all over the country.

In fact, measures such as the Postal Service Enforcement Regulation (*Yubin-ho Seko Kisoku*) and the Postal Network Enforcement Regulation (*Yubinkyoku Kabushikikaisha-ho Seko Kisoku*) regulate nationwide services, require uniform charges, and formulate criteria for setting up mailboxes and post offices.

Ishii (2005b) notes that the policy of having uniform charges for postal services is reasonable in some ways. If this policy had not been chosen, charging according to distance might have been an alternative, but such a system would require obtaining detailed information from customers and making complicated calculations as to dispatch length, etc. In short, information costs might be huge. Therefore, uniform charges or zone charges appear more reasonable for postal services.

4   LIBERALIZATION OF POSTAL SERVICES

4.1   Background of Liberalization

The privatization of Japan's postal services differs from the privatization of other public utility industries in Japan in that there has not been the kind of dramatic transformation that occurred in other former monopolies like railways and telecommunications. Transformation has been brought about less by privatization than by changes in the communications industry, with its progression of technological advances such as facsimiles, mobile phones, and e-mails, all of which have drastically lessened the demand for traditional postal services.

Further diminishing the role of the post office in Japan, private parcel companies, which entered the parcel delivery market in the 70s, have developed new kinds of mail services called 'light parcel mail (*Meiru-bin*),' focusing on the delivery of relatively light booklets such as commercial magazines, catalogues, brochures, and direct-mail items, all of which are considered neither parcels nor letters, but something in between. The private parcel delivery company Yamato started delivering these items in 1997, and the market has expanded rapidly since then, as Table 8.5 shows.

With the development of new postal services and the increased participation of private companies, the price of mail is expected to decrease and liberalization to progress further.

Table 8.5 Trends in Light Parcel Mail Services

Year	Companies	Number of mail items
2000	6	59.0
2001	7	777.8
2002	10	907.2
2003	10	1,344.8
2004	10	1,736.8
2005	11	2,068.2
2006	11	2,310.1
2007	12	4,834.3 (2,578.1)

[Note]:
(1) This table was written by the author and is based on information from the Ministry of Land, Infrastructure and Transport, and Ishii (2005b).
(2) The number of mail items in 2007 includes those of Japan Post. The numbers in parentheses are values excluding Japan Post.

4.2   Major Liberalization in Postal Service

Three major points characterize the liberalization of the postal service industry in Japan. The first two occurred simultaneously: the establishment of the Japan Post public corporation and the deregulation of entry into the market for personal correspondence mail services. The third feature is the privatization of the Japan Post. In this section, I will explain these liberalization policies.

(1) April 2003 ~ March 2007

One important point of postal services' liberalization was the establishment of the Japan Post. From its beginning in 1871 as a governmental body, the Post Office had been operated as a postal services monopoly. The Post Office became a public corporation known as Japan Post, a more commercialized and independent organization separated from the government.

Concomitant with the founding of the Japan Post, the Personal Correspondence Mail Service Law (*Shinshobin-ho*) was enacted in April 2003 to allow the private sector to enter the postal services market.

(2) April, 2007 ~ now

An important feature of the postal service industry liberalization is that the Japan Post was privatized in accordance with a law passed in October 2005, stipulating that the organization be made private in April 2007.

Characteristics of the privatization scheme taken by the government are as follows. First, the Japan Post was reorganized into one stockholding company (the Japan Post Holding Company) and four postal service providing companies (Japan Post Service, Japan Post Bank, Japan Post Insurance, Japan Post Network). Second, the privatization procedure was to be carried out over a period of 10 years. Third, in order to maintain regional local services, the 'Social and Regional Maintenance Fund (*Shakai Chiiki Koken Kikin*)' would be established. Details of the Post Office privatization are given in a separate chapter.

5   REMAINING ISSUES REGARDING POSTAL SERVICES

5.1   Was General Personal Correspondence Service Liberalized?

Personal correspondence mail was liberalized in April 2003. Deregulation created two types of services: the general personal correspondence mail service supplying nation-wide demand and the special personal correspondence mail service supplying specific demand.

However, this deregulation was met with criticism, especially regarding criteria for permission for entry into the general personal correspondence mail services market. One criterion is that mailboxes must be built in order to protect the privacy of senders. For potential entrants, building mailboxes all over the nation would require extra, formidably huge costs. Even if the market is technically deregulated, the mailbox criterion creates unfair competition against potential new entrants. In fact, Yamato Corporation, Japan's biggest parcel delivery company, claimed that the new law was not well designed and that Yamato would not enter the market.

Table 8.6 shows that in the five years after deregulation, no company has entered the market, which suggests that this particular criterion might be an example of managed deregulation, as Tsuru (2002) points out.

Table 8.6   Number of Personal Correspondence Mail Service Companies

Year	2003	2004	2005	2006	2007
General correspondence mail service	0	0	0	0	0
Special correspondence mail service	41	111	159	213	253
Total	41	111	159	213	253

[Note]: This table was written by the author and is based on information from a 2008 White Paper on Information and Communications by the Ministry of Internal Affairs and Communications.

5.2   Issues Related to 'Special Post Offices'

Before the privatization of the Japan Post, many people voiced concern that the existence of the special post office is problematic in modern Japan. Among Japanese public utility industries, the special post office system is unique. Its problems, summarized below, have yet to be solved.

Appointment of the Special Post Office Postmaster

Unlike postmasters of ordinal post offices, postmasters of special post offices are appointed from outside the ranks of general career government officials, and special post office postmasters enjoy several advantages unavailable to postmasters of ordinal post offices. For example, retirement age is 65 for special post office postmasters but 60 for general post office officials (Segawa, 2005). Furthermore, a special post office requires at least 8.9 million yen solely for the salary of the postmaster.

At a summary post office of the same size, only 4.2 million yen is needed for all expenses (Segawa, 2005).

Buildings and Facilities of the Special Post Office

While all buildings housing ordinal post offices were owned by the Japan Post Public Corporation, even now there are many cases in which buildings housing special post offices are privately owned. Many of the special post offices in fact double as residences for the postmaster owner, and a substantial number of special post offices are located in heritable property. By the end of March 2003, there were 18,942 special post offices, of which only 1,436, or 7.6%, were owned by Japan Post. On the other hand, the number of special post offices in which the buildings are rented by Japan Post from private owners is 17,506, or 92.4%. Of these 17,506 post offices, cases in which buildings are owned by the postmaster himself number 5,788, or 33.1% (Harada, 2004).

There have been complaints that rental fees paid to special post office owners may exceed the market price, and because the Post Office has not published detailed information disclosing rental cost, it is natural that there is suspicion. Quite recently, according to the Nihon Keizai Shinbun (2006), rental fees paid by the Japan Post Public Corporation were on average 4.75 million yen per special post office. If this estimate is correct, it would indicate a monthly rental fee of about 396 thousand yen, certainly in most cases considerably higher than the market price.

Management System

Human resource allocation for the special post office is decided by Japan Post. The running expenses of the post office are also determined by its size. A postmaster of a special post office cannot allocate employees or decide running expenses himself. And because the financial independence of the postal service is judged from the point of view of the entire postal system, theoretically it does not matter to Japan Post whether each individual special post office's management is efficient. An individual post office has no incentive to run efficiently, regardless of whether it is a special or an ordinal post office. Furthermore, most special post offices are small.[1] There are 13,698 special post offices with less than five employees, accounting for 72.5% of the total.

Another distinctive feature of the special post office is that there was until recently a category of expense which applied only to it. Originally intended to be used to cover the expense of lighting, fuel, or equipment, the '*watashikiri-hi*' (free-use allowance) was provided annually to postmasters of special post offices.   There were no restrictions on the use of this money or requirements that its use be accounted for.   The amount of '*watashikiri-hi*' was about 91.2 billion yen for the entire postal system, or an average of about one million yen per postmaster in 2000 (Tanaka, 2004).   However, according to Segawa (2005), postmasters serving as regional section chiefs received much higher amounts of '*watashikiri-hi*.'   Although the post office has an audit system, categories of expenses such as '*watashikiri-hi*' create room for vagueness and inefficiency in the postal service.   In 2003, the '*watashikiri-hi*' was abolished after many complaints about its lack of transparency.

After the privatization of the Japan Post, the issue of the special post office remains.   However, it may take time for this problem to be resolved, as political power rests with many of the groups associated with the established postal companies.

NOTE

[1] According to Tanaka (2004, p.126), at the end of March 2003, the size distribution of the special post office was as follows: 2-employee (2,363 post offices, 12%); 3-employee (4,049 post offices, 21%); 4-employee (4,265 post offices, 23%); 5-employee (3,014 post offices, 16%); 6-employee (1,143 post offices, 6%); 7-employee (739 post offices, 4%); and 8-employee (336 post offices, 18%).

9 Telecommunications

1 INTRODUCTION

This chapter will give an overview of the industrial structure and regulatory scheme of the telecommunications industry in Japan. While there is a huge array of companies populating the telecommunications industry, large companies such as NTT and KDDI are few.

Technological progress in this industry is rapid, compared with advances in other public utility industries. Since the Nippon Telegraph and Telephone public corporation was privatized in 1985, regulatory reforms have been enacted with dramatic results. Among the several privatizations of formerly state-owned organizations, that of the telecommunications industry has experienced the most deregulation, with telecommunications facing the most severe intra-industry competition of all the formerly public entities.

After the introduction, in the second section, the market structure of the telecommunications industry in Japan is explained, with information regarding market size, the number of telephone customers, and the major telecommunications companies. In the third section, regulation regarding telecommunications is summarized, with explanations of entry, price, and inter-connection regulations, as well as regulators. The fourth section focuses on liberalization in the electric power industry, with a description of regulatory reforms since the privatization of NTT in 1985, subsequent to which event major changes have occurred four times in the telecommunications industry: in 1985, 1999, 2001, and 2003.

2 STRUCTURE OF THE TELECOMMUNICATIONS INDUSTRY

2.1 Market Structure

Table 9.1 shows the market size of the telecommunications industry and the number of related companies. In terms of total sales, the market size of the industry was about 14.6 billion yen in 2006.   Included in the industry are fixed-line telephone companies, mobile telephone companies, internet protocol companies, and related companies.   There were about 14 thousand companies in this industry in 2007, although there were few large telecommunications companies such as NTT.   In terms of sales share, the fixed-line telephone is no longer in the majority.   As this table shows, in 2007 about 60% of telephone sales was for mobile phones.

Table 9.1   Market Size and Number of Telecommunications Companies

Fiscal year	2002	2003	2004	2005	2006	2007
Sales	16,220	16,140	14,577	14,554	14,591	n.a.
Sales share of mobile telephone	55.1%	58.0%	57.7%	57.3%	57.8%	59.0%
Number of companies	11,318	12,518	13,090	13,774	14,296	14,495

[Note]:
(1)   This table was written by the author and is based on information from the Ministry of Internal Affairs and Communications (2008).
(2)   Unit of sales: billion yen.
(3)   Sales share of mobile telephone is calculated based on total sales of both fixed-line and mobile telephones.

Table 9.2 shows trends in the number of customers seeking telephone services.   As this table shows, the fixed-line telephone is decreasing yearly while mobile and IP telephone market share increases each year.   In 2007, the number of mobile phone customers became more than twice that of fixed-line telephone customers.

Table 9.2   Number of Customers in the Telephone Industry

Fiscal year	2002	2003	2004	2005	2006	2007
Fixed-line telephone	60.8	60.2	59.6	58.1	55.2	51.2
Mobile telephone	81.1	86.7	91.5	96.5	101.7	107.3
IP telephone	n.a.	5.3	8.30	11.5	14.5	17.5

[Note]:
(1)   This table was written by the author and is based on information from the Ministry of Internal Affairs and Communications (2008).
(2)   Unit: million persons.
(3)   These figures are registered numbers.
(4)   IP telephone: Internet Protocol telephone.

2.2   Major Telecommunications Companies

The telecommunications industry itself is changing dramatically due to rapid technological progress.   The main actors in the industry are the three major company groups: NTT, KDDI and Softbank.

First, the NTT group derives from the former Nippon Telegraph and Telephone, known as the NTT public corporation, which was privatized in 1985 and restructured into several companies in 1999.

Figure 9.1 shows the major companies of the NTT group. Under the NTT Stockholding Company are five service companies.   NTT East Japan and NTT West Japan are both fixed-line telephone companies within individual prefectures.   NTT East Japan covers cities in eastern Japan such as Sapporo, Sendai, Tokyo, Yokohama and Chiba, while NTT West Japan covers western cities such as Nagoya, Kyoto, Osaka, Hiroshima and Fukuoka. These companies' annual sales are similar: 2,003 billion yen (NTT East Japan) and 1,901 billion yen (NTT West Japan) in 2007.   NTT Communications provides inter-prefecture, international, and IP network services, with annual sales of about 1,155 billion yen in 2007.   NTT Data provides system integration and network system services, with sales of about 1,074 billion yen in 2007.   Although Docomo, NTT's mobile telephone company, has a short history, its business is growing rapidly, with sales in 2007 of about 4,712 billion yen. However, NTT Docomo has been facing severe competition with other mobile telephone companies.   Total sales of NTT group companies combined were about 10,681 billion yen in 2007.

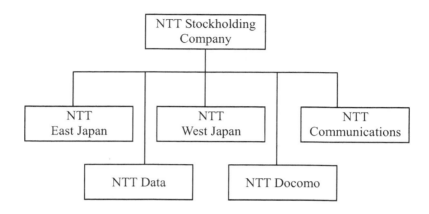

Figure 9.1   Major Companies of the NTT Group

KDDI, the second important telecommunications group, began as an amalgamation of KDD, DDI and IDO in 2000.   KDD was an international telephone company existing before the privatization of NTT in 1985.   DDI was established to replace NTT when it was privatized, and its main shareholder was Kyocera.   IDO was established in 1987 by Toyota, along with electric power companies such as Tokyo Electric Power.   Also included in this group is the mobile telephone company named au.   The KDDI group had sales of about 3,596 billion yen.

Last, the Softbank group of telecommunications companies has recently been growing.   This group consists of fixed-line telephone, e-commerce, broadband infrastructure, Internet culture, mobile telephone services, and so on.   Softbank's mobile telephone service began when it purchased Vodaphone Japan in 2006.

3 REGULATIONS IN THE TELECOMMUNICATION INDUSTRY

3.1 Entry Regulation

A registration scheme applies to telecommunications companies that have more than a certain level of service area and a certain network size. Other smaller telecommunications companies are not required to register but must report only upon starting their business.

As for exit regulations, telecommunications companies need only report the termination of their business to the regulator. There is no stringent exit regulation.

The current entry and exit regulations are much lighter than those in place at the end of the 90s.

3.2 Price Regulation

The Telecommunications Business Law (*Denki Tsushin Jigyo-ho*) was heavily revised in 2003 and enacted in April 2004. With the revised law, except for charges at NTT East and NTT West, prices were largely deregulated. Table 9.3 shows a summary of price regulation in the telecommunications industry.

As Table 9.3 shows, except for special services, basic services and specified services, there is no price regulation. According to the Ministry of Internal Affairs and Communications (2005), regulation classifies telecommunications services into four categories.

First, 'special services,' comprised of basic charges and charges for a call using NTT's fixed line telephone system, are defined as telecommunications services which strongly affect users' benefit. The government regulates the price level of these services according to the price-cap regulation.

'Basic services' are defined as universally necessary services such as fixed-line, public, and emergency telephones. And 'specified services' are those provided by a company with bottleneck facilities, where there is no alternative service available from others. User charges for these services must be described as contract articles and must be reported. If the regulator deems the user charges unfair or unreasonably high, the regulator has the option of ordering the telecommunications company to alter its contract articles.

Table 9.3   Price Regulation in the Telecommunications Industry

Type of services	Basic service	Specified service	Special service	Others
Examples	Basic charge and charge for a call, etc. by NTT	Basic charge and charge for a call, etc. by NTT	Basic charge and charge for a call, etc. by NTT	Mobile telephone and internet connection, etc.
Kind of items related to price	Contract article	Contract article	Price level	—
Price regulation	Ex ante report	Ex ante report	Approval (Price-cap regulation)	No regulation
Reservation of order to change	Yes	Yes	—	Yes

[Note]:
(1) This table was written by the author and is based on several sources, including the Ministry of Internal Affairs and Communications (2005), Kurashino Risachi Senta (2004), Bukka Seisaku Antei Kaigi (2005) and Fuke (2005).
(2) Regulation distinguishes three service types: 'special services' are those affecting users' benefit; 'basic services' are universally necessary services; and 'specified services' are those provided by a company with bottleneck facilities, where there is no alternative service available from others.

There is no price regulation for services other than the abovementioned three.

As noted above, the price-cap regulation has been applied to the main services of NTT East and West companies since October 2000. The price-cap regulation is applied to each basket of service (i.e. fixed-line telephone and ISDN service, and exclusive line service). According to the Ministry of Internal Affairs and Communications (2005), the standard price index is obtained as follows:

$$P_t = P_{t-1} \cdot (1 + \Delta CPI_{t-1} - X_t + EF_t) \qquad (9.1)$$

Where P_t : standard price index,

P_{t-1} : standard price index in the previous period t-1,

ΔCPI_{t-1} : rate of change of consumer price index in the previous period t-1,

X_t : expected productivity growth rate

EF_t : external factors.

If a telephone rate determined by a telecommunications company is lower than the standard price (price cap level), then the rate need only be reported to the regulator. For rates higher than the standard price level, however, the regulator must grant approval.

3.3 Regulation for Inter-connections among Telecommunications Companies

In general, telecommunications companies with essential facilities are obligated to connect with other telecommunications companies, when requested to do so by those companies. Figure 9.2 shows regulations for inter-connection.

Telecommunications companies with users of fixed-line telephones (the first type of telecommunications facilities) are considered as those with essential facilities and are required to provide contracts describing inter-connection rules, rates for connection, separate costs related to accounts, and so on. NTT East Japan and NTT West Japan fall into this category.

Companies with mobile telephone facilities for users (the second type of telecommunications facilities) have some requirements as well. These companies must give reports regarding contracts for inter-connection and their accounts for essential facilities. The Ministry of Internal Affairs and Communications has appointed NTT Docomo, KDDI and Okinawa Cellular as this type of company.

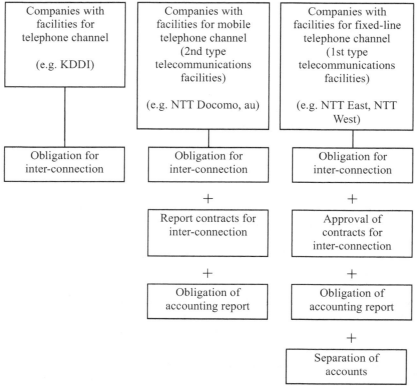

Figure 9.2   Regulation for Inter-Connection

3.4   Regulators

The Ministry of Internal Affairs and Communications is responsible for making regulations and formulating policy.   As mentioned above, telephone prices must be reported to this regulator as well as matters related to compliance with several contract rules.

In addition to this ministry, the Telecommunications Business Dispute Settlement Commission (*Denki Tsushin Jigyo Funso Syori Iinkai*) was established on November 30, 2001, with the role of ensuring a fair and expeditious resolution of disputes.   The commission consists of five members   appointed   by   the   Minister   of   Internal   Affairs   and Communications.

4 REGULATORY REFORMS IN THE TELECOMMUNICATIONS INDUSTRY

4.1 The Telecommunications Business Law of 1985

A dramatic change in the telecommunications industry occurred in 1985, prior to which time services had been monopolized by two organizations, Nippon Telegraph and Telephone Public Corporation in the domestic telecommunications market and Kokusai Denshin Denwa (KDD) Co, Ltd., in the international market. In 1985, Nippon Telegraph and Telephone Public Corporation was privatized, and the new Telecommunications Business Law was established. It was assumed that these actions would bring about competition in the telecommunications industry.

The Telecommunications Business Law classifies telecommunications companies into three categories to which differing regulations apply. Table 9.4 shows a summary of regulations.

Table 9.4   Classification of Telecommunications Companies and Major Regulations

Categories of companies	1st type companies	2nd type companies (special)	2nd type Companies (general)
Definition	Use own lines	Rent other companies' lines (large scale)	Rent other companies' lines (small scale)
Entry regulation	Permission	Registration	Report
Exit regulation	Permission	Ex-post report	Ex-post report
Service regulation	Approval	Ex-ante report	No regulations
Price regulation	Approval	Ex-ante report	No regulations

[Note]: This table was written by the author and is based on information from Fuke (2005) and the Telecommunications Business Law.

The first type of company is one which provides telecommunications services using its own lines. Entry and exit regulations require organizations in this category to obtain permission from the Minister of Posts and Telecommunications, which also must approve the services and prices of these companies.

The second type of company does not hold its own network facilities, providing services to users by borrowing the network of the first type company. As Table 9.4 shows, companies in this category are divided into two groups according to whether they are large-scale or small-scale organizations.

Companies of the second type are lightly regulated, compared with those in the first category. According to Fuke (2005), the government intentionally made regulations light for the second category to encourage new entrants into the telecommunications market, creating competition for the formerly monopolistic companies in the first category. It is deemed that strict regulations should apply to first category companies for reasons of consumer protection, as companies in this category are closed to end-users.

Potential entrants into the telecommunications industry may engage in business after meeting three criteria. First, the company must have the financial and technological ability to conduct telecommunications services. Second, the start-up plan must be feasible. Third, it is judged that fair competition can be maintained after the new company enters the market.

The adjustment of supply and demand is also considered. This policy option is applied to cases in which there is an imbalance between supply and demand. If there is excess supply, the government takes action to limit supply. According to Fuke (2005), however, there has been concern that the regulator might use this regulation arbitrarily. Fuke (2005) maintains that the main reason why new entrants such as pocket-bell companies and PHS companies did not survive in the market was the arbitrary application of the adjustment of supply and demand.

During the regulatory reform in 1985, rules for network access were not well designed. Because essential facilities such as city telephone networks were owned by NTT (an incumbent) monopoly, new entrants could not access the network fairly, and this situation created considerable conflict between NTT and new entrants. At this time, the priority policy of the government was the privatization of NTT. The government did not adequately develop the rules of interconnection between different organizations.[1]

4.2 Major Regulatory Reforms between 1986 and 1999

Since 1985, the Telecommunications Business Law has been gradually revised. Major regulatory reforms up to 2000 can be summarized as follows, according to the Ministry of Internal Affairs and Communications (2005), and Fuke (2005).

First, telephone rates were deregulated in several ways. In 1995, for example, on telephone rates for additional services such as telephone lines for push phones, regulations were changed to a system requiring only reporting to the regulator. Likewise, in 1996, the telephone rate regulation for mobile telephones was changed to a reporting system. In 1998, the price-cap regulation was applied to the telephone rate for basic services such as the domestic telephone services of NTT, while telephone rates for other services, such as non-basic services of NTT and services provided by non-NTT companies, changed into an *ex ante* reporting scheme.

As for entry regulation, in 1997 the adjustment of supply and demand scheme was abolished. Unhindered by arbitrary intervention, entrants were able to enter the telephone service market more easily. Moreover, rules were formulated regarding network access, which became more open in November 1997.

Ownership was also deregulated in February 1998, prior to which the maximum limit of stock shares by foreign investors in the first type of telephone company was at most one third of total shares. In 1997, the limitation on foreign ownership was abolished in the case of first type telephone companies other than NTT and KDD. In 1998, the limitation on foreign ownership of all first type telephone companies was completely eliminated.

4.3 Major Regulatory Reforms between 1999 and 2003

During this period, two major reforms took place. First, NTT was reorganized into several companies. Even though it was privatized in 1985, NTT underwent little reform in the following years. In 1999, NTT was subdivided into 6 companies: NTT Stockholding, NTT East Japan, NTT West Japan, NTT Communications (i.e. intercity telephone company), NTT Docomo (i.e. mobile telephone company), and NTT Data. As Fuke (2005) notes, however, while the rationale for the division of NTT into several companies was to create conditions for fair competition, because these companies are still owned by NTT Stockholding, a truly competitive environment has not been achieved.

Table 9.5   Summary of the Dominant Carrier Regulations

Kind of company	Dominant company		Non-dominant company
	Fixed-line telephone	Mobile telephone	
Rate for service	Price-cap	Report	Report
Service contract terms	Approval	Approval ↓ Report	Approval ↓ Report
Mutual connection	Approval for contract terms of connection, announcement	Approval for contract terms of connection, announcement ↓ Report for contract terms of connection, announcement	Approval for contract terms of connection ↓ Report for contract terms of connection
Providing conditions for fair competition	(i) Install fire wall scheme (e.g. limit on holding board members in different companies, etc.)		(Option for business improvement order)
	(ii) Prohibition of use of connection information for other purposes, prohibition of unfair preferential treatment, etc. (Option for stop and change services)	Prohibition of use of connection information for other purposes, prohibition of unfair preferential treatment, etc. (Option for stop and change services)	

[Note]:
  (1) *This table was written by the author and is based on information from the Ministry of Internal Affair and Communications for the year 2002.*
  (2) *Shaded areas indicate changes resulting from the 2001 regulatory reform.*

Second, the Telecommunications Business Law was revised in 2001 and the dominant carrier regulation, known as the asymmetrical regulation in Japan, was formulated. The basic policy behind the dominant carrier regulation is as follows. First, regulations applying to non-dominant companies in the market are considerably loosened. Second, regulations for dominant companies are retained as is, except for those related to service contract conditions. Last, options for preventing or eliminating unfair competition are provided. The dominant carrier regulation is summarized in Table 9.5.

With regard to the dominant carrier regulation, companies with more than a 50% market share in individual prefectures are considered the dominant company for fixed line telephone services in those areas. As for mobile telephone services, companies with more than a 25% market share are considered dominant. Dominant companies complain that they are regulated much more strictly than non-dominant companies.

Two other important reforms were the establishment of the Telecommunications Business Dispute Settlement Commission and the establishment of the fund for universal service obligation.

First, the Telecommunications Business Dispute Settlement Commission, a body independent of the regulator, was established in November 2001. Five commission members, subject to Diet approval, are appointed by the Minister of Internal Affairs and Communications. The main role of the commission is to resolve disputes fairly and rapidly.

Second, the fund for universal service obligation was established. The universal service obligation, details of which are explained in a separate chapter, was applied to NTT East and NTT West only at the beginning.

4.4   The Revision of the Telecommunications Business Law in 2003

A notable recent reform in the telecommunications industry was the revision of the Telecommunications Business Law in July 2003. According to Fuke (2005), the main reason for the revision was to ease the transition from the telephone to the Internet era. Because a myriad of telecommunications companies would be providing many kinds of services, it was deemed advisable to reconsider regulations for entry and service provision.

The most drastic change within the revision was that the distinction between the first and second types of telecommunications companies was eliminated. Before the revision, telecommunications companies were classified according to whether or not they owned their own network facilities. With the revision, companies are distinguished according to the size of their service areas.

As for entry regulation, a registration scheme is applied to telecommunications companies with more than a certain level of service area and a certain size of network. Other smaller telecommunications companies report only upon the start-up of their business operations and are not required to register.

Price regulation has been scrapped except with regard to the rates of NTT East and NTT West. The rate and articles of contract for basic services such as fixed line telephones and public telephones must be reported to the regulator and published for users. For other services, it is unnecessary to report to the regulator, and dealing directly with users has become possible. However, bodies have been established and provisions made to deal with conflicts that may arise in the deregulated market.

NOTE

[1] According to Fuke (2005), in order to maintain fair competition in telecommunications, there are two approaches: the US-style 'structural separation' scheme, and the UK/EU-style 'behavioral regulation' scheme. In Japan, structural separation was considered when NTT was privatized in 1985. However, the government made the deicison to formulate the rules after the fact, once privatization had been carried out.

10   Broadcasting

1   INTRODUCTION

Changes in the broadcasting industry have not been as rapid or dramatic as those in telecommunications, but the distinction between these two industries has blurred. With the constant advances in telecommunications technology, especially in the last ten years, it is quite possible that barriers between broadcasting and telecommunications will soon disappear altogether, and the two industries will merge.

There are still regulations, however, which apply only to the broadcasting industry. Reforms in broadcasting have been milder than in the telecommunications industry. This chapter will outline the characteristics of the Japanese broadcasting industry and the regulatory reforms that have affected it.

After the introduction, in the second section, the industrial structure of the broadcasting industry in Japan is explained, with attention to characteristics such as market size and the kinds and numbers of broadcasting companies. The third section contains a summary of broadcasting industry regulations, the most important of which are the Radio Law (*Denpa-ho*), the Broadcast Law (*Hoso-ho*) and the Cable Television Broadcast Law (*Yusen Terebijon Hoso-ho*). Along with entry regulations, price regulations and so on, oligopoly regulations are explained. The fourth section deals with regulatory reforms in the broadcasting industry, focusing on important measures carried out according to the de-concentration principle of the mass media, cable television, and the satellite television industry.

2   INDUSTRIAL STRUCTURE

2.1   Classification of Broadcasting Industry

The broadcasting industry in Japan is classified into private broadcasting companies and one publicly owned broadcasting organization, just as in

Europe and the US.   The main revenue sources for private broadcasting companies are advertising revenues and user fees for program content, while the publicly owned broadcasting organization, Nihon Hoso Kyokai (NHK) gets most of its revenue from viewing fees that must be paid by every household in possession of a television set.

Television broadcasting in Japan is classified into three categories: ground broadcasting, satellite broadcasting and cable television.   Table 10.1 shows the market size as total sales of these television industries, and Table 10.2 shows trends in the number of broadcasting companies. The television broadcasting industry is expanding and becoming more competitive because users now have the option of accessing television programs directly from the Internet or their mobile phones.

Table 10.1   Market Size as Total Sales

Fiscal year	2000	2001	2002	2003	2004	2005	2006
Ground broadcasting	2,647	2,596	2,486	2,523	2,615	2,614	2,616
Satellite broadcasting	189	234	277	300	316	341	353
Cable television broadcasting	246	272	308	333	353	385	405
NHK	656	668	675	680	686	675	676
Total	3,738	3,769	3,736	3,836	3,970	4,015	4,049

[Note]:
(1)   This table was written by the author and is based on information from the Ministry of Internal Affairs and Communications (2008).
(2)   NHK: Nihon Hoso Kyokai (Japan Broadcasting Public Corporation).
(3)   Unit: billion yen.

Table 10.2   Number of Broadcasting Companies

Fiscal year	2000	2001	2002	2003	2004	2005	2006	2007
Ground broadcasting	336	346	358	362	371	385	400	414
Satellite broadcasting	149	145	135	135	135	133	127	126
Cable television broadcasting	512	516	528	571	548	535	530	522
NHK	1	1	1	1	1	1	1	1
Total	998	1,008	1,022	1,068	1,054	1,054	1,058	1,063

[Note]: This table was written by the author and is based on information from the Ministry of Internal Affairs and Communications (2007d).

2.2   Ground Broadcasting

Privately owned broadcasting companies have formed nationwide networks, all with Tokyo-based key stations. The ground broadcasting market has been an oligopoly for more than 50 years. Table 10.3 is a summary of the major private broadcasting networks in Japan.

In the television broadcasting industry, the minimum unit of broadcasting area is in general one individual prefecture. Therefore, each private TV broadcasting company provides broadcasting services to users in its prefecture, with the exception of the three largest metropolitan areas Tokyo, Osaka and Nagoya, where broadcasting companies are allowed to serve several prefectures at once. Tokyo's broadcasting area includes seven prefectures (Gunma, Tochigi, Ibaraki, Saitama, Tokyo, Chiba, Kanagawa), Osaka's area includes six prefectures (Shiga, Kyoto, Nara, Osaka, Hyogo, Wakayama), and Nagoya's area includes three prefectures (Aichi, Gifu, Mie).

Table 10.3 Network of Private Broadcasting Companies

Affiliated group	JNN	ANN	NNN	FNN	TXT	Independent U station
Related newspaper company	Mainichi	Asahi	Yomiuri	Sankei	Nikkei	—
Numbers of broadcasting companies	28 stations	26 stations	30 stations	28 stations	6 stations	—
Hokkaido	HBC	HTB	STV	UHB	TVH	—
Aomori	ATV	ABA	RAB	—	—	—
Iwate	IBC	IAT	TVI	MIT	—	—
Miyagi	TBC	KHB	MMT	OX	—	—
Akita	—	AAB	ABS	AKT	—	—
Yamagata	TUY	YTS	YBC	SAY	—	—
Fukushima	TUF	KFB	FCT	FTV	—	—
Gunma						GTV
Tochigi						GYT
Ibaraki						—
Saitama						TVS
Tokyo	TBS	EX	NTV	CX	TX	MXTV
Chiba						CTC
Kanagawa						TVK
Nigata	BSN	NT21	TeNY	NST	—	—
Nagano	SBC	ABN	TSB	NBS	—	—
Yamanashi	UTY	—	YBS	—	—	—
Shizuoka	SBS	SATV	SDT	SUT	—	—
Toyama	TUT	—	KNB	BBT	—	—
Ishikawa	MRO	HAB	KTK	ITC	—	—
Fukui	—	FBC		FTB	—	—
Gifu					—	GBS
Aichi	CBS	NBN	CTV	THK	TVA	—
Mie					—	MTV
Shiga					—	BBC
Kyoto					—	KBS
Nara					—	TVN
Osaka	MBS	ABC	YTV	KTV	TVO	—
Hyogo					—	SUN
Wakayama					—	WTV
Tottori	BSS	—	NKT		—	—
Shimane		—		TSK	—	—
Okayama	RSK			OHK	TSC	—
Kagawa		KSB	RNC			—
Tokushima	—	—	JRT	—	—	—
Ehime	ITV	EAT	RNB	EBC	—	—
Kochi	KUTV	—	RKC	KSS	—	—
Hiroshima	RCC	HOME	HTV	TSS	—	—
Yamaguchi	TYS	YAB	KRY	—	—	—

(continued)

Fukuoka	RKB	KBC	FBS	TNC	TVQ	—
Saga	—	—	—	STS	—	—
Nagasaki	NBC	NCC	NIB	KTN	—	—
Kumamoto	RKK	KAB	KKT	TKU	—	—
Oita	CBS	OAB	TOS		—	—
Miyazaki	MRT	UMK		—	—	—
Kagoshima	MBC	KKB	KYT	KTS	—	—
Okinawa	RBC	QAB	—	OTV	—	—

[Note]:
(1) This table was written by the author and is based on information from sources such as Nihon Minkan Hoso Renmei (2003).
(2) Broadcasting companies are listed in Appendix 2.

As shown in Table 10.3, there are five major privately owned ground broadcasting network companies in Japan: JNN (Japan News Network), ANN (All-Nippon News Network), NNN (Nippon News Network), FNN (Fuji News Network) and TXT (TV Tokyo).

In general, these private broadcasting companies are subject to two kinds of agreements, one related to business and the other to news.   First, the business agreement covers such matters as the time schedule for nationwide broadcasting, the contents of broadcasts by key stations, money distribution, and sales methods in marketing.   News agreements cover matters related to news and information programs.   Japan's private broadcasting networks are strongly connected with the five major nationwide newspaper companies: the Mainichi, Asahi, Yomiuri, Sankei and Nikkei newspapers.

2.3   Satellite Broadcasting

The satellite broadcasting industry in Japan is divided into two groups: BS (Broadcasting Satellite), which uses a satellite system for broadcasting, and CS (Communication Satellite), which uses a satellite system for telecommunications.   Technologically, there is not much difference between the two.

BS analogue broadcasting was initially developed by NHK in 1989. Since then, a private pay channel called WOWOW, specializing in providing movie contents, has entered the market, with its total number of viewers reaching about 20 million in 2000.   BS digital broadcasting began in 2000.   According to Nakamura (2005), the total number of viewers was about 8 million households in March 2005.   CS analogue broadcasting began in 1992, followed by the addition in 1996 of CS digital broadcasting, further expanding the CS market due to the increasing access to a greater number of TV channels.

2.4 Cable TV Broadcasting

Cable TV started in Japan in 1955, two years after the advent of ground broadcasting TV. Originally, cable TV was introduced as a way to provide service to customers who lived in areas where geographical conditions made on-air service distribution difficult, for example areas surrounded by mountains. As the number of regional cable TV stations has increased, these stations have gradually begun to produce their own programs. In urban areas as well, cable TV companies providing widely varied contents and multi-channel programs entered the market. In 1996, Japan's first cable TV Internet company came into being. As mentioned before, the market size of the cable TV industry was 385 billion yen in terms of total sales in 2005, about 15% of the ground broadcasting industry.

In Japan, so-called 'Urban-type cable TV' companies, or those with more than ten thousand terminals, more than 5 channels for broadcasting their own programs and interactive cable television, are expected to grow in the future. According to the Ministry of Internal Affairs and Communications (2008), both the number of cable TV internet companies and their users have been increasing rapidly, as Table 10.4 shows.

Table 10.4   Number of Cable TV Internet Companies and Number of Users

Year	2002	2003	2004	2005	2006	2007
Number of companies	282	307	372	377	385	385
Number of users	2,069	2,578	2,959	3,309	3,610	3,874

[Note]: This table was written by the author and is based on information from the Ministry of Internal Affairs and Communications (2008).

2.5   Nihon Hoso Kyokai (NHK)

The predecessor of Nihon Hoso Kyokai (NHK) was established in 1925, when radio broadcasting began in Tokyo, Osaka and Nagoya, although its formal starting date is 1926. The public corporation took its present organizational form as NHK in 1950, when the Broadcast Law (*Hoso-ho*) was established.

Being a public corporation, NHK is run by a management committee composed of members appointed by the Prime Minister of Japan and approved by the Diet. Furthermore, the budget and closing accounts of NHK must be approved by the Diet.

Unlike private broadcasters, NHK does not rely on advertising revenues but depends instead mainly on viewing fees from users. The payment of viewing fees is mandatory according to the Broadcast Law, and the amount charged must be approved by the Diet. Thus, the management of NHK is strongly regulated by the government.

NHK has many kinds of broadcasting means and media: ground TV, satellite TV, radio, production of contents, and so on. A huge organization, NHK alone accounted for 25% of the entire ground broadcasting industry in terms of total sales in 2006.

3   REGULATION

3.1   Major Regulations

Because broadcasting industry services have the characteristics of public goods, the industry is subject to many regulations, among which are the Radio Law (*Denpa-ho*), the Broadcast Law (*Hoso-ho*), and the Cable Television Broadcast Law (*Yusen Terebijion Hoso-ho*).

First, the Radio Law, enacted in 1950, regulates the fair and efficient use of radio waves in order to further the interests of the public. This law describes rules regarding matters such as the allocation of radio wave frequency and an organization's business plan for using radio waves. One important point in the Radio Law is its stipulation that in order to conduct business, a broadcasting organization must obtain a license, which is valid for 5 years, after which the license must be renewed.

Second, the Broadcast Law was enacted in 1950. While the Radio Law describes technological regulations such as those regarding the allocation of radio wave frequency, the Broadcast Law regulates what the broadcasting business should be. Broadcasting organizations are free to draw up programs and produce their own content, but the Broadcasting

Law includes clauses to protect the public interest, such as prohibitions against violating public order and decency, giving unfair political advantage, reporting falsehoods, and providing prejudicial and one-sided treatment of controversial issues.

Last, the Cable Television Broadcast Law regulates broadcasting organizations using cables. All cable television companies are subject to this law.

Table 10.5 gives a summary of broadcasting industry regulations.

Table 10.5   Broadcasting Industry Regulations

	Ground Broadcasting Company	Cable Television Company	
		Ordinary	Small
Major law	Radio Law Broadcast Law	Cable TV Broadcast Law	Cable TV Broadcast Law
Entry regulation	License	Permission	Report
Price regulation	Approval	Report	Report
Regulation on foreign ownership	Yes	No	No
Regulation on programs	Yes	Yes	Yes
Deliberative body of broadcasting program	Yes	Yes	Yes
Reservation of broadcasting program	Yes	No	No
Efforts for universal service	Yes	No	No
Emergency broadcasting in case of disaster	Yes	No	No

[Note]:
(1)   This table was written by the author and is based on information issued by the Ministry of Internal Affairs and Communications.
(2)   Small cable TV companies are those with less than 500 cable users or those provided by cable TV facilities holder companies.

3.2 Regulation for Oligopoly

Because having too small a number of providers in the broadcasting industry might result in the propagation of biased, misleading, or insufficient contents, the industry is regulated to avoid limiting the number of broadcasters and to limit the power and influence of those in the market.

The oligopoly regulation is described as a ministerial ordinance, called the 'Basic Standard of Establishment of Broadcasting Stations (*Hosokyoku Kaisetsu no Kihonteki Kijun*),' by the Ministry of Internal Affairs and Communications. According to this regulation, a company is allowed to own and manage only one broadcasting station. This regulation, based on what is called in Japan 'the principle of de-concentration of the mass media (*Masu Medhia Syuchu Haijo Gensoku*),' also restricts the percentage of shares one organization can hold in a broadcasting company.

The principle of de-concentration of the mass media embodies two important ideas with regard to an individual broadcasting area. The first important point is related to the shareholding limit. The regulation stipulates that one organization is prohibited from holding voting shares of more than 10% in more than one broadcasting company located in the same broadcasting area. The second important point of the de-concentration principle relates to shareholding in different broadcasting areas. An organization cannot hold voting shares of more than 20% in a broadcasting company if that organization holds voting shares in a broadcasting company in a different broadcasting area. Basically, a broadcasting area is an individual prefecture, with the aforementioned exceptions of the three large metropolitan areas of Tokyo, Osaka and Nagoya.

There is an exception to maintaining the principle of de-concentration of the mass media, and that would be the case of one organization simultaneously holding shares of companies with different broadcasting means, such as a TV broadcasting company and a radio broadcasting company. Asahi Hoso (ABC) in Osaka is one such exception to the principle of de-concentration of the mass media.

4 REGULATORY REFORMS IN THE BROADCASTING INDUSTRY

4.1 Reforms of the Principle of De-concentration of the Mass Media

De-concentration of the mass media was clearly the goal of a ministerial ordinance in October 1988, but related regulations have been loosened in subsequent years. In March 1995, the de-concentration principle was slightly altered to allow a broadcasting company to own voting shares of less than 20% in more than one broadcasting company, as long as the companies' broadcasting areas do not overlap.

More recently, in March 2004, the principle has been deregulated with regard to two points. First, in the case of companies cooperating with other broadcasting companies in an area encompassing seven surrounding broadcasting areas, the shareholding limitation was deregulated. Before deregulation, one organization could not hold voting shares of more than 20% in a broadcasting company in a different broadcasting area. With deregulation, the limit on voting shares was raised to 33.3%. Second, when a broadcasting company in a local area experiences management difficulties, it becomes exempt from limitations on the percentage of voting shares it may hold, and from the rule forbidding board members to hold posts in more than one broadcasting organization.

Regulations regarding de-concentration of the mass media have been lightened. Traditionally, the means of broadcasting—by TV and radio, for example—were very limited in number. However, with technological progress there has been rapid expansion in the industry, with the appearance of BS broadcasting, CS broadcasting, cable TV, the Internet, and mobile phones. All this is in addition to printed media such as newspapers and magazines. With all these mass media venues, it has become the opinion of the majority that heavy regulation should be eliminated and managerial freedom allowed among broadcasting organizations. As a result, deregulation has occurred.

4.2 Reforms of Cable TV

Regulatory reforms of cable TV have also been carried out in many ways. For example, in June 1987, cable TV was limited to being a regional provider only. This regulation changed in December 1993, when the requirement for cable TV companies to be only regional providers was abandoned and they were allowed to serve wider areas.

More drastic reforms relate to foreign ownership. Since the advent of the cable TV industry in January 1973, neither foreign companies nor domestic companies with more than 20% of voting shares held by foreign investors were allowed to own cable TV companies.

However, in December 1993, deregulation changed the allowed level of foreign ownership from 20% to 33.3%, making foreign ownership in the cable TV industry easier. Furthermore, in February 1998, a company owning a class 1 telecommunications company became exempt from the foreign ownership limitation. Finally, in June 1999, the limitation on foreign ownership in the cable TV industry was completely eliminated. Since then, foreign investors can own cable TV companies on an equal footing with their domestic counterparts.

4.3 Reforms of the Satellite TV Industry

In Japan, BS broadcasting and CS broadcasting are treated institutionally differently. When BS broadcasting services first began to be offered, a hardware broadcasting company owning its own broadcasting facilities and a software broadcasting company that produced the contents of broadcast programs were considered one and the same organization. That is, BS broadcasting companies produced broadcasting programs as well as managing and maintaining broadcasting facilities.

However, in 1989, one year before CS broadcast services began, both the Radio Law and the Broadcast Law were reformed so that it was no longer necessary for broadcasting companies that use communications satellites (CS) to own their own communications satellite facilities. That is, it became possible for software companies to be separated from hardware companies in the CS broadcasting industry in Japan, in a system called 'Trust-Entrust Broadcasting System (*Jutaku-Itaku Hoso Seido*)' (see Figure 10.1).

In this system, a software broadcasting company, which produces program contents (trustee), entrusts a hardware broadcasting company, which has its own broadcasting facilities (entrustee), with distributing broadcasting services. The Trust-Entrust Broadcasting System is used in both BS digital broadcasting services and CS broadcasting services. This system was installed mainly to foster conditions conducive to new companies' entering the market, even if they do not own their own satellite facilities.

In January 2002, 'Broadcasting System by Use of Telecommunications Services (*Denki Tsushin Ekimu Riyo Hoso Seido*)' began. In this system, broadcasting companies provide broadcasting services to users by using the facilities of others, such as satellite owners without their own broadcasting license. This system aims to make it easier to use telecommunications facilities for broadcasting.

(1) Ordinal broadcasting company

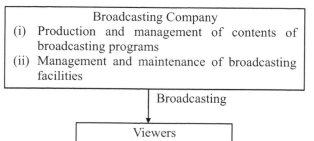

(2) Trust-Entrust Broadcasting System

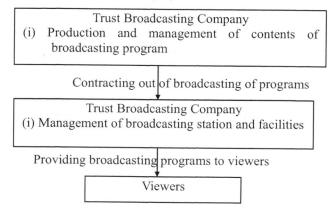

(3) Broadcasting System by Use of Telecommunications Services

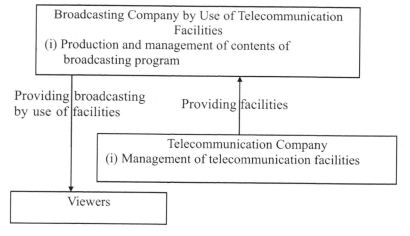

Figure 10.1   Major Kinds of Broadcasting Systems

Thus, structural changes in the satellite broadcasting industry can be summarized with attention to three characteristics, according to Nakamura (2005). First, the vertical separation policy in the broadcasting industry—the separation of broadcasting program companies from broadcasting facility companies—promotes more competition and causes expansion in the content-providing market.

Second, CS broadcasting created a new type of organization called a 'platform company,' or one which mediates between the trust broadcasting company and the entrust company. The platform company's role is the coordination of broadcasting programs, marketing activities, collecting viewing fees from viewers, and so on. This intermediate organization is interesting in that it reduces transaction costs.

Last, the introduction of the Broadcasting System by Use of Telecommunication Services augurs further unification of the telecommunications and the broadcasting industries.

PART V

Selected Topics on Regulatory Reforms in Japan

11   Yardstick Regulation

1   INTRODUCTION

Japanese public utility industries seek to improve firms' managerial efficiency by applying incentive regulations.   In Japan, the most common way to encourage efficiency improvement is through the use of yardstick regulation, a regulatory method whereby the regulator evaluates firms' performance and gives rewards or penalties according to firms' efficiency level.   The firms are in general located in different markets, so that they are not in direct competition.   However, competition can be created among these firms by subjecting them to common assessment measures in the form of yardstick regulation, which in Japan is generally used at the price-setting stage and applies to the following public utility industries: electric power, gas, rail, and bus service.

This chapter consists of five sections.   Following the introduction, the second section, an overview of yardstick regulation, gives a definition of yardstick regulation, explains its theoretical background, outlines the necessary conditions for its application, and identifies the industries to which it is applied.   The third section is a summary of how yardstick regulation is applied in practice to four Japanese public utility industries—electric power, gas, rail, and bus service.   The fourth section is a discussion, based on previous empirical research, of the effectiveness of yardstick regulation.   The last section summarizes points important to the design of yardstick regulation.

2   OVERVIEW OF YARDSTICK REGULATION

2.1   Yardstick Regulation

Yardstick regulation is an incentive regulation whereby a regulator assesses firms' performance by imposing common evaluation measures on plural firms operating in geographically different markets. Although these firms are not directly competing with each other in the market, indirect competition can be created among them through the use of yardstick regulation, which is designed to increase their internal efficiency.

The idea of yardstick regulation is not new. For example, according to Uekusa (2000), the economic advantages of yardstick regulation gained attention when Littlechild recommended applying the scheme to the water supply industry in the UK in 1986, since which time yardstick regulation has apparently worked well in this industry and has been widely recognized for its practical value.

In Japan, while the actual phrase 'yardstick regulation' has not been used, in fact a scheme similar to what this phrase denotes has existed in the rail industry in Japan since the 1970s, having been applied to 15 large private railway companies since that time. In the Japanese rail industry, yardstick regulation is used to assess rail companies when they seek to revise their fares. Details will appear in a later section, but the essence of yardstick regulation is as follows. The regulator evaluates each individual firm's performance by using such information as the firm's average cost. If a firm outperforms others, the regulator will grant approval for a fare revision. To the contrary, if a firm's performance is inferior to others, approval for fare revision will be withheld until the less efficient firm reduces its costs.

2.2   Theoretical Background for Yardstick Regulation

There is much theoretical research on yardstick regulation—Shleifer (1985), Armstrong et al. (1994), Dalen (1998), Sobel (1999), Tangerås (2002). The most important among these is Shleifer (1985), which gives a theoretical foundation for yardstick regulation. In this section, using Uekusa (2000) as a basis, I will explain the essence of the theory.

There are n firms. Each individual firm is located in a different geographical market and each firm is assumed to be a local monopoly. Each firm is supposed to face its demand function, $q(p)$, where q: service output, p: price. This monopoly firm is supposed to invest a certain amount of z in order to reduce the firm's cost. As a result, the firm's marginal cost $c(z)$ decreases by z. A government sets up the service price, p, as equal to the marginal cost of the firm. However, as the firm creates deficits, the government gives lump-sum subsidies, T, to the firm. Under these conditions, the firm's profit, π, is expressed as follows: $\pi = (p - c(z))\, q(p) - z + T$. On the other hand, the government maximizes social welfare, W, which consists of the consumer's and the producer's surplus, under the zero profit condition of the firm. That is, $max_{p,z,T} W = \int q(x)dx + (p - c(z))q(p) - z$.

Under these conditions, optimal solutions are summarized as follows. First, price is equal to the marginal cost, $p^* = c(z^*)$. Second, a certain amount of investment to reduce the marginal cost is equal to lump-sum subsidies, $z^* = T^*$. Third, cost reduction efforts by investment occur until the marginal benefit of cost reduction is equal to the marginal cost of effort (investment), $-c'(z^*) q(p^*) = 1$.

However, the solution does not introduce cost reduction behavior of a firm because the government does not know the optimal level of the firm's marginal cost $(c(z))$. Furthermore, whatever the cost reduction effort (z) level, the firm can be guaranteed to have zero profit. Therefore, the firm has no incentive to reduce marginal cost to the lowest possible level.

In order to solve the problem, Shleifer proposes that the marginal cost of firm i and the cost reduction effort of firm i should be the average value of those of other firms. That is, $\check{c}_i = \Sigma_{j \neq i} c_j /(n-1)$ for the marginal cost and $\check{z}_i = \Sigma_{j \neq i} z_j /(n-1)$ for the cost reduction investment. And by setting a rule such that $p_i = \check{c}_i$ and $T_i = \check{z}_i$, the government can induce firms to engage in behavior that will incur the minimum marginal cost $(\check{c}_i = c_i^*)$.

Thus, Shleifer provides a theoretical foundation for how yardstick regulation works. Since then, theoretical studies have been carried out exploring questions such as what results might occur when preconditions are changed.

2.3 Necessary Conditions for Yardstick Regulation to Work

For yardstick regulation to be effective, it must be applied to firms operating in different geographical markets, where they are competing not directly but indirectly, although even in geographically separated markets natural competition is not altogether nonexistent. In this section, I will summarize the conditions necessary for yardstick regulation to work.

In general, the following five points are important, as noted by Ito and Miyazone (1994), Uekusa (1996), and Ishii (1996): (i) there exist plural firms, (ii) the firms are homogeneous, (iii) there is no collusion, (iv) a regulator has evaluation measures by which comparison of firms' performance is possible, (v) an incentive system is designed whereby firms improve their performance based on evaluation results.

First, as yardstick regulation evaluates firms' performance, it is necessary that plural firms exist. Although monopolies are common in public utility industries, the existence of at least two firms is necessary. However, even two firms may not be enough, according to Price (2003), who notes that yardstick competition is generally difficult to apply unless there is a large number of units and data are easily verifiable.

Second, it is necessary that firms be homogeneous. As many researchers point out, theoretically yardstick regulation cannot be applied if homogeneity among firms does not hold. Practically, if firms are very different, it is difficult to compare their performance, and yardstick regulation does not work well, as noted by Sobel (1999). Furthermore, Kridel et al. (1996) argue that the reason yardstick regulation is used so sparingly in the telecommunications industry is that there is such wide variation among firms.

Third, it is necessary that there be no collusion. If a relatively more efficient firm shirks increasing its efficiency level due to collusion with a less-efficient firm, then the entire industry becomes inefficient. Obviously, collusion should be prevented.

Fourth, it is important that there be measures and sufficient data for a performance comparison of firms. Price (2003) argues that if measures for performance comparison are constructed based on poor or unreliable data sets, there is a risk of producing the wrong results, as poor measures distort a firm's incentive to increase efficiency.

Last, the performance evaluation stipulated by yardstick regulation must promote incentives for firms to increase their efficiency, such as by imposing penalties on inefficient firms and awarding bonuses to highly efficient firms.

2.4 Public Utility Industries Subject to Yardstick Regulation

Yardstick regulation is widely applied to public utility industries, a typical example being the rail industry in Japan. Since the 1970s, in order to determine rail fare levels, the national government has used yardstick regulation for large privately owned railways. Moreover, in 1997, yardstick regulation became more systematically applied to 6 passenger JR companies and 10 subway organizations in addition to 15 large private railways. While information is lacking as to what extent yardstick regulation is applied in foreign rail industries, Bouf and Péguy (2001) contend, based on an analysis of western European railways, that the yardstick competition scheme is desirable.

Although not named as such, 'yardstick regulation' seems to be in effect in the bus industry in Japan as well. The standard cost for each region is set and each bus company's cost is evaluated through a comparison with standard cost. Incidentally, outside Japan, the yardstick regulation scheme is used in Norway's bus industry as well (see, for example, Dalen and Gómez-Lobo (2003)).

As for Japan's energy-providing electric power and gas utility industries, yardstick regulation has been in use, particularly since 1996, when it began to be applied to these industries on a systematic basis. Details of the scheme will appear in the next section, but in general, yardstick regulation is used for 10 general electricity companies in the electric power industry and 240 gas utility companies, divided into 16 groups, in the gas utility industry. Outside Japan, in Sweden, other Scandinavian countries and the UK, yardstick regulation is applied to the electric power and gas utility industries (see, for example, Kumbhakar and Hjalmarsson (1998), Price (2003), Agrell et al. (2005) and Weyman-Jones (2003)).

Although yardstick regulation is used in the water supply industry in the UK (e.g. Cowan (1997)), it has not yet been applied to Japan's water supply industry.

Yardstick regulation is also applied to other activities in various countries, such as port services (e.g. Estoche, González and Trujillo (2002)), the inspection of automobiles (e.g. Ylvinger (1998)), and pipelines (e.g. Hillman (1991)). Furthermore, as Lawrence, Houghton and George (1997) show, the yardstick scheme, with its several performance measures, can be used for evaluating infrastructure development. Dormont and Milcent (2005) propose extending the model of Shleifer's yardstick competition scheme in order to apply it to the medical payment system in order to increase hospitals' efficiency.

3   THE PRACTICE OF YARDSTICK REGULATION IN JAPAN

3.1   The Electric Power Industry

Referring to studies by Ito and Miyazone (1994), Yamaya (1996) and Yokokura (1996), as well as interviews with the Agency of Natural Resources and Energy, in this section I will summarize yardstick regulation's application to the electric power industry in Japan.

Yardstick regulation in the electric power industry has been systematically applied since January 1996. Although yardstick regulation had existed before this date, the scheme was revised to increase efficiency by introducing competition among general electricity companies.

Ten general electricity companies are subject to yardstick regulation, including Tokyo Electric Power Company and Kansai Electric Power Company. Unlike organizations in the gas utility and railway industries, general electricity companies are not divided into groups but are all subject to the same measures of yardstick regulation. Furthermore, although deregulation in the electric power industry has been gradually progressing, the government does not yet apply yardstick regulation to new-entrant electricity providing companies (PPS).

Yardstick regulation is applied for the assessment of electricity prices in Japan. Pricing has two stages, and the yardstick regulation scheme comes into play at the second stage. At the first stage, a general electricity company's electricity prices are individually evaluated according to the validity of the individual company's cost performance relative to real material prices, price increase ratios, and so on. The yardstick scheme is used at the second stage.

As for relative assessment among general electricity companies, evaluation categories are divided according to three items: (i) capital cost related to facilities for gleaning power resources, (ii) capital cost related to other facilities such as power transmission facilities and substations, and (iii) general variable costs. For these three items, two evaluation measures are used: (i) the cost level of each category (yen per kwh), and (ii) the rate of change of each category (%). According to Yamaya (1996), figures from the three years preceding the evaluation are used.

As the ten general electricity companies vary in size and demand conditions, certain problems arise if yardstick regulation is applied without modification. Therefore, in Japan the measures are adjusted in several ways to remove noise unrelated to managerial efficiency, with corrections made on the following four points: (i) facilities of power resources, (ii) inter-regional usage, (iii) Okinawa, (iv) regional differences. These corrections are summarized in Table 11.1.

First, corrections are made with regard to power resource facilities in order to correct for energy cost differences due to differing power resources. Nuclear power generation, thermal power generation by coal, and hydroelectric power generation have cost-saving advantages over thermal power generation by petroleum and gas. Savings attributable to fuel costs are deducted from base-costs.

Second, corrections are made to costs related to the inter-regional transmission of electricity, which are also deducted from base-costs.

Third, corrections on Okinawa are made to reflect Okinawa prefecture's disadvantage in holding a considerable number of remote, isolated islands, a fact which drives up its providing costs in comparison with such costs in other prefectures.

Last, using regression results, corrections in regional difference are made in order to equalize providing conditions. Half the difference between actual values and estimated values based on regression results for each electricity company is considered to represent regional specific factors unexplained by the regression. These become the base of coefficients for corrections in regional differences.

Table 11.1   Corrections in Costs in Electric Power Service

Item of corrections	Explanation
Corrections in facilities of power resources	This is to correct energy cost differences among power resources such as nuclear, coal, and hydroelectric power generation.
Corrections in inter-regional usage	This is to correct facility related costs for inter-regional usage.
Corrections on Okinawa	This is to correct cost disadvantages related to Okinawa's many remote islands.
Corrections in regional differences	This is to correct regional cost differences. The regression result is used for the correction. Explanatory variables for the correction include the following: (i) demanded electric energy per contracted household or firm, (ii) ratio of highly populated areas, (iii) ratio of low-voltage and high-voltage demand, (iv) number of contractors per supply area of 1 km^2, (v) demanded electric energy per 1 km of power transmission line, (vi) maximum electric energy at initial power reception.

[Note]: This table was written by the author and is based on information from the Agency of Natural Resources and Energy.

After the costs of each general electricity company are corrected with regard to the four items mentioned above, evaluation scores are calculated.   The scores are obtained based on the efficiency level of each electricity company.   Table 11.2 shows details of the scoring system.

As this table shows, scores are obtained for three items under evaluation: (i) facilities for power generation; (ii) facilities for transmission and substations; and (iii) other general costs.   For these three items, scores are calculated in terms of both quantity and rate of change.   A score of 100 points is awarded to the most efficient company, 0 points to the least efficient, and between 0 and 100 to companies with mid-range efficiency.   Total scores are located between 0 points (lowest) and 200 points (highest).

*Table 11.2   Evaluation Method for Yardstick Regulation
          in the Electric Power Industry*

Evaluation item	Facilities for power generation	Facilities for transmission and substations	Other general costs
Evaluation measure	Capital stock per electricity volume	Capital stock per electricity volume	Costs per electricity volume
Specified measure (Quantity)	0~100 points	0~100 points	0~100 points
Specified measure (Rate of change)	0~100 points	0~100 points	0~100 points
Total scores	0~200 points	0~200 points	0~200 points
Category for evaluation	I~III	I~III	I~III

[Note]: This table was written by the author and is based on information from the Agency of Natural Resources and Energy.

Finally, each general electricity company is categorized into one of three groups based on its total score. Group I (more than 121 points) is categorized as most efficient, Group II (less than 120 points and more than 80 points) is in the medium range of efficiency, and Group III (less than 79 points) is the least efficient group. Finally, as Table 11.3 shows, electric power companies are expected to improve their efficiency levels based on their category, with highest expectations for steep cost reductions being placed on the least efficient group.

Table 11.3 Categories for Evaluation and Goals of Management Effort in Yardstick Regulation: the Case of the Electric Power Industry

Category	Group I	Group II	Group III
Total score	121~200 points	80~120 points	0~79 points
Evaluation	Firms attaining higher efficiency level	Firms attaining average efficiency level	Firms remaining at lower efficiency level
Management Goal	Not necessary to set a clear goal	1% cost reduction	2% cost reduction

[Note]: *This table was written by the author and is based on information from the Agency of Natural Resources and Energy.*

3.2 The Gas Utility Industry

In the gas utility industry, a comprehensive yardstick regulation scheme was established in January 1996. As in the electric power industry, this comprehensive yardstick regulation was a revision of the former yardstick regulation scheme aiming to introduce competition among firms and attain managerial efficiency. This section contains a summary of the main points of the yardstick regulation scheme in the gas utility industry, based on previous studies by Yamaya (1996) and Yokokura (1994, 1996), as well as interviews with the Agency of Natural Resources and Energy.

First, the yardstick regulation scheme in the gas utility industry divides organizations for evaluation into 16 groups and applies yardstick regulations to each group. While the electric power industry, with only 10 power companies, is not subdivided, the gas utility industry encompasses more than 240 companies, and among those companies there is wide variation as to type of ownership, size, kinds of gas resources, and quantity of heat. Gas companies are divided based on three criteria: (i) ownership (private or public), (ii) raw material and the manufacturing process of gas, and (iii) region.

As in the electric power industry, the evaluation process for the gas utility industry takes place in two stages, the first of which is to evaluate each individual company's costs, and the second of which is to evaluate relative efficiency among gas companies. Yardstick regulation is applicable at the second stage.

As for relative assessment among gas companies, evaluation categories are divided into two items: (i) capital costs related to facilities, and (ii) general variable costs. For these two items, two evaluation measures are used: (i) the cost level of each category (yen per m^3), and (ii) the rate of change of each category (%).

Although evaluation measures are corrected in the gas utility industry as they are in the electric power industry, the correction method is different, with the gas utility industry focusing on the following two points: (i) individual corrections, and (ii) common corrections. Individual corrections are conducted for each individual gas company for investment in the construction of large-scale facilities such as LNG stations and main pipes. On the other hand, common corrections are conducted for all gas companies of each group in order to correct for providing conditions. In the corrections, regression results are used. The corrected items for the regression are scale of demand size, unit volume of demand, and the rate of change in demand.

After the costs of each gas company are corrected, evaluation scores are calculated, based on the efficiency level of each gas company. Table 11.4 shows the details of the scoring system. As this table shows, scores are obtained for two evaluation items: (i) capital costs for facilities, and (ii) other general costs. For these items, scores are calculated in terms of both quantity and rate of change. A score of 100 points is awarded to the most efficient company, 0 points to the least efficient, and between 0 and 100 to companies with mid-range efficiency. For each item, total scores are located between 0 points (lowest) and 200 points (highest).

Finally, each gas company is categorized into one of three groups according to its total score. Group I (more than 121 points) is categorized as most efficient, Group II (less than 120 points and more than 80 points) is in the medium range of efficiency, and Group III (less than 79 points) is the least efficient group. Finally, as Table 11.5 shows, gas companies are expected to improve their efficiency levels based on their category, with the least efficient group being expected to achieve the biggest reductions in cost.

Table 11.4   Evaluation Method for Yardstick Regulation
in the Gas Utility Industry

Evaluation item	Capital costs for facilities	Other general costs
Evaluation measure	Capital costs per gas volume	Costs per gas volume
Specified measure (Quantity)	0~100 points	0~100 points
Specified measure (Rate of change)	0~100 points	0~100 points
Total scores	0~200 points	0~200 points
Category for evaluation	I~III	I~III

[Note]: This table was written by the author and is based on information from the Agency of Natural Resources and Energy.

Table 11.5   *Categories for Evaluation and Management Goals in Yardstick Regulation: the Case of the Gas Utility Industry*

Category	Group I	Group II	Group III
Total score	121~200 points	80~120 points	0~79 points
Evaluation	Firms attaining higher efficiency level	Firms attaining average efficiency level	Firms remaining at lower efficiency level
Management Goal	Not necessary to set a clear goal	0.5 % cost reduction	1 % cost reduction

[Note]: This table was written by the author and is based on information from the Agency of Natural Resources and Energy.

3.3   The Rail Industry

Ten years after the privatization of the Japan National Railways, regulatory reform in the rail industry was carried out. One important reform was the application in 1997 of comprehensive yardstick regulation, which in practice had been applied to fare revision in fifteen large private railways since the 1970s. The regulator, the Ministry of Land, Infrastructure and Transport, had used yardstick regulation to increase efficiency among existing railway companies. According to Fujii and Chujo (1992), this scheme used three measures to evaluate rail operators' performance: the improvement rate of (i) fare revenue, (ii) productivity, and (iii) operating costs. Yardstick regulation was applied to only 15 large private railway companies until the 1997 revision, which I will explain based on Ishii (1996), and Okabe (1997, 2004).

While the former yardstick regulation scheme applied to only 15 large private railway companies, the 1997 revised regulation increased that number to 31 railway companies, divided into three different groups: 15 large private railways, 6 passenger JRs, and 10 public subway systems (Okabe, 2004).

Yardstick regulation comes into play when rail companies seek to revise their fares. The regulator evaluates the cost level of a company, and if the actual cost of the railway is higher than the standard cost, then the rail company is considered a less efficient rail operator and can be expected reduce actual costs. On the other hand, if the actual cost of the railway company is lower than the standard cost, it need not reduce costs. Moreover, half the difference between actual and standard costs is remitted to the efficient rail operator as a reward. Standard cost is set by the yardstick competition scheme.

To set up standard cost for yardstick regulation, operating costs are separated into five sub-components: (i) track costs, (ii) catenary costs, (iii) rolling stock costs, (iv) train operating costs, and (v) station operating costs. Standard costs (*Kijun Hiyo*) for these five measures are obtained by considering each railway company's providing conditions, such as vehicle-km, number of passengers, route-km, and stations. In fact, this information is made public as a regression formula to calculate standard unit cost.

In sum, yardstick regulation is used to promote competition among regulated railway companies. Because the less efficient rail company in the yardstick group is forced to reduce costs, railway costs in general are expected to decline over time if this regulation works well.

3.4 The Bus Service Industry

Although not as clearly stated or formulated as for the rail industry, a yardstick regulation scheme is in use in the bus service industry in Japan for the purpose of setting a benchmark cost for efficiency comparisons among bus companies when bus fare is assessed. That is, according to Fujii and Chujo (1992), the mean value of the operating costs of all bus service companies is defined as the standard cost. An individual company's efficiency level is evaluated according to whether or not its cost is lower than this standard cost. In a case where an individual bus company's operating cost exceeds the standard cost, the difference between these two costs becomes the amount the bus company is penalized. On the other hand, if a company's cost is lower than the standard cost, the difference becomes a bonus in the assessment of bus fare level.

In the bus service industry, evaluation is conducted for 21 regions. The standard cost is obtained as weighted average costs per vehicle kilometer of each region's bus companies. Publicly owned bus companies and small private bus companies (with less than 30 vehicles) are excluded when calculating standard costs.

Personnel expenses, fuel costs, vehicle repair costs, and vehicle depreciation are included in the standard cost of each region. However, this raw standard cost also includes regional variations faced by individual bus companies and is therefore corrected before the fare assessment. In fact, the standard cost of each region is defined as the mean value of the raw standard costs and the real operating costs of its bus companies. It is worth noting that the raw standard cost of private bus companies is used for the calculation of the standard cost of publicly owned bus companies.

4   EMPIRICAL RESULTS REGARDING THE EFFECTIVENESS OF YARDSTICK REGULATION

Although Shleifer (1985) presents a theoretical foundation for yardstick regulation, empirical studies are few on the subject of whether or not yardstick regulation works to improve efficiency. This section contains a summary of empirical results from both Japan and other countries.

4.1   Public Utility Industries in Japan

The Electric Power Industry

First of all, Ito and Miyasone (1994) investigate the effect of yardstick regulation on the electric power industry in Japan. There are ten general electricity companies, and yardstick regulation has been applied to all ten. However, comprehensive yardstick regulation was not applied to companies in the electric power industry until 1996, so that Ito and Niyasone's study is an analysis of the effect of the less comprehensive yardstick scheme in existence before that time. In essence, their study evaluates the effect of yardstick regulation by using time series data. As yardstick regulation is used in the assessment of price setting, it follows that if it works properly, then each general electricity company will increase its efficiency due to the competitive pressure presumably created by the regulation. Therefore, the authors conjecture some index showing organizational efficiency improvement over time, if yardstick competition works effectively. They evaluate whether or not companies' performance index improves, and indeed the authors note a lessening in variation among the 10 indexes they examine, such as the labor productivity for 9 general electricity companies, over 36 years between 1955 and 1990. The fact that 6 out of 10 indexes indicate performance improvement and that the variation among companies has shrunk makes the authors conclude that yardstick regulation has been working effectively. However, this study's considerable weak point is the lack of evidence that efficiency improvement is caused by yardstick regulation, in light of the fact that yardstick regulation is applied to all general electricity companies in Japan.

Ida and Kuwahara (2004) compare efficiency among general electricity companies in Japan. In their study, the translog cost function is estimated for an efficiency comparison by using a data set for the years between 1978 and 1998. Due to the substantial variation in efficiency measures among companies, their estimation results show no clear evidence that yardstick regulation works well.

The Railway Industry

Mizutani (1997) investigates the effectiveness of yardstick regulation for large private railways by using a data set from the years 1980 to 1993, prior to the time when comprehensive yardstick regulation was formally enacted but when it was nevertheless applied to some extent. The conclusion reached is that yardstick regulation does not cause large cost reductions but that it works to some degree because average costs decline and the fare level falls between the price under perfect competition and the monopoly price.

The Committee of the Regulatory Impact Study on Government-Regulated Public Service Charges (2005) investigates the effect of the comprehensive yardstick regulation introduced into the rail industry in 1996. In this study, the demand forecast model is used for the analysis. Simulation results are compared for two cases: with and without yardstick regulation. In this analysis, user benefits and producer benefits are calculated for the year 2000. According to this study, the suppression effect on fare increase due to yardstick regulation was 1.1 to 5.5 yen per passenger, so that total user benefits in the Tokyo metropolitan areas were 5.3 billion yen in 2000. One weak point of this study is that it remains unclear whether the effects were caused by yardstick regulation.

More recently, Mizutani et al. (2009) investigated the effectiveness of yardstick regulation by using a data set of rail companies in Japan and estimating the variable frontier cost function. In their study, both the coefficient of the yardstick regulation dummy and the coefficient of the competitive pressure outside the industry show the negative sign with statistical significance in the cost function. Therefore, they conclude that the introduction of yardstick regulation and competition tend to decrease a rail company's variable cost. They found that railways to which yardstick regulation was applied improved cost efficiency by about

11.5% between 1995 and 2000.

4.2   Other Examples

Dalen and Gómez-Lobo (2003) analyze what kind of regulation method is beneficial to the performance of bus operators in Norway. In their study, the contract type is analyzed and as an example the yardstick competition method for contracts is included. They use 1136 observations from 142 Norwegian bus operators for the 11 years from 1987 to 1997 and estimate frontier cost function. In cost inefficiency differences, the yardstick competition effect is included. The authors conclude that the adoption of a more high-powered scheme based on a yardstick type of regulation significantly reduces operating costs.

Kumbhakar and Hjalmarsson (1998) analyze productive efficiency in Swedish retail electricity distribution by using data from 1970 to 1990 in order to find differences according to ownership. In their analysis, they use several statistical methods, including DEA (Data Envelopment Analysis) and the stochastic frontier model for labor input. Their conclusion is that privately owned companies are relatively more efficient. They interpret persistent efficiency differences between private and publicly owned firms as a strong indication of the impact of yardstick competition. They also mention that this yardstick type of regulation seems to offer weak incentives for cost minimization in municipal firms located in densely populated regions.

Estoche, González and Trujillo (2002) analyze productive efficiency by applying the stochastic production frontier function to Mexican ports for the years from 1996 to 1999. They note that the analytically sound performance rankings allowed by port-specific efficiency measures can help in promoting yardstick competition. However, again this study also does not show a direct relationship between yardstick competition and an increase in efficiency.

By using a 1993 data set, Ylvinger (1998) analyzes productive efficiency in the operation of Swedish motor-vehicle inspections. His method is to measure the efficiency level by applying DEA to the data set. He concludes that the fairly high level of technical efficiency might be explained by the extensive practice of yardstick competition in the industry, but unfortunately a clear link is not established between the results and the application of yardstick competition.

To test the theory of yardstick competition, Jürges et al. (2005) apply it to the schooling system in Germany and conclude that yardstick competition has a positive effect on the quality of teaching. However, this study's disadvantage is that because other factors are not controlled, it does not measure the effect of yardstick competition to the exclusion of other factors.

Thus, most previous studies suggest that yardstick regulation has an effect on productive efficiency but they fail to distinguish the yardstick regulation effect from other factors.

5 THE DESIGN OF YARDSTICK REGULATION

5.1 Firms to which Yardstick Regulation is Applied

It is not easy to apply yardstick regulation to utility industries consisting of few firms.   For yardstick regulation to be applied, it is necessary that there be multiple firms, that the firms be subject to similar outside conditions, and that the firms be homogeneous.   We cannot specify how many firms are required in order for yardstick regulation to be advisable, but if there are too few firms in a public utility industry, the regulator faces difficulties in equalizing outside conditions, and firms might tend to be more likely to engage in collusion.

As a method of creating conditions conducive to the application of yardstick regulation, it is possible to subdivide a firm into several different smaller ones.   Bouf and Péguy (2001) discuss the possibility of using yardstick regulation to horizontally separated organizations in the rail industry.   In fact, in the case of the Japan National Railway privatization in 1987, horizontal separation of the passenger service division (i.e. subdivision into 6 regional passenger JR companies) was carried out, thereby creating the minimum condition for applying yardstick regulation.

5.2 The Prevention of Collusion

One important consideration with regard to yardstick regulation is the prevention of collusion among regulated firms.   Although yardstick regulation is widely applied to public utility industries in Japan, the issue of preventing collusion has been largely ignored.

One way to decrease the likelihood of collusion is to apply yardstick regulation to a great number of firms in the industry, making it more difficult for firms to organize any effort to collude.

A second possible way of preventing collusion is to withhold information about the identities of the firms to which yardstick regulation is being applied.   Currently, there is an attitude that matters related to government regulation should be completely transparent and that no information should be withheld from the public. However, in Japan, there is a multitude of firms in the bus industry, subdivided into smaller groups to which yardstick regulation is applied. Each firm knows to which group it belongs, and this knowledge possibly creates the opportunity for collusion, a problem that might be ameliorated if yardstick groups were shuffled on a periodic basis.

A third way to decrease the possibility of collusion is to treat the most efficient and the least efficient firms very differently, by giving generous rewards to the most efficient and imposing penalties on the least efficient.

Thus, the chance of collusion is largely dependent upon the design of the yardstick regulation. Potters et al. (2004), by using the method of experimental economics, investigate the differences between cases of the same yardstick method and cases of different yardstick methods.

The relationship between privatization and collusion is also important. Bös (1991) pointed out that privatized firms tend to have a higher chance of collusion because information such as that concerning contracts among firms is not open to the public. Even if collusion is not clearly identifiable, customs common prior to privatization might prevail, producing inefficient behavior similar to what existed before privatization.

5.3   Method for Controlling Outside Factors

Many factors affect a firm's costs. The most common method for controlling outside factors is regression analysis, which Filipini and Wild (2001), for example, use to control heterogeneity among firms in the electric supply industry in Switzerland. They correct the cost function for the assessment by estimating the average cost function.

In the electric power industry and the rail industry in Japan, a similar method is used, as mentioned above. An explanation of the essence of the method can be found in Yokokura (1996), who defined three categories of factors affecting the cost structure of a firm: (i) a firm's common environmental factor (X), comprising outside factors affecting firms in general, and (ii) a firm's individual environmental factor (Y), comprising outside factors affecting a specific firm, (iii) a firm's effort factor (Z), which is its internal effort factor. Yokokura specifies the cost of firm-i as $C_i = \alpha + \beta X_i + \gamma Y_i + \delta Z_i + e_i$. In this equation, he mentions that e_i is a coincidental factor and that in this equation, as Y_i is affected on a case by case basis for each individual firm, we cannot recognize it clearly by using other firms' information. Therefore, the only possible factor to control the firm's heterogeneity is X_i by using the regression analysis. Therefore, we estimate the equation $C_i = \alpha + \beta X_i + e_i$, and obtain the predicted value of firm-i, which is $\underline{C_i} = \alpha + \beta \underline{X_i}$. The difference between the predicted and actual values, $\underline{C_i} - C_i$, could be a measure of firm-i's effort level. However, as this measure also includes a firm's individual environmental factor (Y), Yokokura proposes a partial adaptation. That is, $\mu (\underline{C_i} - C_i)$ $(0 \leq \mu < 1)$. For example, if a regulator takes $\mu = 0.5$, half of the factors is considered as a firm's effort factor. In fact, an individual firm's standard cost (C_i^*) for yardstick regulation in Japan is specified as $C_i^* = \mu (\underline{C_i} - C_i)$.

5.4 Evaluation Method for Managerial Effort

Yokokura (1996) also classifies evaluation methods for managerial effort into two types: 'the cardinal approach,' whereby real values such as firms' average cost are used for the evaluation; and 'the ordinal approach,' whereby categorized order is used.

Yokokura (1996) notes that there are three possible targets for the evaluation. The first is the current situation of a firm. In this case, the target cost of the firm (C^*) is the current cost level of the firm (C_i). Therefore, the target cost of the firm is $C^* = C_i$. If the firm reduces its current cost level of C_i, the firm will receive a reward. The second kind of target is the most efficient firm's level. In this case, the target cost of the firm (C^*) is the minimum cost level of the firms $(min (C_1 \cdot \cdot \cdot C_N))$. Therefore, the target cost of the firm is $C^* = min (C_1 \cdot \cdot \cdot C_N)$. The third kind of target is the average level of firms. In this case, the target cost of the firm (C^*) is the average cost level of the firms $(\Sigma C_i/N)$. Therefore, the target cost of the firm is $C^* = \Sigma C_i/N$. Among public utility industries in Japan, the cardinal approach to evaluation is used in the rail industry.

As for the ordinal approach, firms are categorized into different groups according to their efficiency level. If firms are divided into three groups, for example—the most efficient group, the average group and the least efficient group—rewards are given and penalties applied to each group. Among public utility industries in Japan, the electric power industry and the gas utility industry are subject to the ordinal approach to evaluation.

It is important to adhere strictly to evaluation rules, even if the least efficient firm faces management difficulties, as Bös (1991) points out. If the regulator deals leniently with the least efficient firm without holding management liable for inefficiency, a serious moral hazard arises, and the smooth functioning of yardstick regulation is impeded.

5.5 Organizational Form and Incentive

While not much attention has yet been paid to this question, it is also important to consider the organizational form in which yardstick regulation works. The M-form and U-form are typical of organizations in the public utility industry. According to Maskin, Qian and Xu (2000), an M-form organization tends to give more desirable incentive because yardstick competition can be introduced among divisions.

Finally, it is important to consider how yardstick regulation affects firms' investment incentive, as Dalen (1998) notes.

12 Universal Service Obligation

1 INTRODUCTION

Although it has been much less examined and discussed than issues related to efficiency, the universal service system is important to public utility industries in Japan. The universal service system has been comprehensively adopted by the postal service and telecommunications industries, which have recently been undergoing rapid transformation. The Japan Post Public Corporation was privatized in 2007, leading to progress in competition in the postal services industry. In telecommunications, new companies have entered the market, generating severe competition for traditional telecommunications companies such as NTT. With all the recent rapid changes, the idea of universal service is no longer relevant only to traditional incumbent telecommunications companies but to many new types of organizations as well.

This chapter lists the characteristics of the universal service system in Japanese public utility industries. First, there is a definition of universal service in Japan and a justification of its use. Second, there follows an explanation of universal service as related to postal services, with attention to the object and range of universal service, service standards, and major comparisons with other countries. Third, there is an account of universal service as applied to the telecommunications industry, with an explanation of historical change in the system, the structure of the universal service obligation system, and the calculation method of universal service costs. Last, empirical results related to universal services in Japan are summarized.

2   UNIVERSAL SERVICE IN JAPAN

Although there is no concrete definition of the term, there seems to be consensus about what universal service means.   For example, Hayashi and Tagawa (1994) define it as service available regardless of users' location (geographical universality) and income level.   The definition of universal service in telecommunications in the UK, according to OFTEL, is the provision of affordable access to a basic voice telephone or its equivalent for all those reasonably requesting it, regardless of where they live (Garnham, 1997).   A report by the OECD (1991) defined universal service as having four components: (i) Universal Geographical Access, (ii) Universal Affordable Access, (iii) Universal Service Quality, and (iv) Universal Tariffs.

Based on these ideas, universal service in Japan is defined by the Council on Economy and Fiscal Policy (CEFP) as the obligation to provide services of good quality to all users at uniform and affordable prices.

The universal service obligation has been accepted and has met no clear opposition in certain specific industries.   Yamashige (2004) justifies the universal service obligation system as a way to achieve efficiency and equity.   First, efficiency is related to network externality. Services with more users are desirable because the value of network services increases as users become more numerous.   Because individual users are generally unaware of network externality, however, network service might turn out to be smaller than the social optimum, a problem that might be obviated by the imposition of the universal service obligation on service providers (Yamashige, 2004).

Second, a system whereby the government guarantees a minimal service level to all citizens is equitable, allowing all users to enjoy access, no matter where they live.

Ida (2001) also lists characteristics of network externality and merit goods in public utilities such as telephone service.

Among public utility industries in Japan, those in which the universal service obligation is explicitly mentioned are the postal service and telecommunications industries.   Of course, in other public utility industries such as broadcasting and transportation, certain kinds of universal service exist, but the application of the universal service obligation is not as explicitly stated or applied as it is in the postal and telecommunications industries.

3 UNIVERSAL SERVICE IN THE POSTAL SERVICE INDUSTRY

3.1 Object and Range of Universal Service

According to the Ministry of Internal Affairs and Communications (2007a,b,c), universal service is specified in the Postal Law (*Yubin-ho*) as follows: 'the purpose of postal business is to increase the public welfare by providing postal services as cheaply and fairly as possible throughout the country.' Even with the privatization and division of the Japan Post Public Corporation into several corporations in October 2007, postal service companies continue to follow the universal service doctrine.

In Japan, the object of universal service is identified according to postal service categories, of which there are three: (i) domestic, (ii) international, and (iii) special mail services. Domestic postal services include letters (first-class mail), postal cards (second-class mail), periodical literature (third-class mail), and braille for blind people (fourth-class mail). Second, international postal services include normal letters, parcels and EMS (Express Mail Service). Third, special mail services include registered mail and component-certified mail. These three kinds of postal services are defined as 'mail' in Japan and are subject to the universal service obligation.

However, after the privatization of the Japan Post Public Corporation, parcel services were excluded from items subject to the universal service obligation because parcels were no longer categorized as mail according to the Postal Law (*Yubin-ho*).

3.2 Service Standards of Universal Service

Criteria of service quality addressed here are frequency of mail delivery to each customer, the number of delivery days it takes mail to reach customers, the price of sending mail, and facilities and locations for posting mail.

First, the frequency and speed of mail delivery is specified in Postal Law (*Yubin-ho*) Article 70. In general, the frequency of mail delivery is ruled as '6 days a week and once-a-day delivery.' The speed of mail delivery is ruled as 'within 3 days of the day subsequent to posting.' Mail sent to isolated islands with limited transportation access is exempt from the three-day rule, but mail delivered to remote areas must nevertheless be delivered within two weeks.

Second, the Postal Service Enforcement Regulation (*Yubin-ho Seko Kisoku*) Article 30 stipulates that mail be delivered to each address, with delivery guaranteed to each house anywhere in Japan, the only exception being areas made inaccessible by heavy winter snowfall or remote dam construction sites in the mountains.

Third, Postal Law Article 67 describes postage rates, which it rules must be 'uniform in Japan and as low as possible.' For example, postage rates for first- and second-class mail 'must not differ from place to place.' The Ministry must approve postage rates for third and fourth-class mail, one criterion being that rates must be uniform.

Fourth, Postal Law Article 70 states that public mailboxes must be installed to facilitate the posting of mail. The Postal Service Enforcement Regulation Article 30 stipulates that public mailboxes be installed nationwide. Article 5 of the Postal Network Law (*Yubinkyoku Kabushikikaisha-ho*) stipulates that numerous post offices be established nationwide. Article 2 specifies that each municipality must have at least one post office.

Thus, there are three requirements for universal service quality in postal services in Japan: frequency and speed of delivery, uniform postage rates, and access to posting facilities.

3.3   Comparison with Major Countries

Table 12.1 shows an international comparison of the universal service obligation system in postal services.

It can be seen that countries have adopted similar approaches. Items to which the universal service obligation applies are mainly letters, the frequency of delivery is generally 6 days per week, and flat postal rates apply nationwide.

When new entrants were allowed into the postal service market, the Japanese government, citing the universal service obligation, stipulated that they be required to install an enormous number of mailboxes. Other countries also impose stringent rules regarding mailboxes, requirements that present what often seems to be an insurmountable barrier to entrance into the market, due to the huge initial capital costs that installing so many mailboxes would incur.

Table 12.1 *International Comparison of the Universal Service Obligation System in the Postal Service Industry*
(Part-1)

	Provider	Managerial Form	Items for Universal Service Obligation
Japan	Japan Post Service, Japan Post Network	Corporation (100% shares held by the government)	Letters under 4kg, periodicals, postal matters in braille, registered mail
UK	Royal Mail	Corporation (100% shares held by the government)	Postal matters under 20kg, registered mail, guaranteed mail
France	La Poste	Public Organization	Letters under 2kg, parcels under 20kg, newspapers, magazines, registered mail, guaranteed mail
Germany	German Post	Corporation (30.6% shares held by government-related financial institution)	Letters under 2kg, parcels under 20kg, newspapers, magazines, registered mail, guaranteed mail, cash on delivery mail, express delivery mail
USA	US Post (USPS)	Public Corporation	Services provided by USPS

(Part-2)

	Frequency of Delivery	Delivery Days	Mailbox
Japan	6 days per week	Within 3 days	Maintain about 180 thousand mailboxes[a]
UK	6 days per week	Aims for next-day delivery: 93%	99% of Users can access a mailbox within 500m.
France	6 days per week	Aims for next-day delivery: 85%	Unlimited access Mailboxes installed on streets.
Germany	6 days per week	Aims for next-day delivery: 80%	Users can access mailboxes within 1km in cities.
USA	—	—	—

(Part-3)

	Post Office	Post Office Density [b]	Rate
Japan	Establish post offices around the country	1.93 65.3	Nationwide flat rate
UK	95% of Users can access a post office within 5km.	2.46 60.1	Nationwide flat rate
France	Post offices are established to provide services around the country.	2.81 30.7	Nationwide flat rate
Germany	More than 12,000 post offices (5,000 are directly owned by the postal organization)	1.58 36.5	Nationwide flat rate
USA	Postal facilities are established in accessible places.	1.25 3.9	Affordable rate

(Part-4)

Financial Backing for the Universal Service Obligation	
Japan	Fund: A portion of Japan Post Holding company profits
UK	Tax Privilege: Exemption from Value Added Tax (VAT) Subsidies: Support for maintaining post offices in rural areas
France	Subsidies: Support for newspapers, magazines and periodicals Fund: Contributing fund by organization with some amount of sales Tax Privilege: Exemption from Value Added Tax (VAT)
Germany	Fund: Bear Fund by licensed organizations with a certain amount of sales Tax Privilege: Exemption from Value Added Tax (VAT)
USA	Subsidies: For postal services for blind people and for absentee voting

[Note]:
(1) Information and numbers appearing in this table were obtained from several sources such as the Ministry of Internal Affairs and Communications (2007a, 2007b, 2007c).
(2) In item (a), 180 thousand mailboxes have already been installed.
(3) In item (b), Upper part: Per 10,000 population, Lower part: Per area (1,000 km².)

3.4   Future Issues related to Universal Service

Inadequate Definition of Universal Service

Objections have been raised concerning the vague definition of universal service. Even though the concept of universal service is outlined in the Postal Law, the doctrine is quite ambiguously defined. Yamashige (2004) notes that 'good quality,' 'basic service,' and 'reasonable rate,' phrases often used when referring to universal service, need to be more concretely defined. Without a consensus about what 'universal service' means, it is impossible to say whether the government is right to claim that universal service is being maintained in the postal industry. Especially after privatization, as the term 'universal service' remains unclear, the issue of postal rates is likely to be troublesome.

4   UNIVERSAL SERVICE IN THE TELECOMMUNICATIONS INDUSTRY

4.1   Overview of the Universal Service System

According to the Ministry of Internal Affairs and Communications (2007b), the basic features of universal service in the telecommunications industry are essentiality, affordability, and availability. Essentiality means that the services are indispensable in daily life, affordability means that everyone is offered services at reasonable prices, and availability means that services are available to everyone regardless of regional differences. Based on these three concepts, universal service in the telecommunications industry is described in Article 7 of the Telecommunications Business Law (*Denki Tsushin Jigyo-ho*).

The universal service obligation was clearly stipulated when Nippon Telegraph and Telephone (NTT) was reorganized in July 1999 into NTT East Japan and NTT West Japan, both of which are obligated to provide universal service.

The service range of the universal service obligation is described in Article 14 of the Enforcement Regulation of the Telecommunications Business Law (*Denki Tsushin Jigyo-ho Shiko Kisoku*). The main obligation services are subscriber telephone service, public telephone service, and emergency call services to police (110) and fire stations (119). Although no longer required, a local call service was included in the universal service obligation until April 2006. Dubbed as the Universal Service System in Telecommunications, the current system was instituted in April 2006. Not only do NTT East and West Japan support this system, but other telephone companies do so as well, sharing the costs to provide universal service.

Figure 12.1 shows changes in providers of universal service.

The current universal service obligation system was installed mainly because the former NTT (later NTT East and NTT West) had been expected to shoulder too much of the financial burden of providing universal service, as Figure 12.1 shows. Now, universal service obligation costs in rural or mountainous areas are no longer borne only by NTT East and NTT West but also by the many companies that, due to the recent sharp increase in the use of mobile phones, have entered the industry and proliferated, bringing about severe competition for market share.

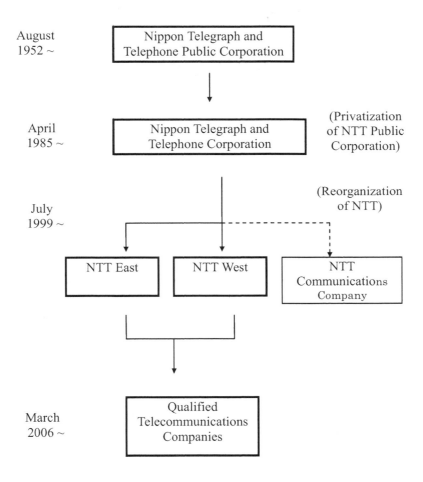

August
1952 ~

Nippon Telegraph and
Telephone Public Corporation

April
1985 ~

Nippon Telegraph and
Telephone Corporation

(Privatization
of NTT Public
Corporation)

(Reorganization
of NTT)

July
1999 ~

NTT East   NTT West   NTT
Communications
Company

March
2006 ~

Qualified
Telecommunications
Companies

Figure 12.1   Change in Providers of Universal Service

For example, an NTT West (2006a) comparison of the costs of telephone offices reveals the characteristics of the universal service situation in Japan, a summary of which can be seen in Table 12.2.

Telephone offices with higher costs accounted for only the top 4.9%

in terms of numbers of subscribers but have been required to cover almost half the nation.   The number of offices considered as having higher costs account for 43% of the total.   The unit cost per telephone line of these telephone offices is 2.57 times higher than the average of all telephone offices.

Because of this situation, it was agreed that costs for maintaining the universal service obligation should be borne by the entire telecommunications industry.

Table 12.2   *The Situation in Areas with Higher Costs*

	Areas Not Needing Support (Low-Cost Areas)	Areas Needing Support (High-Cost Areas)	Total
Number of subscribers	48,300 (95.1%)	2,500 (4.9%)	50,800 (100.0%)
Covered areas (thousand km^2)	134 (52.3%)	122 (47.7%)	256 (100.0%)
Subscriber density	360	20	200
Number of telephone offices	4,090 (57%)	3,070 (43%)	7,160 (100%)
Unit cost per subscriber (yen)	2,225 (0.92)	6,222 (2.57)	2,421 (1.00)

[Note]:
(1)   This table was written by the author and is based on information from NTT West (2006b).
(2)   Numbers in this table are for 2003.
(3)   'Subscriber density' is defined here as the number of subscribers per area.

4.2 Structure of the Universal Service Obligation System

Figure 12.2, a summary of the current system of universal service, shows the flow by which grants are given to those providing universal service.

In the current universal service system, NTT East and NTT West are universal service providers. First, these two companies submit basic data for universal service costs calculation to the Telecommunications Carrier Association (TCA) (*Denki Tsushin Jigyo Kyokai*), an independent neutral institution comprised of both government and telecommunications companies. After reviewing the submitted data, the TCA calculates the amount to be granted to NTT East and NTT West, along with the amounts of universal service costs to be borne by telecommunications companies. The TCA submits documentation of calculations to the Ministry of Internal Affairs and Communications and applies for a grant for universal service. After an assessment, the Minister may approve the application. After obtaining the approval of the ministry, the TCA informs those telecommunications companies using the lines of the universal service providers (NTT East and NTT West), of the amount due for their share of the cost of universal service. The TCA collects the money and disperses it as grants to the universal service providers. This is the general flow of the universal service system in the telecommunications industry.

Telecommunications companies deemed responsible for bearing the incidence of universal service costs are in general companies whose lines are connected with those of NTT East and NTT West. These cost-sharing telecommunications companies are fixed line telephone companies other than the two NTTs, as well as mobile telephone, PHS and IP telephone companies. According to the Ministry of Internal Affairs and Communications (2007b), the criteria for holding telecommunications companies responsible for bearing a portion of universal service costs are as follows:

(i) The company had revenues of more than 1 billion yen in the previous year.
(ii) The company assigns a telephone number to each customer.

The item regarding company revenues is included in order to ensure that the company has the ability to pay. In 2006, there were 56 telecommunications companies required to pay universal service costs, which the companies passed on to users as service fees.

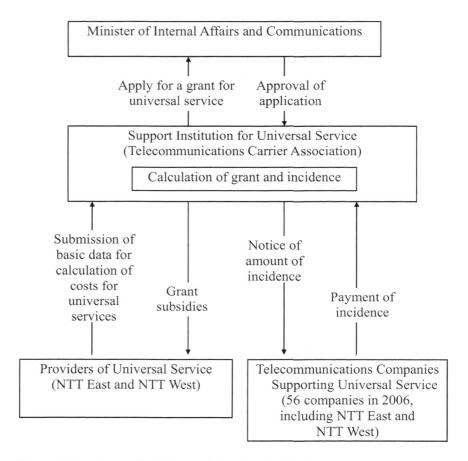

Figure 12.2   System for Universal Service Application

[Note]: This figure was written by the author and is based on several sources from organizations such as the Ministry of Internal Affairs and Communications (2007b)

4.3   Calculation Method of the Incidence of Universal Service Costs

Universal service costs are calculated as follows.   First, both NTT East and West identify costs they consider to be universal service costs. These are reported to the Telecommunications Carrier Association (TCA), which evaluates them and decides the payment per telephone subscriber. The incidence of universal service costs for each telecommunications company is determined according to the company's total numbers of subscribers.

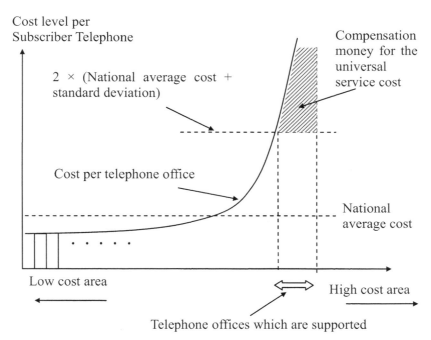

Figure 12.3   System of Support for Universal Service Costs

This is the general method for the calculation of universal service costs. However, according to the Telecommunications Carrier Association (2007), there are three methods used for different service items in order to calculate universal service costs.

(i) Subscriber telephone, basic charge: As a benchmark, standard cost, which is twice the level of 'average cost + standard deviation,' is set up. Total costs exceeding standard cost are defined as the universal service costs, as shown in Figure 12.3.

(ii) Subscriber telephone, emergency costs: Unit costs per telephone subscriber of the top 4.9% of telephone offices in terms of basic charge level.

(iii) Public telephone: Difference between costs and revenues.

Table 12.3 shows the total amount of compensation for universal service costs provided to NTT East and NTT West as of January 2008. This amount, which includes administrative costs of the Telecommunications Carrier Association (TCA), was about 13,628 million yen.

Table 12.3   *Compensation Money for Universal Service Obligation Costs*

Item	NTT East	NTT West	TCA	Total
Subscriber Telephone: Basic charge	5,770	3,473	—	9,243
Subscriber Telephone: Emergency	45	28	—	73
Public Telephone	2,151	2,094	—	4,245
Total	7,966	5,595	—	13,561
Administration Costs for Supporting Institution	—	—	67	13,628

[Note]:
(1) The numbers in this table were obtained from information released by the Telecommunications Carrier Association on October 9, 2007.
(2) TCA: Telecommunications Carrier Association.
(3) Unit: million yen.

The unit rate for the universal service obligation charged to each user is obtained as follows:

Unit price for the USO per subscriber telephone =
(Compensation money for NTT East + Compensation money for NTT West + Administration costs by TCA) / Number of subscriber telephones / 12 months.

In summary, as total costs for the universal service obligation are 13,628 million yen and the number of subscriber telephones is 183 million, the unit rate for the universal service obligation is 6 yen/month. As the number of subscriber telephones varies over time, the numbers are reviewed every six months.

5 EMPIRICAL STUDIES ON UNIVERSAL SERVICE IN JAPAN

Although there are few empirical studies related to universal service in Japan, Mizutani and Uranishi (2006) and Uranishi (2007) have examined universal service costs in the postal service industry.

There are two main approaches to estimating the universal service obligation (USO) cost: the net avoidable cost (NAC) approach and the entry pricing (EP) approach. With the NAC approach, USO costs are defined as those an organization need not incur if it does not provide services, that is, costs created in unprofitable areas. With the EP approach, in the case where universal service is provided under the condition of revenues-costs equivalence, USO costs are defined as profit reduction in profitable areas caused by the introduction of competition. Using the NAC approach, there are Castro and Maddock (1997), Mizutani and Uranishi (2006) and Uranishi (2007). On the other hand, Bradley and Colvin (2000) and Robinson and Rodriguez (2000) use the EP approach. This section will explain Uranishi (2007), which is similar to Mizutani and Uranishi (2006).

Uranishi (2007) estimates the USO costs of the postal service and evaluates whether or not universal service could be maintained after the privatization of the Japan Post. Basically, cost estimation is carried out on a prefecture basis, so that the areas considered unprofitable are the less crowded prefectures, where the unit cost of postal matter exceeds its price. Uranishi (2007) concludes as follows. First, the annual USO costs are about 260 billion yen and account for about 13.6% of postal service revenues. Second, if new entry occurs in the postal service market and causes cream skimming, universal service by the Japan Post cannot be maintained when the output of the Japan Post decreases to less than 85% of the current level. Thus, Uranishi (2007) raises concerns that it might be impossible to maintain universal service in the postal industry if competition becomes more intense.

Theoretical work on the universal service obligation and cream skimming by Laffont and Tirole (2000) suggests that larger subsidies are required under competitive pressure than under regional monopoly. Even with increased competition, the postal service market in Japan would remain at the current price level.

13   Privatization and Structural Reforms

1   INTRODUCTION

In the Japanese public utilities market, the private sector plays a vital role, but this has not always been the case.   Table 13.1 shows the extent to which privatization has been taking place in several public utilities industries in Japan.   There have been two massive trends in privatization schemes.   During the first period in the late 1980s under the leadership of Prime Minister Nakasone, three national public corporations were privatized: Nippon Telegraph and Telephone (NTT) in 1985; the Japan Monopoly Public Corporation (Tobacco and Salt) in 1985; and the Japan National Railway (JNR) in 1987.   The second wave of privatization occurred more recently during the tenure of Prime Minister Koizumi in the early 2000s, with the most notable cases being the privatization of three public corporations: the Teito Rapid Transit Authority (Tokyo Metro) in 2004; four highway public corporations in 2005; and the Japan Post Public Corporation in 2007.

These organizational reforms in Japan, especially the privatization of the JNR, differ from those in other industrial countries, especially European countries.   The privatization of the Japan National Railway (JNR) in 1987 marked the first sweeping reform of a state railway in the world.   Since then, privatization has been accomplished in various ways in different countries.   For example, in Europe, a vertical separation scheme was selected, but vertical integration was chosen in Japan. While the reform process differs from country to country, this chapter aims to explain the characteristics of the Japanese approach to the restructuring of public enterprises.

As examples, I have chosen to explain the Japan National Railways, the public highway corporations and the Japan Post Public Corporation, for the following reasons.   First, the recent privatization schemes taken in the highway industry and postal services are typical of the current

Japanese approach.   Second, JNR's case is a classic example of the basic Japanese philosophy to restructuring, as compared with that of other counties, especially in Europe.   Third, more than twenty years have passed since the reform of the JNR, providing ample time to glean information and results for performance evaluation.

As background for an explanation of privatization in Japan, Table 13.1 shows the current situation of major providers in Japanese public utility industries.

Table 13.1   *The Current Situation of Major Providers and the Privatization Scheme in Japan*

Public utility industry	Major providers	Current privatization scheme
Electric power supply	10 regional private companies	—
Gas utility	3 large and many private companies	—
Water supply	Many municipal public organizations	—
Railway	Many private companies and 9 public subway organizations	JNR Privatization in 1987, Privatization of the Teito Rapid Transit Authority (Tokyo Metro) in 2004
Bus	Private companies and municipal organizations	—
Highway	6 highway companies	Privatization of 4 public highway corporations in 2005
Telecommunications	Private companies	Privatization of NTT in 1985
Broadcasting	One public corporation (NHK) and many private companies	—
Post	5 post related companies	Privatization of Japan Post in 2007

As for the organization of this chapter, after the introduction, three cases are explained: the JNR, the public highway corporation, and the Japan Post Public Corporation. In each case, the main reasons for privatization and the main features of organizational reform are explained. Finally, there is a summary of performance results after reform, focusing mainly on the case of JNR, followed by a discussion of features common to various cases of restructuring.

2 JNR PRIVATIZATION

2.1 The Reasons for and the Process of Privatization

Along with the privatization of two other huge public corporations (Nippon Telephone and Telegraph and the Japan Monopoly Public Corporation (Tobacco and Salt)) in the late 1980s, JNR began the process of privatization in 1987, when it was divided into six regional passenger companies and one nationwide freight company.

Because of apparently insoluble problems both within and outside the organization, it was felt that JNR could be saved only through the radical reform of privatization. First, within the organization, complacency and the lack of a sense of crisis left problems ignored and unsolved. The hostile relationship between management and labor unions negatively affected the morale of the organization, leading to a decline in service quality, which in turn led to a decrease in the number of JNR users. These internal problems significantly weakened the financial health of JNR. Problems also arose from outside pressure. Even in the face of insufficient rail demand, new rail lines were constructed for merely political reasons. Rail fares were set not for any rational economic reason but for the benefit of certain political groups. There was also the unfavorable business environment of users expecting JNR to provide rail services even when demand was inadequate.

For these reasons, in 1964 JNR showed operating losses for the first time in its history, beginning a decline that continued into the late 1970s and early 1980s. JNR did take measures to improve its performance to some degree, but these efforts proved too little and too late. When it became obvious that radical steps would be necessary, a special committee was formed of several political entrepreneurs and pro-privatization managers inside JNR, who drew up a plan for the divestiture of the national railway.

One important aspect of the JNR privatization process was that it was not accomplished all at once but was carried out in several stages.

At the beginning of privatization in 1987, all stock shares of the six newly established regional JRs and the one freight JR were held by the government, or, more precisely speaking, by a newly founded governmental organization called the Japan National Railway Settlement Corporation (JNRSC) (*Nihon Kokuyu Tetsudo Seisan Jigyodan*). This organization was an important part of the plan of extending the JNR privatization process over a period of several years, a course considered prudent under the circumstances. With regard to the initial stock offering, because JNR's performance before privatization had been widely known to be poor, the government feared that JNR's reputation for waste and inefficiency would stimulate embarrassingly little interest among investors in acquiring the newly created railway companies' stock. Therefore, the government postponed offering it to the public until the various new companies could begin to turn the tide of public opinion.

Among the seven JR companies, JR East's stock first went public in 1993, when 62.5% of its stock was offered for sale. Three years later, in 1996, a portion of JR West shares (68.3%) went on the market, followed by JR Central shares (67.0%) in 1997. All shares of the other four JR companies, however, are still held by the government, and a specific plan for their issue has not been determined (Mizutani and Nakamura, 2000). Since then, the three large JR companies—JR East, JR West and JR Central—were fully privatized in 2002, 2004 and 2006, respectively. In contrast, the government still holds all shares of the four weaker JR companies—JR Hokkaido, JR Shikoku, JR Kyushu and JR Freight—and a specific plan for their issue has not been announced.

2.2   The Main Features of Privatization

The Japanese approach to state railway restructuring is different from that of other countries, especially European countries, notably regarding the following seven points: (i) horizontal separation (or regional subdivision); (ii) functional separation (or passenger-freight distinction); (iii) vertical integration (or operation and infrastructure integration); (iv) lump-sum subsidies for low density JRs; (v) establishment of an intermediary institution; (vi) allowance of non-rail service; and (vii) yardstick regulation. For further details, please see previous articles such as Mizutani (1999a) and Mizutani and Nakamura (1997, 2000, 2004). Figure 13.1 summarizes the changes in organizational structure brought about by the privatization of the JNR.

(1) Before Privatization

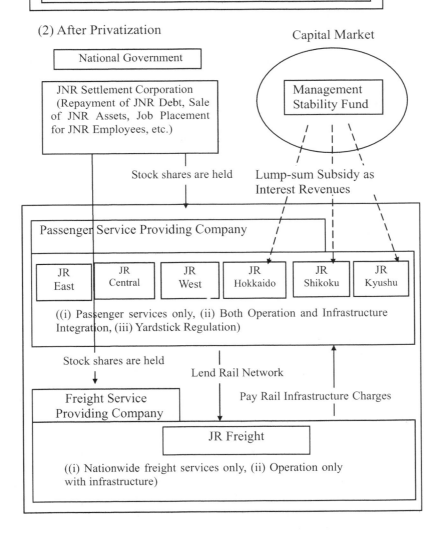

Figure 13.1   Structural Changes with the Privatization of
the Japan National Railway

Horizontal Separation (Regional Subdivision)

One important feature of the Japanese approach to rail restructuring is that horizontal separation of nationwide passenger services was chosen. As the JNR had been too large an organization to be managed properly, upon privatization, passenger services were separated into six regional passenger companies. Before privatization, the JNR had often been criticized for ignoring regional needs, so that with privatization and subdivision came the expectation that such needs would be recognized and met.

Several possible options had been discussed about how to divide the nationwide JNR passenger service network, with intercity and urban passenger separation, or Shinkansen (rapid train) and regular train service separation being considered. Ultimately, regional subdivision by geographical demand was chosen because of the expectation that 95% of all trips would be completed within the borders of each separate railway company. Under these circumstances, the smaller subdivided regional companies could focus on meeting their users' local needs. It is worth noting that far fewer regional subdivisions were created in the Japanese scheme than in the British case. With regional separation, 25 franchise areas were created when British Rail was privatized, while subdivision in Japan resulted in six regional JR passenger companies: JR Hokkaido, JR East, JR Central, JR West, JR Shikoku and JR Kyushu.

Functional Separation (Passenger-Freight Distinction)

In contrast to passenger services, freight services were not separated by region but were to be provided by a single nationwide freight service company called JR Freight. This functional distinction is similar to that outlined by European rail policy. The rationale for the distinction of freight from passenger services by separating them into independent companies was to clarify the management responsibility of each service.

The newly created independent JR Freight rail company does not hold its own rail network. By borrowing tracks from the infrastructure-holding JR companies, the JR Freight rail company can avoid the costs of constructing and maintaining its own tracks. These cost savings have become especially important with the completion of Japan's national highway system, which has made the trucking industry more powerful, posing a severe threat to the survival of the rail freight business. Another threat to JR Freight is that, especially in rural areas, rail demand for passenger transport is insufficient, so that unprofitable lines are in danger of being abandoned by the rail network. Because JR

Freight does not hold its own tracks, it is vulnerable to the exigencies of the JR passenger companies. If JR passenger companies choose to discontinue low usage lines, the freight service network provided by JR Freight cannot be sustained.

Vertical Integration (Operation and Infrastructure Integration)

Vertical integration in the Japanese restructuring approach is a feature which distinguishes it from the European approach. Since the privatization of JNR, the newly established six JR rail passenger companies have provided both rail operation and infrastructure services.

Although the vertical separation policy is standard in the European rail industry, vertical integration is quite common in the Japanese railway industry: in fact, about 150 rail operators operate rail services while holding their own tracks. Because the practice is so widespread in Japan, a vertical separation policy was hardly considered as an option before privatization (Suga (1997)).

Lump-sum Subsidies for low density JRs

The fourth distinguishing feature of Japanese rail restructuring is that the lump-sum subsidy scheme, called the Management Stability Fund (MSF) (*Keiei Ankei Kikin*), was created to support smaller JR companies such as JR Hokkaido, JR Shikoku and JR Kyushu. These three JR companies are in charge of the Management Stability Fund (MSF), whose interest revenues become subsidies to the smaller JRs.

Before privatization, because subsidies were given to the JNR after revenues and costs were realized, JNR had no incentive to decrease costs, and subsidies continued to escalate. On the contrary, with the newly created MSF, the amount of subsidies is almost fixed because the fund is fixed, compelling the three smaller JRs to control cost escalation. If the capital market is weak, interest revenues generated by the fund decrease, creating incentives for efficient management in the organizations dependent on the fund.

Establishment of an Intermediary Institution

The fifth distinguishing feature is the establishment of an intermediary institution, the Japan National Railway Settlement Corporation (JNRSC), whose main role was to ease the effect on the JRs of the sharp changes caused by privatization.

The actual role of this institution was to repay the debts of the JNR and to find new jobs for its redundant employees. While the newly established JR companies took on some of the debt of the former JNR, a need was felt for the creation of the JNRSC to lessen the burden on the new companies.

Allowance of Non-Rail Service

Sixth, newly established JR companies were permitted to engage in non-rail business, as private rail companies have been doing in Japan for decades. To increase demand for rail transportation, private rail companies build housing projects and shopping centers along their lines, promote tourism, and operate complementary modes of transportation such as buses. These businesses undoubtedly benefit the railway companies by which they are set up, but accounting laws strictly prohibit cross-subsidization between rail and non-rail businesses.

Yardstick Regulation

Last, a yardstick competition scheme was introduced. Under this scheme, rail operators compete with each other to improve performance, the regulator assesses the operators' performance by using common measures, and the results of the assessment are used when fare revision is being considered.

3   HIGHWAY PRIVATIZATION

3.1   Reason for Privatization

The privatization process of public highways began on October 1, 2005, when four public highway corporations were privatized: the Japan Public Highway Corporation, the Metropolitan Expressway Public Corporation, the Hanshin Expressway Public Corporation and the Honshu-Shikoku Bridge Authority. This reform brought about the subdivision of the Japan Public Highway Corporation into three companies.

According to the Ministry of Land, Infrastructure and Transport (2005), the main purposes for the privatization of the four public highway corporations are as follows:

   (i)   to secure repayment of interest-bearing debts, amounting to 381 billion US dollars (40 trillion yen);
   (ii) to construct, without delay, genuinely needed expressways with a minimum burden on the general public, while paying due

respect to the autonomy of the companies; and
(iii) to provide diverse and flexible prices and services by utilizing the private sector's expertise.

In general, when a national highway network plan is approved by the Diet, the Ministry of Land, Infrastructure and Transport orders the public highway corporations to build the highway. This procedure has sparked protests that public highway corporations have been building prohibitively expensive new highways for political reasons and that construction projects have been inefficiently managed. The total amount of highway construction debt remains tremendous (381 billion US dollars or 40 trillion yen), and highway tolls remain expensive.

Under these circumstances, Prime Minister Koizumi resolved to reform public highway corporations, appointing a Committee for Promoting the Privatization of Four Highway-related Public Corporations. On December 6, 2002, the committee issued its final opinion report, in which it recommended vertical separation (management and infrastructure holding separation). The privatization of public highway corporations was approved in the Diet on June 2, 2004 (Ministry of Land, Infrastructure and Transport, 2005).

3.2 Important Features of Highway Privatization

When the privatization of the four public highway corporations was considered, the committee took into account experiences related to the privatization of Japan National Railway in 1987. There are several similarities between the highway and railway privatizations.

Figure 13.2 summarizes the organizational structure changes brought about by the privatization of the public highway corporations. Among several features, the most important characteristics of the organizational reforms of these four public expressway corporations are regional subdivision and vertical separation (management-holding separation). For details regarding highway privatization, please see, for example, Mizutani and Uranishi (2008).

(1) Before Privatization

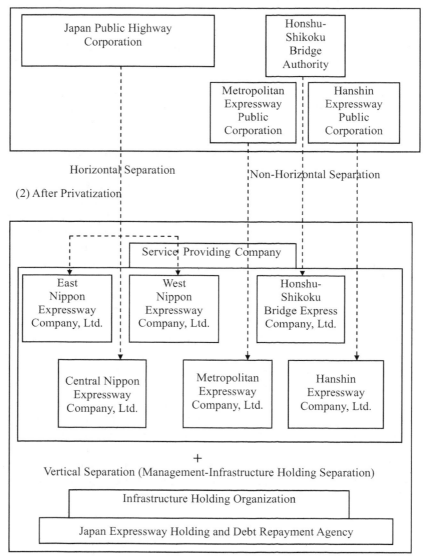

*Figure 13.2   Organizational Change by Privatization:
            Four Highway-related Public Corporations*

*[Note]: This figure was written by the author and is based on Mizutani and Uranishi
         (2008).*

Horizontal Separation

Public highway corporations originated as six regional expressway companies. The policy taken for regional subdivision was similar to that of the JNR privatization, with subdivision applying only to the Japan Public Highway Corporation, which upon privatization in October 2005, was regionally separated into three expressway companies: East Nippon Expressway Company, Ltd., Central Nippon Expressway Company, Ltd. and West Nippon Expressway Company, Ltd.

The three other pre-existing public corporations were privatized without further subdivision: the Metropolitan Expressway Company, Ltd. (formerly the Metropolitan Expressway Public Corporation), the Hanshin Expressway Company, Ltd. (formerly the Hanshin Expressway Public Corporation), and the Honshu-Shikoku Bridge Express Company, Ltd. (formerly the Honshu-Shikoku Bridge Authority). The Metropolitan Expressway Company provides services in the Tokyo metropolitan area, while the Hanshin Expressway Company does so in the Osaka metropolitan area.

Vertical Separation (Management and Infrastructure Separation)

The second characteristic of highway reform is that the vertical separation policy was taken. As mentioned before, the meaning of 'vertical separation' in the highway industry differs from that in the railway industry, where vertical separation refers to the separation of rail service operation and infrastructure maintenance. In the case of Japanese highway service, the separation is between the highway service provider and the infrastructure holding organization.

The main role of these six regionally separated expressway companies is to provide expressway services through the administration and maintenance of highway roads and service areas, which are rented from the new public organization, the Japan Expressway Holding and Debt Repayment (JEHDR) Agency (*Nihon Kosoku Doro Hoyu Saimu Hensai Kikou*). The responsibility of the JEHDR Agency therefore is to hold highway facilities and lease them to expressway companies. Incidentally, there is a plan that Honshu-Shikoku Bridge Express Company, after its management is stabilized, be merged with West Nippon Expressway Company.

The Infrastructure Management Public Organization

As explained above, the JEHDR Agency holds highway facilities and leases them to expressway companies.   In addition to this role, this JEHDR Agency holds the highway assets and debts of four highway-related public corporations, repaying the debts by collecting highway fees from six companies.   When repayment is completed in 45 years, the JEHDR Agency will be dissolved.   This public organization was created in part to reduce the financial burden on highway companies and to support the successful operation of highway services by highway companies.

Other Features

These six companies are joint-stock companies but all shares are still held by the government.   Although the privatization plan remains incomplete, in the future these highway service providing companies are expected to be fully privatized, despite current laws which impose several obstacles to full   privatization.   For   example,   the   Highway   Company   Law (*Kosokudoro Kaisha-ho*) stipulates that the government hold one third of the shares of highway service providing companies (Doro Horei Kenkyukai (2004)).   According to the Doro Horei Kenkyukai (2004), the main justification for partial public ownership is that the highway network itself is a public asset with public benefits.

Other important points are that the new highway providing companies need approval for various management decisions from the Ministry of Land, Infrastructure and Transport.   For example, appointing representative directors of new companies, issuing corporate bonds, and borrowing for long-term debts all require government approval.

4   THE PRIVATIZATION OF POSTAL SERVICES

4.1   Reasons for Privatization

The last case summarized here involves the privatization of the Japan Post Public Corporation.   Several years prior to the privatization, when the April 2007 target date was announced, political chaos ensued.   The law requiring the privatization of Japan Post was finally passed in October   2005,   after   having   been   approved   in   the   House   of Representatives and subsequently rejected in the House of Councilors in August 2005.   To establish political support, Prime Minister Koizumi dissolved the House of Representatives and held a snap election. Voters overwhelmingly supported the privatization of the Japan Post Public Corporation in a landslide victory for the LDP. After the election, Koizumi's plan for postal reform passed both houses without resistance and the Japan Post Public Corporation was privatized in April 2007.

Although there were several reasons put forward for the privatization of Japan Post, the following three points are important. First, several services provided by Japan Post were already being provided by various private companies. Savings accounts (postal savings) and insurance (postal insurance) are cases in point. For example, the saving service offered by the post office does not significantly differ from that available at private banks. The same applies to insurance: the kind of insurance offered by the post office is available from private insurance companies. Furthermore, even such ordinal postal services as parcel delivery can be obtained from private companies. Thus, there is no need for the public sector to provide all services heretofore monopolized by the post office.

The second rationale for the post office privatization was that the deficits of many unprofitable post offices had customarily been subsidized by more profitable post offices. The Japan Post Public Corporation did not create deficits as a whole, but many post offices in rural areas were creating deficits. In Japan, post offices are spaced even more densely than elementary schools (Japan Post (2003)). Moreover, these post offices were mostly special post offices, which were complicated cases whereby private property was rented and the postmaster specially appointed. These institutions were more expensive to maintain than other types of post offices in Japan (Mizutani and Uranishi (2006)). Privatization would create a situation whereby Japan Post would be free to reform expensive, inefficient, and perhaps superfluous special post offices.

The third goal of post office privatization was to stop the money flow to special corporations. Before privatization, money made by the government through postal savings was used for investment in special corporations. The amount of postal savings is huge, supplying special corporations with a flood of investment money, many of it inefficiently channeled into the construction of unnecessary highways or other public works projects.

Of course, there have been many objections to the privatization of the Japan Post Public Corporation (e.g. Tanaka (2004), Takigawa (2004)). Some have objected that privatization will prevent universal service from being maintained and that services provided by the post office were not limited to only what might be called postal services. However, over these objections, voters showed clear support for the privatization policy proposed by Prime Minister Koizumi, leading to the privatization of Japan Post.

4.2   The Main Features of Postal Privatization

The privatization scheme of the Japan Post taken by the government is summarized in Figure 13.3.   Among several characteristics of the privatization, the following three are important.

Functional Separation

The Japan Post Public Corporation was reorganized into one stockholding company (Japan Post Holding Company) and four postal service providing companies: Japan Post Network Company, which holds the post office buildings; the Japan Post Service Company; the Japan Post Bank Company; and the Japan Post Insurance Company.   The Japan Post stockholding company owns these four companies.

Creating a Network Organization

In addition to the three former postal businesses (postal services, banking, and life insurance), a customer service company was created.   The Japan Post Network Company provides postal customer services such as counter transactions.   These services are accomplished by contracting-in from the three other postal business companies.

Procedure to Full Privatization

The road map to full privatization is quite new among regulatory reforms in Japan.   The privatization procedure will be carried out in two steps over a period of ten years.

At the end of the preparation stage, the first step in postal privatization was the creation of five new private companies in 2007. This stage, when the government owns all shares of both the stockholding company and the service providing companies, can be considered as a transition period toward full privatization.

(1) First Stage: October 2005 Postal Business Privatization Law

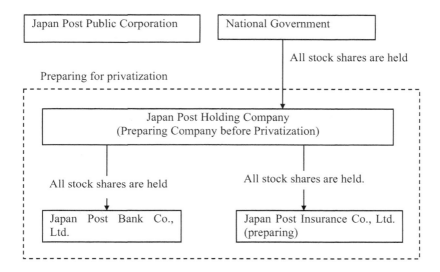

(2) Second Stage: October, 2007 Postal Business Privatization

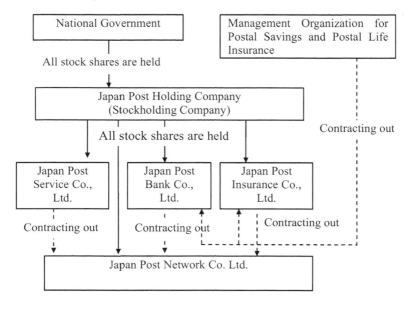

Figure 13.3   Process for the Full Privatization of Postal Businesses

(3) Third Stage: By the end of September, 2017   Full Privatization

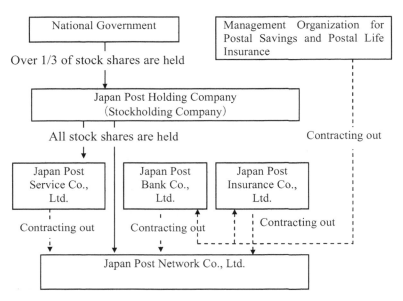

Figure 13.3   (continued)

When this transition period ends in 2017, privatization will be completed.   During the second stage, all shares of both the Japan Post Bank Company and the Japan Post Insurance Company will be sold to the private sector.   However, as for the Japan Post Service Company and the Japan Post Network Company, it is planned that the shares be held by the Japan Post Stockholding Company.   Furthermore, at the second step, one third of the shares of the Japan Post Holding Company will be held by the National Government.   Therefore, the Japan Post Network and the Japan Post Service Company will continue to be regulated by the government as a partially privatized company, a special corporation under Japanese law.

Universal Service Obligation Fund

Last, in order to maintain regional local services, the 'Social and Regional Maintenance Fund (*Shakai Chiiki Koken Kikin*)' will be established (Ishii

(2005)). This fund has yet to be created but is expected to be about one trillion yen (about $US 8.5 billion), the main source of which will come from the proceeds of stock sales of the postal saving company and the postal life insurance company. The Japan Post Network company and the Japan Post Service company plan to use the revenues from this fund in the capital market to maintain postal services in local areas, in a scheme similar to that of the Management Stability Fund for the JNR privatization.

5 CONCLUDING REMARKS

5.1 Performance Results: The Case of JNR

Two decades have passed since the Japan National Railway (JNR) was privatized and separated into several passenger and freight railway JR companies. The overall performance of the JR companies has improved and the privatization of JNR can be deemed a success in having apparently brought about many changes for the better.

As for service quality and demand, service quality factors such as speed and frequency seem to be improving overall. The most important fact is that while rail fare increased almost every year leading up to privatization, in the twenty years since privatization fare has increased only once for JR East, JR Central, JR West and JR Freight, and only twice for JR Hokkaido, JR Shikoku and JR Kyushu.

As for productivity, privatization has increased efficiency. According to Mizutani and Uranishi (2007), TFP growth after privatization was annually 2.97%, and privatization contributed to a 1.62% annual increase in TFP growth. Moreover, privatization certainly helped reduce costs among the JR companies. The former JNR was over-capitalized, with 75% more capital capacity than the optimal amount. Privatization seems to have solved the problem of excess capitalization.

5.2 Characteristics of the Japanese Approach to Privatization

The Japanese approach to the privatization of public enterprises has certain common characteristics: (i) structural separation, (ii) step-by-step restructuring, (iii) competition and support systems, and (iv) separation from former financial burdens.

The first common feature is that structural separation was selected when the privatization scheme was installed. In the case of the JNR, regional and functional separation plans were chosen. In the case of public highway corporations, regional and vertical separation plans were selected. In the case of the Japan Post Public Corporation, functional separation was chosen. Thus, the reform of public enterprises is not limited to the ownership transformation inherent in the definition of privatization, but the reforms chosen determine the quality of change in organizational structure. As for structural change, it is worth noting that the Japanese approach does not follow the majority when it comes to the selection of reform options. For example, in railway reform, vertical integration was chosen, although vertical separation is common in Europe. In postal reform, a customer service company was newly created in addition to companies providing postal, bank, and insurance services. The Japanese approach tends to favor flexible options.

The second characteristic of Japanese privatization is its step-by-step approach. In the UK, the reform of public enterprises was rather sudden, with British Railways being fully privatized from the beginning. In Japan, reform is slow but steady.

The third characteristic of Japanese privatization is that seemingly contradictory policies such as competition and supporting systems are chosen at the same time. The competition policy is in general yardstick competition. Horizontal or regional separation of public enterprises aims to promote yardstick competition among newly established organizations. The six passenger JRs, for example, are expected to engage in yardstick competition. The same is expected to occur in the newly privatized highway companies, though the yardstick policy has not been explicitly stated. In addition to competition, a supporting system is also prepared for the more managerially unstable organizations. For example, although the yardstick regulation applies to them as well, the smaller JR companies have been supported by the Management Stability Fund in order to compensate for their handicap with regard to larger JR companies. In the case of the post office, the Universal Service Fund was instituted in order to help with the cost of maintaining post offices in rural areas.

Last, Japanese privatization is characterized by its willingness to relieve newly created organizations of any financial burdens remaining from pre-privatization days. In the case of the JNR privatization, the JNR Settlement Corporation was established in order to repay leftover JNR debts, reducing the number of managerial duties at the privatized companies. The same approach applies to highway privatization. Japan Expressway Holding and Debt Repayment Agency's only role is to repay the debt remaining from the Japan Highway Public Corporation, leaving managers of the newly created organizations free to concentrate on building more productive, efficient private companies.

14 Private Sector Involvement

1 INTRODUCTION

At both the national and local levels in Japan, industries in the public sector have several important goals: to foster efficient government, to restructure the government budget, and to reestablish trust in government.

With these goals in mind, the Ministry of Internal Affairs and Communications issued new guidelines for use in the general inspection of public corporation management and the promotion of reforms among local public corporations. The basic concepts are summarized in a white paper published by the Ministry of Internal Affairs and Communications in 2006.

First, it must be determined whether or not services currently provided by local public corporations are truly necessary. It is also necessary to examine whether or not it is the public sector's role to provide existing services.

Second, even if it is concluded that the public sector should indeed provide existing services, the white paper maintains that to the extent possible, 'private sector style management'[1] should be promoted, with such strategies as the Designated Manager System (*Shitei Kanrisha Seido*), the Local Independent Administrative Institution Scheme (*Chiho Dokuritsu Gyosei Hojin Seido*), the Private Finance Initiative (PFI), and Comprehensive Outsourcing (*Hokatsuteki Gaigu Itaku*).

Third, in order to develop transparent management in local public corporations, medium-term management plans should be formulated, job performance evaluations must be carried out, and disclosure of information must be made mandatory. Furthermore, data regarding salary, service prices, and so on should be made public so that these may be compared with data from other similar organizations.

Of these three basic concepts, this chapter focuses on the second, the improvement of management in the public sector in Japan. After the introduction, there follows an explanation of what the phrase 'private sector style management (*Minkanteki Keiei*)' means in Japan. The third section contains an explanation of Japanese style PFI, which is followed by a description of Comprehensive Outsourcing to the private sector and a discussion of the characteristics of this scheme. The fifth section deals with the designated manager system—its characteristics, applications, and current situation. Last is an explanation of the local independent administrative institution scheme, which is designed to allow for increased managerial flexibility.

2   'PRIVATE SECTOR STYLE MANAGEMENT' IN JAPAN

The Private Sector Style Management Scheme (*Minkanteki Keiei Syuho*) refers to a system whereby the main body of the service provider is publicly held but the private sector is to some degree involved in its management.

According to several researchers, Private Sector Style Management in Japan encompasses a wide range of management methods. For example, Kishii (2002) defines Private Sector Style Management by the public sector as the methods by which the private sector cooperates with or is used by the public sector. Kishii's definition includes such activities as outsourcing, PFI (Private Finance Initiative), PPP (Public Private Partnership), Governmental Franchising, and voucher systems. Others, for example Kakizaki (2002) and Furukawa (2002), consider Private Sector Style Management to include a wider range of methods.[2] For example, privatization is regarded as a manifestation of Private Sector Style Management. Kakizaki (2002) maintains that management buyout, which is considered a privatization method, is included in the category.

The phrase 'Private Sector Style Management,' used in the institutional reforms of public corporations in Japan especially since the late 90s, indicates a process involving the following four items: (i) PFI, (ii) Comprehensive Outsourcing (*Hokatsuteki Gaibu Itaku*), (iii) Designated Manager System (*Shitei Kanrisha Seido*), and (iv) Local Independent Administrative Institution (*Chiho Dokuritsu Gyosei Hojin*).[3]

PFI began in Japan with the 1999 enactment of the PFI Law. A comprehensive outsourcing system was established when the Waterworks Law (*Suido-ho*) was revised in 2002. Moreover, the Local Independent Administrative Institution Law was enacted in 2004. Because these items are all related to the institutional reform of public corporation law and are not limited to matters related to management style, hereafter I will use the term 'Private Sector Involvement' rather than 'Private Sector

Style Management.'

Private sector involvement in pubic corporations existed to some degree before institutional reform, the most typical case being the outsourcing of certain services, but traditional outsourcing to the private sector was done on a much smaller scale than the activity generated by recent measures to increase private sector involvement.

3   JAPANESE-STYLE PFI

3.1   The Introduction of PFI to Japan

PFI, or Private Finance Initiative, uses the private sector's know-how and funds for the construction, maintenance and management of public facilities.   The PFI method has been developed in and applied to various public services in the UK, whose success with the approach sparked interest in Japan.

PFI was introduced in Japan in July 1999 with the enactment of the PFI law,[4] whereby formerly publicly funded public facility projects are allowed to be funded privately.   According to the Cabinet Office (2005), as of the end of March 2005, national and local government projects to develop public facilities through the PFI scheme numbered more than 180. Of these projects, in 43 cases the construction stage is complete and operations have begun.

There are variations in PFI, but in general its first goal is to create as little need as possible for public involvement while making use of the private sector's originality and ingenuity.   Traditionally, for public works project schemes, specifications have been concretized at the early design stage in the course of the project.   With PFI, on the other hand, specifications for public facilities can be changed on a flexible basis, in accordance with the private sector's know-how and creativity.

Second, the PFI can develop public facilities efficiently by adequately distributing project risks. In traditional public works projects by the public sector, all project risks have been borne only by the public sector, which naturally seeks to avoid risk by choosing only options perceived as safe.   The private sector can evaluate project risks skillfully by combining the knowledge and experience of several private finance-related companies in the form of a consortium, which provides funds for the PFI project and evaluates its feasibility and stability.   In the planning stage, in general, financial corporations evaluate project risks and assess methods for dealing with such risks, and at the operational stage utilize accurate forecasting techniques to reduce risks such as unanticipated decreases in revenue.   Thus, with its capacity to distribute risk, the PFI scheme appears superior to traditional public works project schemes.

In turn, it is the public sector's role to evaluate the consortium's work to ensure the quality of facilities resulting from PFI projects.   In fact, PFI contracts should cover not only matters related to price but also issues regarding maintenance strategy, administrative ability, risk sharing, technological know-how, planning skills, and so on.   General competitive bidding could be based on comprehensive evaluation of such matters.

3.2   Current Situation of PFI in Japan

According to the Cabinet Office, PFI projects are adopted mostly in the field of waste-disposal, which accounted for 11 cases as of March 2005. Other PFI projects include welfare facilities for the elderly (11 cases), elementary and junior high schools (6 cases), and waste heat utilization facilities (6 cases).   PFI has not been applied significantly to projects involving infrastructure such as roads.

The most often applied PFI project methods are (i) BTO, (ii) BOT, (iii) BOO, (iv) RO.[5]   First, BTO refers to a project built by a consortium of private companies, which continues to operate the facility after construction is complete, but which transfers ownership of the facility to the public sector.   Second, BOT refers to a case where the private consortium builds and operates the facility, and upon completion of the PFI project, the facility is transferred to the public sector.   Third, BOO refers to a case where the private consortium builds, owns and operates the facility, and upon completion of the PFI project, the facility is torn down and removed.   Finally, RO refers to a case where the private consortium rehabilitates and operates the facility until the project is complete.

As for the financing of the PFI project, there are three types of PFI: (i) the purchasing service type, (ii) the self-supporting finance type, and (iii) the composite type.   Figure 14.1 shows the type of financing for PFI projects.   First, for the purchasing service type, the public sector pays private companies to build and manage the PFI facility.   The private company provides service to users.   Second, for the self-supporting finance type, the private consortium builds and operates the PFI facility after the public sector gives permission for the project.   The private consortium provides service to users of the facility and is paid by charging user fees.   Last, the composite type combines features of the first two types.

(a) Purchasing Service Type

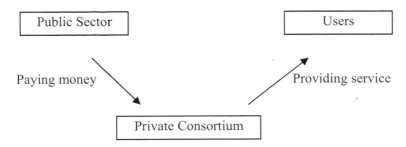

(b) Self-Supporting Finance Type

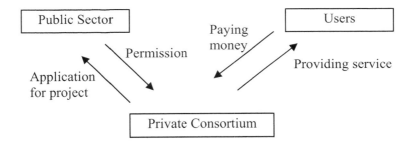

(c) Composite Type

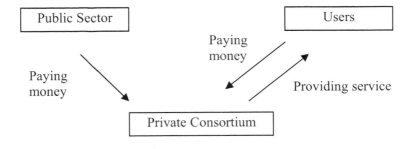

Figure 14.1   Types of Financing for PFI Projects

The situation of PFI projects conducted by local municipal governments as of March 2005 is summarized in Table 14.1, which shows that BTO is the most commonly adopted PFI project method, accounting for about 60% among the four project methods.   As for type of financing, the purchasing service type is the most common, accounting for about 65%.

Table 14.1   The Current Situation of PFI Projects

PFI method	Type of financing				
	Purchasing service	Self-supporting	Composite	Others	Total
BTO	49	6	19	10	84
BOT	21	7	8	0	36
BOO	3	2	1	1	7
RO	2	0	0	0	2
Others	—	—	—	—	13
Total	75	15	28	11	142

[Note]:
(1)   Numbers in this table were obtained from the Cabinet Office (2005, p.21).
(2)   The PFI projects counted in this table are projects conducted by local municipal governments as of March 2005.

4   COMPREHENSIVE OUTSOURCING

4.1   Comprehensive Outsourcing in Japan

In Japan, 'comprehensive outsourcing (*Hokatsuteki Gaibu Itaku*)' includes a wide range of activities related to service provision contracted out to private companies, and the meaning of the phrase may vary according to the individual sub-fields of the public utilities to which it is applied, such as the water supply and sewerage industries (e.g. see Chusho Kibo Jougesuido Kenkyukai (2005)). This section focuses on comprehensive outsourcing, especially with regard to the water supply industry.

When the Waterworks Law was revised in 2002, comprehensive outsourcing was introduced in the water supply industry to help smaller public organizations that were facing financial difficulties, staff shortages, and other problems. Many water supply organizations have a limited number of employees and are moreover forced to provide service under tight budget constraints. In addition, when permanent employees in the technology division of the water supply organization are due to retire, their positions are often phased out because of financial concerns, further exacerbating a manpower shortage. It was with these difficulties in mind that the new system of outsourcing was introduced and is now used in various undertakings such as the operation and management of water purification plants.

4.2 Characteristics of Comprehensive Outsourcing

In contrast to the former practice of informal small-scale outsourcing, with comprehensive outsourcing, the government emphasizes the following three points. The first regards the range of services that may be outsourced. Traditional outsourcing in the public corporation was limited to dispensable or contingent activities carried out in the process of service provision. The scale of outsourcing was not large, with outsourcing to the private sector being considered a task complementary to public provision. However, what most distinguishes the new outsourcing system from the old is that the private sector is allowed to be involved in core activities, such as the operation and management of water purification plants, as well as the maintenance and management of water intake facilities, pump plants, and reservoirs.

The second difference between the old and the new systems is that in traditional outsourcing, contracts were generally for only one year and had to be renewed annually, whereas comprehensive outsourcing allows longer terms of contract with the private sector. With multiple-year contracts, more efficient management can be expected.

The third point of contrast is the nature of activities subject to outsourcing. Although it is now permissible to outsource a wider range of activities, outsourcing is still limited to activities controlled by technology, such as the operation and management of water purification plants, and does not include matters related to the general management of water supply services, such as pricing. The same trend can be seen in the sewerage industry. According to Chusho Kibo Jougesuido Kenkyukai (2005), comprehensive outsourcing in the sewerage industry is limited to the operation and management of sewerage treatment plants, to the exclusion of other management activities.

Last, even if a public corporation makes use of comprehensive outsourcing, final responsibility for activities and to users remains with the head of the public corporation. Outsourcing is different from governmental franchising, whereby the private sector receives a contract from and is monitored and supervised by the public sector.

In summary, the comprehensive outsourcing system continues the traditional system of outsourcing that previously existed on a limited scale, but has been revised to allow the private sector to engage in a wider range of activities and for longer terms.

5   DESIGNATED MANAGER SYSTEM

5.1   Characteristics of the Designated Manager System

The designated manager system (*Shitei Kanrisha Seido*) was established in accordance with the Local Autonomy Law (*Chiho Jichi-ho*) in July of 2003. The essence of this system is that individuals from outside organizations can be appointed by local governments to manage public facilities as designated managers. This system was generated in December 2002 by the Council for Regulatory Reform (*Sogo Kisei Kaikaku Kaigi*) in a report stipulating that openings for the position of public facilities managers, whose responsibilities include decision making about such matters as fare revision, be made available not only to current public officials but also to individuals from private companies. Based on this report, the Local Autonomy Law was revised in July 2003. The designated manager system is closely related to comprehensive outsourcing, explained in the previous section.

The designated manager system has several characteristics, the first of which is related to the type of manager. In the old system, there were multiple constraints to becoming a manager. Because outsourcing in the old system was limited to public institutions in which the local government invested, it was impossible for individuals from the private sector to become public facilities managers. With the new system, individuals from private institutions may become managers after being approved by local diets.

The second point concerns the responsibility of the manager of the public facilities. Although the contracted institution is responsible for the operation of facilities under contract with local governments, the final responsibility for management decisions still lies with the local government. Therefore, it is necessary for the manager to get permission on various matters from local governments. On the other hand, management responsibility and ownership are clearly separated. The local government, as owner of the public facility, has supervisory responsibility whether or not the designated manager adequately manages the facility. If the local government encounters problems with management, it can order corrections or even under certain circumstances revoke approval of the designated manager. In the new system, designated managers are given more leeway to make management decisions.

The third point concerns managers' term of service. In the old system, an annual contract was the norm. The new system makes possible a multiple-year contract, which provides more flexibility in matching the needs of individual public facilities.

The fourth point is related to the selection of public facility managers. The new system stipulates that the designated manager of public facilities be decided at the local assembly. It is expected that the designated manager be selected from among plural candidates after an evaluation of the management plan. As selection from plural candidates encourages competition, it would be considered desirable.

The last point is about public facility user fees. In the old system, the manager of public facilities was simply the head of an institution following a specific contract to manage the organization within a budget. There was no room for incentive to improve efficiency. To the contrary, in the new system, because user fees of the public facilities are the direct revenues of the contracted institution, the designated manager has a strong incentive to improve management. Such a situation presumably fosters managerial originality and ingenuity.

5.2   Application of the Designated Manager System

Tables 14.2 through 14.6 show the characteristics of the designated manager system. The Ministry of Internal Affairs and Communications (2004) reported the number of organizations that had adopted the designated manager system 10 months after the new system was introduced in 2003.

As Table 14.2 shows, the designated manager system has not been widely adopted, although every prefecture has applied it to some facilities.

Second, the majority of organizations for which designated managers are appointed are public institutions, which account for 57.4% of the total, with the private sector (i.e. limited companies and limited liability companies) accounting for only 13.4%. These statistics suggest that the public sector is still conservative, which means that the public is still hesitates to employ the private sector in Japan. Apparently, it will take time for the public sector to become comfortable with using private sector management.

Third, as for kinds of facilities applying the designated manager system, facilities for medical and social welfare are most numerous, accounting for 35.4%. Facilities for education, recreation, and sports are also among those adopting the system. In constrast, the new system was adopted in only 8.8% of public utility and infrastructure facilities.

Fourth, as for opening the selection of designated manager positions to the public, even though candidates should be selected through a process of giving notice of openings and gathering a diversified candidate pool, less than half of the organizations advertised openings publicly (i.e. 44.5%), and even then, selection by outside committee was only 8.6%. The majority of candidates selected as managers were from within public organizations.

Table 14.2   The Degree of Adoption of the Designated Manager System

Number of facilities and organizations which adopt the system	Average number of facilities and organizations per prefecture
1,550 facilities	33 facilities per prefecture
393 organizations	8.4 organizations per prefecture

[Note]:
(1) Numbers in this table were obtained from the Ministry of Internal Affairs and Communications (2004, pp.1-2).
(2) These numbers are as of December 2004.

Table 14.3   Organization Type with regard to Designated Manager

Type of organization	Numbers	Percentage
Limited company	90	10.7%
Limited liability company	23	2.7%
Incorporated foundation	121	14.4%
Incorporated association	36	4.3%
Public institution	483	57.4%
NPO	44	5.2%
Others	44	5.2%
Total	841	100.0%

[Note]:
(1) Numbers in this table were obtained from the Ministry of Internal Affairs and Communications (2004, p.3).
(2) These numbers are as of December 2004.

Table 14.4   Kinds of Facilities Adopting the Designated Manager System

Kinds of facilities	Numbers	Percentage
Recreation and sports	352	22.7%
Promotion of industries	133	8.6%
Public utility and infrastructure	136	8.8%
Education	380	24.5%
Medical and social welfare	549	35.4%
Total	1,550	100.0%

[Note]:
(1) Numbers in this table were obtained from the Ministry of Internal Affairs and Communications (2004, p.3).
(2) These numbers are as of December 2004.
(3) 'Facilities of public utilities and infrastructure' include parking lots, parks, water supply facilities, sewage treatment facilities, and so on.

Table 14.5   The Designated Manager Selection Method

Selection method		Number of organizations	Percentage
Applications open to the public	Selected by outside committee	38	8.6%
	Selected by public organizations	116	26.2%
	Selected by other above-mentioned methods	43	9.7%
Not open to the public	Select traditional contracted manager with applications closed to the public	73	16.5%
	Others	173	39.1%
Total		443	100.0%

[Note]:
(1)   Numbers in this table were obtained from the Ministry of Internal Affairs and Communications (2004, p.4).
(2)   These numbers are as of December 2004.

Table 14.6   Terms of Appointment of Designated Managers

Appointed term	Number of facilities	Percentage
1 year	328	21.2%
2 years	152	9.8%
3 years	548	35.4%
4 years	62	4.0%
5 years	269	17.4%
6~9 years	28	1.8%
More than 10 years	163	10.5%
Total	1,550	100.0%

[Note]:
(1) Numbers in this table were obtained from the Ministry of Internal Affairs and Communications (2004, p.4).
(2) These numbers are as of December 2004.

Last, as for the term of appointment, 3-year contracts were most often selected, accounting for 35.4%. Although multiple-year contracts have become possible with the new system, cases of 1-year contracts still account for 21.2%. A longer-term contract was propounded as a way to encourage management originality and ingenuity, but few organizations have so far adopted the multiple-year contract.

6   LOCAL INDEPENDENT ADMINISTRATIVE INSTITUTIONS

The local independent administrative institution scheme (*Chiho Dokuritsu Gyosei Hojin Seido*) was established in July 2003, and the law regulating the institution was enacted as the Local Independent Administrative Law (*Chiho Dokuritsu Gyousei Hojin-ho*). The main purpose of this scheme is to establish an independent agency separate from the municipal government, with the aim of supplying local services deemed necessary for stabilizing the regional economy and society. The local independent administrative institution is considered as having flexibility in management due to its separation from the local government.

The local independent administrative institution has several characteristics, which are, according to Hosotani (2004), (i) self-responsibility, (ii) corporate accounting and term of budget, (iii) disclosure, and (iv) performance-based salary.

First, as for self-responsibility, the traditional public corporation did not have clear goals, plans for accomplishing clear goals, or schemes for self-evaluation. In short, management at traditional public corporations was irresponsible. In contrast, the newly established scheme of the local independent administrative institution calls for setting up clear three- to five-year goals and plans. At the end of each term, the institution conducts a self-evaluation and uses the results to improve or reform its organization and management. Furthermore, in order to avoid complacency, a third party is appointed to evaluate the institution's performance and holds the institution liable in the event of lower than expected results. In extreme circumstances, the directors of the institution may be dismissed.

Second, in the local independent administrative institution, corporative accounting rules such as double-entry bookkeeping and the accrual basis are adopted. Furthermore, the budget term is not limited to one year, unlike that of the traditional local public corporation. Therefore, while the management of the traditional public corporation is conducted generally on an annual basis, the local independent administrative institution is free to enjoy the flexibility of a longer budget term.

Third, the institution is required to disclose information such as medium-term goals, medium-term plans, financial statements, performance records, and employee salaries. Such information was not made available to the public by traditional public corporations.

Last, local independent administrative institutions include a performance-based salary system, unlike the traditional system, which awarded pay increases solely based on age. In the new institution, salary is related to the performance of the institution. Furthermore, employee salaries are reported to the local municipal government and salary information is made available to the public.

In summary, while the local independent administrative institution has more flexibility in its management, it has heavier responsibility for its performance. If performance results do not meet expectations, directors are held accountable.

NOTES

[1] Details regarding 'private sector style management' are given in the next section.
[2] Some research covers topics besides institutional and organizational reforms. For example, Sato (2002) states that evaluation methods of public corporation performance, methods of transparency of the organization, methods of utilization of the assets of public corporations, and management systems of other related services in public corporations should be treated when discussing 'Private Sector Style Management.'
[3] Private sector style management in individual sectors is summarized in *Japan Water Works Association* (2006) for the water supply industry, and in *Municipal Transportation Works Association* (2006) for public transportation.
[4] The PFI Law is legislation for the Promotion of Public Facility Development by Use of Private Finance (*Minkan Shikin Tou no Katsuyou ni Yoru Koukyo Shisetsu Tou no Seibi no Sokushin ni Kansuru Houritsu*).

[5] These abbreviations represent the kinds of action in a PFI project, for example B (Build), O (Operate) or O (Own), T (Transfer), R (Rehabilitate), with the order in which they are written denoting the order in which they are carried out in the PFI project.

Appendix

1 MATHEMATICAL EXPLANATION FOR THE REGULATION OF NATURAL MONOPOLIES

The numerical explanation for regulation of natural monopoly is as follows. First, we consider simple situations. The inverse demand function for the public utility service is $p(Q) = \alpha - \beta Q$, where the price of the service is $p(Q)$, and the quantity of the public utility service is Q. This monopoly firm decides a service output level attaining the maximum profit. The monopoly firm's cost function is expressed as $C(Q) = cQ + f$.

Therefore, the profit of the monopoly firm is expressed as
$$\pi(Q) = p(Q)Q - C(Q) = (\alpha - \beta Q)Q - (cQ + f) \ .$$

The behavior of the monopoly firm is to maximize profit. Therefore, the object function of the firm is as follows.

$$\max_{Q} \ \pi(Q) = (\alpha - \beta Q)Q - (cQ + f). \qquad (A.1.1)$$

The first order condition for profit maximization is

$$d\pi/dQ = (\alpha - 2\beta Q) - c = 0. \qquad (A.1.2)$$

It is worth noting that this profit maximizing condition shows marginal revenues ($MR = \alpha - 2\beta Q$) as equal to marginal cost ($MC = c$).

From the equation above, the service output provided by the monopoly firm, Q_M, and the price, p_M, are

$$Q_M = (\alpha - c)/2\beta \qquad (A.1.3)$$
$$p_M = (\alpha + c)/2. \qquad (A.1.4)$$

As for the social optimal, we assume that social welfare, $W(Q)$, is the sum of consumer surplus, $CS(Q) = \int p(Q)dQ - p(Q)Q$, and the profit of the firm, $\pi(Q)$. Therefore, the welfare function for society is expressed as $W(Q) = CS(Q) + \pi(Q)$.

The regulator decides the service output level to attain social welfare maximization. Therefore, the object function of the regulator is

$$\max_{Q} \quad W(Q) = \int (\alpha - \beta Q) dQ - (cQ + f) \cdot \qquad \text{(A.1.5)}$$

The first order condition for the social welfare function is

$$dW/dQ = (\alpha - \beta Q) - c = 0. \qquad \text{(A.1.6)}$$

It is worth noting that this social welfare maximizing condition shows the demand function ($p(Q) = \alpha - \beta Q$) as equal to the marginal cost ($MC = c$).

From the equation above, the service output decided by the regulator, Q_C, and the price, p_C, are

$$Q_C = (\alpha - c)/\beta. \qquad \text{(A.1.7)}$$
$$p_C = c. \qquad \text{(A.1.8)}$$

Compared with these two cases, the monopoly is clearly less than socially optimal because, $Q_M < Q_C$, $p_M > p_C$.

The government is therefore justified in regulating the natural monopoly firm.

2   LIST OF PRIVATE GROUND BROADCASTING TV COMPANIES

(1) Hokkaido: HBC (Hokkaido Hoso), STV (Sapporo TV Hoso), UHB (Hokkaido Bunka Hoso), HTB (Hokkaido TV Hoso), TVH (TV Hokkaido

(2) Aomori: ATV (Aomori TV), RAB (Aomori Hoso), ABA (Aomori Asahi Hoso)

(3) Iwate: IBC (IBC Iwate Hoso), TVI (TV Iwate), MIT (Iwate Menkoi TV), IAT (Iwate Asahi TV)

(4) Miyagi: TBC (Tohoku Hoso), MMT (Miyagi TV Hoso), OX (Sendai Hoso), KHB (Higashi Nihon Hoso)

(5) Akita: ABS (Akita Hoso), AKT (Akita TV), AAB (Akita Asahi Hoso)

(6) Yakagata: TUY (TV U Yamagata), YBC (Yamagata Hoso), SAY (Sakuranbo TV), YTS (Yamagata TV)

(7) Fukushima: TUF (TV U Fukushima), FCT (Fukushima Chuo TV), FTV (Fukushima TV), KFB (Fukushima Hoso)

(8) Gunma: GTV (Gunma TV)

(9) Tochigi: GYT (Tochigi TV)

(10) Saitama: TVS (TV Saitama)

(11) Tokyo: TBS (Tokyo Hoso), NTV (Nihon TV), CX (Fuji TV), EX (Zenkoku Asahi Hoso), TX (TV Tokyo), MXTV (Tokyo Metropolitan TV)

(12) Chiba: CTC (Chiba TV Hoso)

(13) Kanagawa: TVK (TV Kanagawa)

(14) Niigata: BSN (Niigata Hoso), TeNY (TV Niigata Hoso), NST (Niigata Sogo TV), NT21 (Niigata TV21)

(15) Nagano: SBC (Shinetsu Hoso), TSB (TV Shinshu), NBS (Nagano Hoso), ABN (Nagano Asahi Hoso)

(16) Yamanashi: UTY (TV Yamanashi), YBS (Yamanashi Hoso)

(17) Shizuoka: SBS (Shizuoka Hoso), SDT (Shizuoka Daiichi TV), SUT (TV Shizuoka), SATV (Shizuoka Asahi TV)

(18) Toyama: TUT (Tulip TV), KNB (Kita Nihon Hoso), BBT (Toyama TV)

(19) Ishikawa: MRO (Hokuriku Hoso), KTK (TV Kanazawa), ITC (Ishikawa TV Hoso), HAB (Hokuriku Asahi Hoso)

(20) Fukui: FBC (Fukui Hoso), FTB (Fukui TV Hoso)

(21) Gifu: GBS (Gifu Hoso)

(22) Aichi: CBS (Chubu Nihon Hoso), CTV (Chukyo TV Hoso), THK (Tokai TV Hoso), NBN (Nagoya TV Hoso), TVA (TV Aichi)

(23) Mie: MTV (Mie TV Hoso)

(24) Shiga: BBC (Biwako Hoso)

(25)Kyoto: KBS (Kyoto Hoso)

(26)Nara: TVN (Nara TV Hoso)

(27)Osaka: MBS (Mainichi Hoso), YTV (Yomiuri TV Hoso), KTV (Kansai TV Hoso), ABC (Asahi Hoso), TVO (TV Osaka)

(28)Hyogo: SUN (Sun TV)

(29)Wakayama: WTV (Wakayama TV)

(30)Tottori: BSS (Sanin Hoso), NKT (Nihonkai TV Hoso)

(31)Shimane: TSK (Sanin Chuo TV Hoso)

(32)Okayama: RSK (Sanyo Hoso), OHK (Okayama Hoso), TSC (TV Setouchi)

(33)Kagawa: RNC (Nishi Nihon Hoso), KSB (Setonaikai Hoso)

(34)Tokushima: JRT (Shikoku Hoso)

(35)Ehime: ITV (Ai TV), RNB (Nankai Hoso), EBC (Ehime Hoso), EAT (Ehime Asahi Hoso)

(36)Kochi: KUTV (TV Kochi), RKC (Kochi Hoso), KBS (Kochi Sansan TV)

(37)Hiroshima: RCC (Chugoku Hoso), HTV (Hiroshima TV Hoso), TSS (TV Shin-Hiroshima), MOME (Hiroshima Home TV)

(38)Yamaguchi: TYS (TV Yamaguchi), KRY (Yamaguchi Hoso), YAB (Yamaguchi Asahi Hoso)

(39)Fukuoka: RKB (RKB Mainichi Hoso), FBS (Fukuoka Hoso), TNC (TV Nishi Nihon), KBS (Kyushu Asahi Hoso), TVQ (TVQ Kyushu Hoso)

(40)Saga: STS (Saga TV)

(41)Nagasaki: NBC (Nagasaki Hoso), NIB (Nagasaki Kokusai TV), KTN (TV Nagasaki), NCC (Nagasaki Bunka Hoso)

(42)Kumamoto: RKK (Kumamoto Hoso), KKT (Kumamoto Kenmin TV) TKU (TV Kumamoto), KAB (Kumamoto Asahi Hoso)

(43)Oita: CBS (Oita Hoso), TOS (TV Oita), OAB (Oita Asahi Hoso)

(44)Miyazaki: MRT (Miyazaki Hoso), UMK (TV Miyazaki)

(45)Kagoshima: MBC (Minami Nihon Hoso), KYT (Kagoshima Yomiuri TV), KTS (Kagoshima TV Hoso), KKB (Kagoshima Hoso)

(46)Okinawa: RBC (Ryukyu Hoso), OTV (Okinawa TV Hoso), QAB (Ryukyu Asahi Hoso)

3   ENGLISH-JAPANESE MAJOR TERMS

English	Japanese
Basic Service (in Telecommunication Service)	Kisoteki Denki Tsushin Ekimu
Basic Standard of Establishment of Broadcasting Stations	Hosokyoku Kaisetsu no Kihonteki Kijun
Basic Water Volume System	Kihon Suiryo Sei
Broadcast Law	Hoso-ho
Broadcasting System by Use of Telecommunications Service	Denki Tsushin Ekimu Riyo Hoso Seido
Cable Television Broadcast Law	Yusen Terebijon Hoso-ho
Ceiling Price	Jogen Kakaku
Community Gas Supply Company	Kani Gasu Jigyosha
Community Water Supply Organization	Kani Suido Jigyosha
Comprehensive Outsourcing	Hokatsuteki Gaigu Itaku
Council for Regulatory Reform	Sogo Kisei Kaikaku Kaigi
Delivery Post Office	Shuhaikyoku
Designated Manager System	Shitei Kanrisha Seido
Electric Power System Council of Japan	Denryoku Keito Riyo Kyougikai

(Continued)

Electricity Enterprise Law	Denki Jigyo-ho
Enforcement Regulation of the Railway Business Law	Tetsudo Jigyo Seko Kisoku
Enforcement Regulation of the the Telecommunications Business Law	Denki Tsushin Jigyo-ho Seko Kisoku
Forwarding System of Gas Supply	Gasu Takuso Kyokyu Seido
Gas Transmission and Distribution Company	Gasu Dokan Jigyosha
Gas Utility Enterprise Law	Gasu Jigyo-ho
General Electricity Company	Ippan Denki Jigyosha
General Gas Supply Company	Ippan Gasu Jigyosha
General Water Supply Organization	Josuido Jigyosha
Highway Company Law	Kosokudoro Kaisha-ho
Independent Power Producer Company	Oroshi Kyokyu Jigyosha
Japan Electric Power Exchange	Nihon Oroshi Denryoku Torihikisyo
Japan Expressway Holding and Debt Repayment Agency (JEHDRA)	Nihon Kosoku Doro Hoyu Saimu Hensai Kiko
Japan National Railways	Nihon Kokuyu Tetsudo
Japan National Railway Law	Nihon Kokuyu Tetsudo-ho

(Continued)

Japan National Railway Settlement Corporation (JNRSC)	Nihon Kokuyu Tetsudo Seisan Jigyodan
Japan Post	Nihon Yusei
Japan Post Holding Company	Nihonyusei Kabushikikaisha
Japan Post Network Company	Yubinkyoku Kabushikikaisha
Japan Post Service Company	Yubinjigyo Kabushikikaisha
Japan Post Bank Company	Yuchoginko Kabushikikaisha
Japan Post Insurance Company	Kanposeimeihoken Kabushikikaisha
Japan Post Public Corporation	Nihon Yusei Kosha
JR railways	JR tetsudo
Large private railways	Ote Shitetsu
Large-scale Gas Supply Company	Oguchi Gasu Jigyosha
License System	Menkyo Sei
Local Autonomy Law	Chiho Jichi-ho
Local Independent Administrative Institution Scheme	Chiho Dokuritsu Gyosei Hojin Seido
Local Independent Administrative Law	Chiho Dokuritsu Gyosei Hojin-ho
Local Public Corporation Law	Chiho Koei Kigyo-ho
Local Railway Law	Chiho Tetsudo-ho
Management Stability Fund (MSF)	Keiei Antei Kikin

(Continued)

Ordinal Post Office	Futsu Yubinkyoku
Permission System	Kyoka Sei
Personal Correspondence Mail Service Law	Shinshobin-ho
Postal Law	Yubin-ho
Postal Network Law	Yubinkyoku Kabushikikaisha-ho
Postal Network Enforcement Regulation	Yubinkyoku Kabushikikaisha-ho Seko Kisoku
Postal Service Enforcement Regulation	Yubin-ho Seko Kisoku
Power Producer and Supplier Company	Tokutei Kibo Denki Jigyosha
Princple of De-concentration of the Mass Media	Masu Medhia Shuchu Haijo Gensoku
Private Sector Style Management Scheme	Minkanteki Keiei Shuho
Private Water Supply Organization	Senyo Suido Jigyosha
Radio Law	Denpa-ho
Railway Accounting Regulations	Tetsudo Kaikei Kisoku
Railway Business Law	Tetsudo Jigyo-ho
Report in Advance	Jizen Todokede Sei
Regional Council	Chiiki Kyogikai
Road Transportation Law	Doro Unso-ho

(Continued)

Social and Regional Maintenance Fund	Shakai Chiiki Koken Kikin
Special Electricity Company	Tokutei Denki Jigyosha
Special Law on the Merger of Municipalities	Shichoson no Gappei no Tokurei ni Kansuru Horitsu
Special Post Office	Tokutei Yubinkyoku
Special Service (in Telecommunications Service)	Tokutei Denki Tsushin Ekimu
Specified Service (in Telecommunications Service)	Shitei Denki Tsushin Ekimu
Summary Post Office	Kani Yubinkyoku
Supply-demand Adjustment Regulation	Jukyu Chosei Kisei
Telecommunications Business Dispute Settlement Comission	Denki Tsushin Jigyo Syori Iinkai
Telecommunications Carrier Association	Denki Tsushin Jigyo Kyokai
Trust-Entrust Broadcasting System	Jutaku-Itaku Hoso Seido
Waterworks Law	Suido-ho
Water Supply Organization	Suido Jigyosha
Waterworks	Suido
Wholesale Electricity Company	Oroshi Denki Jigyosha
Wholesale Water Supply Organization	Suido Yosui Kyokyu Jigyosha
Yardstick Regulation	Yahdo Suttikku Kisei

References

Adam, C., W. Cavendish and P. S. Mistry (1992) *Adjusting Privatization,* London, UK : James Currey.

Agrell, P. J., P. Bogetoft and J. Tind (2005) 'DEA and Dynamic Yardstick Competition in Scandinavian Electricity Distribution,' *Journal of Productivity Analysis,* **23** (2), 173−201.

Alchian, A. (1977) *Economic Forces at Work,* Indianapolis, IN, USA: Liberty Press.

Alchian, A. A. and H. Demsetz (1972) 'Production, Information Costs, and Economic Organization,' *American Economic Review,* **62** (5), 777−95.

Alchian, A. A. and H. Demsetz (1973) 'The Property Right Paradigm,' *The Journal of Economic History,* **33** (1), 16−27.

Anayama, T. (2005) *Economics of Electric Power Industry (Denryoku Sangyo no Keizaigaku),* Tokyo, Japan: NTT Syuppan (in Japanese).

Ariu, T. (2001) 'Impacts of Business Customer Services on Electric Power Supplier Choice (Denryoku Kaisya Sentaku ni Okeru Kokyaku Sabisu no Juyosei),' *Journal of Public Utility Economics (Koeki Jigyo Kenkyu),* **53** (1), 29−57 (in Japanese).

Ariu, T. (2003) 'Evaluation of Electric Power Supplier by Japanese Manufacturing Customers: Analysis of Customer Choice Based on Price, Power Reliability and Services (Denryoku Jiyuka ni Okeru Seizougyo Juyouka no Denryoku Kaisya no Sentaku Yoin: Kakaku, Hinshitsu, Shinraisei oyobi Sabisu no Men kara Mita Hyoka),' *Journal of Public Utility Economics (Koeki Jigyo Kenkyu),* **55** (1), 31−40 (in Japanese).

Armstrong, M., S. Cowan and J. Vickers (1994) *Regulatory Reform: Economic Analysis and British Experience,* Cambridge, MA: MIT Press.

Asano, H. (2006) 'Regulatory Reform of the Electricity Industry in Japan: What is the Next Step of Deregulation?,' *Energy Policy,* **34** (16), 2491−7.

Association of Water and Sewage Works Consultants Japan (2004) *Basic Data for Water Works Vision (Suido Bijon Kiso Deta Syu),* Tokyo,

Japan: Association of Water and Sewage Works Consultants Japan (in Japanese).

Atkinson, S. E. and R. Halvorsen (1986) 'The Relative Efficiency of Public and Private Firms in a Regulated Environment: The Case of U.S. Electric Utilities,' *Journal of Public Economics*, **29** (3), 281 – 94.

Averch, H. and L. L. Johnson (1962) 'Behavior of the Firm under Regulatory Constraint,' *American Economic Review*, **52** (5), 1053 – 69.

Bailey, E. E. and R. D. Coleman (1971) 'The Effect of Lagged Regulation in the Averch-Johnson Model,' *Bell Journal of Economics and Management Science*, **2** (1), 278 – 92.

Baldwin, R. and M. Cave (1999) *Understanding Regulation: Theory, Strategy, and Practice*, Oxford, UK: Oxford University of Press.

Baumol, W. J., J. C. Panzar and R. D. Willig (1982) *Contestable Markets and the Theory of Industrial Structure*, New York, NY, USA: Harcourt Brace and Jovanovich.

Bennett, J. T. and M. H. Johnson (1979) 'Public versus Private Provision of Collective Goods and Services: Garbage Collection Revisited,' *Public Choice*, **34** (1), 55 – 63.

Bishop, M., J. Kay and C. Mayer (1994) *Privatization and Economic Performance*, Oxford, UK: Oxford University Press.

Bouf, D. and P. Y. Péguy (2001) 'Is Yardstick Competition Desirable for Western European Railway?' *International Journal of Transport Economics*, **28** (2), 205 – 27.

Bös, D. (1991) *Privatization: A Theoretical Treatment*, Oxford, UK: Clarendon Press.

Bradley M. D. and J. Colvin (2000) 'Measuring the Cost of Universal Service for Posts,' in M. A. Crew and P. R. Kleindorfer (eds.) *Current Directions in Postal Reforms*, Boston, MA: Kluwer Academic Publishers, 29 – 46.

Breyer, S. (1982) *Regulation and Its Reform*, Cambridge, MA, USA: Harvard University Press.

Bruggink, T. W. (1982) 'Public versus Regulated Private Enterprise in the Municipal Water Industry: A Comparison of Operating Costs,' *Quarterly Review of Economics and Business*, **22** (1), 111 – 25.

Bukka Seisaku Antei Kaigi (2005) *Interim Report on the Guideline for Analysis of Regulatory Impact on the Industries Related to Public Utility Charges (Kokyo Ryokin Bunya ni okeru Kisei Eikyo Bunseki Gaidorain Chukan Hokoku)*, Tokyo, Japan: Bukka Anteikaigi, Kokyo Ryokin Bunya ni okeru Kisei Eikyo Bunseki Kento Iinkai (in Japanese).

Byrners, P., S. Grosskopf and K. Hayes (1986) 'Efficiency and Ownership: Further Evidence,' *Review of Economics and Statistics*, **68** (2), 337−41.

Cabinet Office (2005) *Guide of Setting-up PFI Project for the Local Municipal Governments (Chiho Kokyo Dantai ni Okeru PFI Jigyo Donyu no Tebiki)*, Tokyo, Japan: Minkan Shikin-tou Katsuyo Jigyo Suishin Shitsu, Cabinet Office (in Japanese).

Castro, M. and R. Maddock (1997) 'The Universal Service Obligation for Post: Some Australian Calculations,' in M. A. Crew and P. R. Kleindorfer (eds.) *Managing Change in the Postal and Delivery Industries*, Boston, MA: Kluwer Academic Publishers, 258−69.

Caves, D. W. and L. R. Christensen (1980) 'The Relative Efficiency of Public and Private Firms in a Competitive Environment: The Case of Canadian Railroads,' *Journal of Political Economy*, **88** (5), 958−76.

Caves, D. W., L. R. Christensen, J. A. Swanson and M. W. Tretheway (1982) 'Economic Performance of U.S. and Canadian Railroads: The Significance of Ownership and the Regulatory Environment,' in W. T. Stanbury and F. Thompson (eds.) *Managing Public Enterprises*, New York, NY, USA: Praeger, 123−51.

Chujo U. (1992) 'Publicness and Market Intervention (Kokyosei to Shijo Kainyu),' in Y. Fujii and U. Chujo (eds.) *Modern Transportation Policy (Gendai Kotsu Seisaku)*, Tokyo, Japan: the University of Tokyo Press, 45−65 (in Japanese).

Chusho Kibo Jougesuido Kenkyukai (2005) 'Management of Enterprise and Outsourcing to Private Sector (Jigyo Unei to Minkan Itaku),' *Public Corporation (Koei Kigyo)*, **36** (10), 64−75 (in Japanese).

Collins, J. N. and B. T. Downes (1977) 'The Effects of Size of the Provision of Public Services: The Case of Solid Waste Collection in Smaller Cities,' *Urban Affairs Quarterly*, **12** (3), 333−47.

Committee of the Regulatory Impact Study on Government-Regulated Public Service Charges (2005) *Interim Report for Guideline of Regulatory Impact Study on Government-Regulated Public Service Charges (Kokyo Ryokin Bunya ni okeru Kisei Eikyo Bunseki Gaidorain Chukan Hokoku)*, Tokyo, Japan: Price Stability Council (Bukka Antei Kaigi), Cabinet Office, September 26, 2005 (in Japanese).

Cowan, S. (1997) 'Competition in the Water Industry,' *Oxford Review of Economic Policy*, **13** (1), 83−92.

Crain, M. and A. Zardkoohi (1978) 'A Test of the Property-Right Theory of the Firm: Water Utilities in the United States,' *Journal of Law and Economics*, **21** (2), 395−408.

Cubbin, J., S. Domberger and S. Meadowcroft (1987) 'Competitive Tendering and Refuse Collection: Identifying the Sources of Efficiency Gains,' *Fiscal Studies*, **8** (3), 49−58.

Dalen, D. M. (1998) 'Yardstick Competition and Investment Incentives,' *Journal of Economics and Management Strategy*, **7** (1), 105−26.

Dalen, D. M. and A. Gómez-Lobo (2003) 'Yardstick on the Road: Regulatory Contracts and Cost Efficiency in the Norwegian Bus Industry,' *Transportation*, **30** (4), 371−86.

Davies, D. G. (1971) 'The Efficiency of Public versus Private Firms: The Case of Australia's Two Airlines,' *Journal of Law and Economics*, **14** (1), 149−65.

Davies, D. G. (1977) 'Property Rights and Economic Efficiency: The Australian Airline Revisited,' *Journal of Law and Economics*, **20** (1), 223−26.

De Alessi, L. (1974) 'Managerial Tenure under Private and Government Ownership in the Electric Power Industry,' *Journal of Political Economy*, **82** (3), 645−53.

De Alessi, L. (1977) 'Ownership and Peak-Load Pricing in the Electric Power Industry,' *Quarterly Review of Economics and Business*, **17** (4), 7−26

Di Lorenzo, T. J. and R. Robinson (1982) 'Managerial Objectives Subject to Political Market Constraints: Electric Utilities in the U.S.,' *Quarterly Review of Economics and Business*, **22** (2), 113−25.

Donahue, J. D. (1989) *The Privatization Decision: Public Ends, Private Means*, USA: Basic Books.

Dormont, B. and C. Milcent (2005) 'How to Regulate Heterogeneous Hospitals?' *Journal of Economics and Management Strategy*, **14** (3), 591−621.

Doro Horei Kenkyukai (2004) *Privatization Laws of Four Highway Public Corporation (Yokuwakaru Doro Kankei Yonkodan Mineika Kankeiho)*, Tokyo, Japan: Gyosei (in Japanese).

Estoche, A., M. González and L. Trujillo (2002) 'Efficiency Gain from Port Reform and the Potential for Yardstick Competition: Lessons from Mexico,' *World Development*, **30** (4), 545−60.

Ezoe, N. (1994) *Economic Theory of Market and Regulation (Shijo to Kisei no Keizai Riron)*, Tokyo, Japan: Chuo Keizai Sha (in Japanese).

Ezoe, N. (2002) 'Liberalization of an Electric Power Market: Structural Analysis of a Retail Supply Market (Denryoku Shijo no Jiyuka: Kouri Kyokyu Shijo no Kozo Bunseki),' *Journal of Public Utility Economics (Koeki Jigyo Kenkyu)*, **54** (4), 23−34 (in Japanese).

Färe, R., S. Grosskopf and J. Logan (1985) 'The Relative Performance in Publicly Owned and Privately Owned Electric Utilities,' *Journal of Public Economics*, **26** (1), 89 — 106.

Federation of Electric Power Companies Statistics Committee (2005) *Handbook of Electric Power Companies (Denki Jigyo Binran)*, Tokyo, Japan: Japan Electric Association (in Japanese).

Feigenbaum, S. and R. Teeples (1983) 'Public versus Private Water Delivery: A Hednic Cost Approach,' *Review of Economics and Statistics,* **65** (4), 672 — 78.

Filippini, M. and J. Wild (2001) 'Regional Differences in Electricity Distribution Costs and Their Consequences for Yardstick Regulation of Access Prices,' *Energy Economics*, **23** (4), 477 — 88.

Foreman-Peck, J. and R. Millward (1994) *Public and Private Ownership of British Industry 1820 — 1990*, Oxford, UK: Clarendon Press.

Fujii Y. and U. Chujo (eds.) (1992) Modern Transportation Policy (Gendai Kotsu Seisaku), Tokyo, Japan: University of Tokyo Press (in Japanese).

Fujiwara, J. (2005) 'Gas Utility Industry (Gas Jigyo),' in Japan Public Utility Economics Association (ed.) *Public Utility Industries in Japan (Nihon no Koeki Jigyo)*, Tokyo, Japan: Hakuto Shobo, 48 — 59 (in Japanese).

Fuke, H. (2005) 'Telecommunications (Tsushin Jigyo),' in Japan Society of Public Utility Economics (ed.), *Public Utility Industries in Japan (Nihon no Koeki Jigyo)*, Tokyo, Japan: Hakuto Shobo, 81 — 97 (in Japanese).

Furubotn, E. G. and S. Pejovich (1974) 'Introduction of the Economics of Property Rights,' in E. G. Furubotn and S. Pejovich (eds.) *The Economics of Property Rights*, Cambridge, MA, USA : Ballinger.

Furukawa, S. (2002) 'Introduction of Oversea's Literatures Related to Public Corporations: Privatization — International Comparison of Performance (Kaigai no Koei Kigyo Kankei Bunken Shokai: Mineika — Gyoseki no Kokusai Hikaku),' *Public Corporation (Koei Kigyo)*, **34** (5), 50 — 59 (in Japanese).

Garnham, N. (1997) 'Universal Service,' in W. H. Melody (ed.), *Telecom Reform: Principles, Policies and Regulatory Practices*, Lyngby, Denmark: Den Private Ingenior Fond.

Gómez-Ibáñez, J. A. (2003) *Regulating Infrastructure: Monopoly, Contracts, and Discretion*, Cambridge, MA, USA: Harvard University Press.

Gómez-Ibáñez, J. A. and J. R. Meyer (1993) *Going Private: The International Experience with Transport Privatization*, Washington,

D.C., USA: Brookings Institution.

Goto, H. and T. Ariu (2006) 'Customers' Loyalty to Electricity Supplier and Analysis of Relationship between Loyalty and its Factors (Denryoku Kyokyusaki Henko ni Kansuru Kokyaku no Roiyaruti to Yoin Bunseki),' *Journal of Public Utility Economics (Koeki Jigyo Kenkyu)*, **58** (2), 35−46 (in Japanese).

Goto, M. and T. Sueyoshi (2009) 'Productivity Growth and Deregulation of Japanese Electricity Distribution,' *Energy Policy*, **37** (8), 3130−38.

Harada, T. (2004) *True Story of Japanese Special Post Office (Tokutei Yubin Kyoku no Shinjitsu)*, Tokyo, Japan: Daiyamondosya (in Japanese).

Hattori, T. (2004) 'An Empirical Analysis of the Determinants of the Retail Access in the U.S. Electricity Industry (Beikoku ni Okeru Denryoku Kouri Jiyuka no Kettei Yoin no Bunseki),' *Journal of Public Utility Economics (Koeki Jigyo Kenkyu)*, **56** (3), 11−19 (in Japanese).

Hattori, T. (2006) 'A Statistical Analysis of Patenting Behavior of the Japanese Electric Utilities (Denki Jigyo ni Okeru Tokkyo Syutsugan Kodo no Henka ni Kansuru Tokei Bunseki),' *Journal of Public Utility (Koeki Jigyo Kenkyu)*, **58** (2), 1−11 (in Japanese).

Hattori, T. (2007) 'An Empirical Analysis of the Number of Bidders in Competitive Procurement for Electricity Supply Contracts (Denryoku Chotatsu no Kyoso Nyusatsu ni Okeru Shinki Sannyusha no Sanka Kodo),' *Journal of Public Utility (Koeki Jigyo Kenkyu)*, **59** (2), 33−41 (in Japanese).

Hattori, T. and M. Tsutsui (2004) 'Economic Impact of Regulatory Reforms in the Electricity Supply Industry: A Panel Data Analysis for OECD Countries,' *Energy Policy,* **32** (6), 823−32.

Hausman, J. M. (1976) *Urban Water Services Pricing: Public vs Private Firms*, Washington, D.C., USA: Unpublished Ph.D. Dissertation, George Washington University, Department of Economics.

Hayashi. K. and Y. Tagawa (1994) *Universal Service (Yunibasaru Sabisu)*, Tokyo, Japan: Chuo Kouronsha (in Japanese).

Hensher, D. A. (1988) 'Productivity in Privately Owned and Operated Bus Firms in Australia,' in J. S. Dodgson and N. Topham (eds.) *Bus Deregulation and Privatisation*, Aldershot, UK: Avebury, 141−70.

Hillman, J. J. (1991) 'Oil Pipeline Rates: A Case for Yardstick Regulation,' in Michael A. Crew (ed.) *Competition and the Regulation of Utilities*, Norwell, MA, USA: Kluwer Academic Publishers, 71−95.

Hirsch, W. Z. (1965) 'Cost Functions of an Urban Government Service: Refuse Collection,' *Review of Economics and Statistics*, **47** (1), 87 – 92.

Hosoe, N. and S. Akiyama (2009) 'Regional Electric Power Demand Elasticities of Japan's Industrial and Commercial Sectors,' *Energy Policy*, **37** (11), 4313 – 19.

Hosotani, Y. (2004) *Explanatory Diagram the Local Public Corporation Law (Zukai Chiho Koei Kigyo Ho)*, Tokyo, Japan: Daiichi Hoki (in Japanese).

Ida, T. (2001) *Network Economics (Nettowaku Ekonomikusu)*, Tokyo, Japan: Nihon Hyoronsha.

Ida T. and T. Kuwabara (2000) 'The Panel Data Analysis of the Japanese Electric Power Industry (Nihon no Denryoku Sangyo no Paneru Deta Bunseki),' *Journal of Public Utility Economics (Koeki Jigyo Kenkyu)*, **52** (2), 71 – 82 (in Japanese).

Ida, T. and T. Kuwahara (2004) 'Yardstick Cost Comparison and Economies of Scale and Scope in Japan's Electric Power Industry,' *Asian Economic Journal*, **18** (4), 423 – 38.

Ide, H. (2004a) 'Gas Utility (Gasu),' in H. Ide (ed.) *Regulation and Competition in the Network Industries (Kisei to Kyoso no Nettowahku Sangyo)*, Tokyo, Japan: Keiso Shobo, 27 – 49 (in Japanese).

Ide, H. (2004b) 'Postal Services (Yubin),' in H. Ide (ed.) *Regulation and Competition in the Network Industries (Kisei to Kyoso no Nettowahku Sangyo)*, Tokyo, Japan: Keiso Shobo, 139 – 64 (in Japanese).

Ide, H. and T. Okamoto (2004) 'Gas Utility Industry in Japan: Structures and Reforms (Nihon no Gasu Sangyo: Kozo to Henkaku),' in M. Uekusa (ed.) *Reforms in the Energy Industry (Enerugi Sangyo no Henkaku)*, Tokyo, Japan: NTT Syuppan, 211 – 47 (in Japanese).

Ihori, T. (1990) 'Economic Theory of Privatization (Mineika no Keizai Riron),' in NIRA (ed.) *Research on Privatization of Public Corporations (Kosya Kodan to no Mineika no Kenkyu)*, Tokyo, Japan: Sogo Kenkyu Kaihatsu Kiko, 105 – 17 (in Japanese).

Ishii, H. (1996) 'Deregulation of the Rail Industry and Introduction of New Rail Fare Setting Method (Tetsudo Jigyo ni Okeru Kiseikanwa to Atarashii Unchin Settei Hoshiki no Donyu),' *Journal of Public Utility Economics (Koeki Jigyo Kenkyu)*, **48** (1), 43 – 9 (in Japanese).

Ishii, H. (2005a) 'Water Supply Industry (Suido Jigyo),' in Japan Public Utility Economics Association (ed.) *Public Utility Industries in Japan (Nihon no Koeki Jigyo)*, Tokyo, Japan: Hakuto Shobo, 59 – 79 (in Japanese).

Ishii, H. (2005b) 'Postal Services (Yubin Jigyo),' in Japan Society of Public Utility Economics (ed.) *Public Utility Industries in Japan (Nihon no Koeki Jigyo)*, Tokyo, Japan: Hakuto Shobo, 122 – 34 (in Japanese).

Ito, E., T. Ida and S. Kinoshita (2004) 'Productivity Gains in the Japan's Electricity Industry: Following Two Regulatory Reforms (Nihon no Denryoku Jiyuka ga Gijutsuteki Koritsusei ni Ataeta Koka no Jissho Bunseki),' *Journal of Public Utility Economics (Koeki Jigyo Kenkyu)*, **56** (3), 53 – 9 (in Japanese).

Ito, N. and T. Miyazone (1994) 'Yardstick Competition (Yado Sutikku Kyoso),' in M. Uekusa (ed.) *Public Regulation and Industries: Electric Power Industry (Koteki Kisei to Sangyo: Denryoku)*, Tokyo, Japan: NTT Syuppan, 88 – 124 (in Japanese).

Iwasaki, A. (1992) 'Privatization (Mineika),' in Economic Research Institute of Osaka City University (ed.), *Dictionary of Economics (Keizaigaku Jiten)*, Third Edition, Tokyo, Japan: Iwanami Shoten, 1256 – 7 (in Japanese).

Jamasb, T. and M. Pollitt (2007) 'Incentive Regulation of Electricity Distribution Networks: Lessons of Experience from Britain,' *Energy Policy*, **35** (12), 6163 – 87.

Japan Post (2003) *Postal Service in Japan: Annual Report 2003*, Tokyo, Japan: Japan Post.

Japan Post (2005) *Universal Service Cost (USC) of Postal Services (Yubin no Yunibasaru Sabisu Kosuto)*, Tokyo, Japan: Japan Post Public Corporation (in Japanese).

Japan Post (2007) *Postal Service in Japan: Disclosure Annual Report 2007*, Tokyo, Japan: Japan Post (in Japanese).

Japan Water Works Association (2006) *Research Report on the Setting-up of the Private Sector Style Management in the Water Supply Industry (Suido Jigyo ni Okeru Minkanteki Keiei Syuho no Donyu ni Kansuru Chosa Kenkyu Hokokusho)*, Tokyo, Japan: Japan Water Works Association (in Japanese).

Japan Water Works Association (2007) *Water Supply Statistics (Suido Tokei)*, Tokyo, Japan: Japan Water Works Association (Nihon Suido Kyokai) (in Japanese).

Jordan, W. A. (1982) 'Performance of North American Australian Airlines,' in W. T. Stanbury and F. Thompson (eds.) *Managing Public Enterprises*, New York, NY, USA: Praeger, 161 – 99.

Joskow, P. L. and R. G. Noll （1981） 'Regulation in Theory and Practice: An Overview,' in G. Fromm (ed.) *Studies in Public Regulation*, Cambridge, MA, USA: MIT Press.

Jürges, H., W. F. Richeter and K. Schneider (2005) 'Teacher Quality and Incentive: Theoretical and Empirical Effects of Standard on Teacher Quality,' *FinanzArchiv*, **61** (3), 298 − 326.

Kahn, A. E. (1988) *The Economics of Regulation: Principles and Institutions*, Cambridge, MA, USA: MIT Press.

Kaino, K. (2007) *Quantitative Analysis on Regulatory Policy Changes in the Electric Power and the Gas Utility Industry (Denki, Toshi Gasu Jigyo ni Okeru Seisaku Seido Henko no Teiryoteki Eikyo Bunseki)*, RIETI Discussion Paper Series 05-J-034, Tokyo, Japan: Research Institute of Economy, Trade and Industry (in Japanese).

Kakizaki, Y. (2002) 'Management Buyout as a Method to Revitalize Managegement (Keiei Kasseika Syuho to Shiteno Keieisya Baiauto),' *Public Corporation (Koei Kigyo)*, **34** (5), 44 − 9 (in Japanese).

Kamata, S. (1985) 'Comparison Between Public Organization and Private Company Organization (Paburikku Soshiki to Minkan Kigyo Soshiki no Hikaku),' *Organizational Science (Soshiki Kagaku)*, **19** (2), 17 − 26 (in Japanese).

Kanou, Y. (1990) 'Modern Society and Privatization (Gendai Shakai to Mineika),' in Sogo Kenkyu Kaihatsu Kiko (ed.) *Studies on Privatization of Public Corporations (Kosha Kodan no Mineika no Kenkyu)*, Tokyo, Japan: NIRA, No. 900067, 9 − 18 (in Japanese).

Kato, H. (2004) 'Corporate Strategy of JR Bus Companies Before and After Deregulation in Japan (Waga Kuni Basu Shijo ni okeru Kisei Kanwa to JR Basu no Keiei Senryaku),' *Annual Report on Transportation Economics (Kotsugaku Kenkyu)*, **48**, 51 − 60 (in Japanese).

Kemper, P. and J. M. Quigley (1976) *The Economics of Refuse Collection*, Cambridge, MA, USA: Ballinger Publishing.

Kessides, I. N. (2004) *Reforming Infrastructure: Privatization, Regulation, and Competition*, Washington D.C., USA: The World Bank.

Kishii, D. (2002) 'Setting-up the Private Sector Style Management and Contractualisation (Minkanteki Keiei Shuho no Donyu to Keiyakuka),' *Public Corporation (Koei Kigyo)*, **34** (8), 11 − 63 (in Japanese).

Kitchen, H. (1976) 'A Statistical Estimation of an Operating Cost Function for Municipal Refuse Collection,' *Public Finance Quarterly*, **4** (1), 56 − 76.

Kridel, D, D. Sappington and D. Weisman. (1996) 'The Effects of Incentive Regulation in the Telecommunication Industry: Survey,' *Journal of Regulatory Economics*, **9** (3), 269 − 306.

Kumbhakar, S. C. and L. Hjalmarsson (1998) 'Relative Performance of Public and Private Ownership Under Yardstick Competition: Electricity Retail Distribution,' *European Economic Review*, **42** (1), 97−122.

Kurashino Risachi Senta (2004) *Deregulation and System of Public Utility Charges (Kisei Kanwa to Kokyo Ryokin Seido)*, Tokyo, Japan: Kurashino Risachi Senta (in Japanese).

Kusano, S. (2002) 'The Challenge and Prospects of the Japanese Gas Utility Industry Structural Reform (Gasu Jigyo Seido Kaikaku heno Kadai to Tenbo),' *Journal of Public Utility Economics (Koeki Jigyo Kenkyu)*, **54** (1), 45−8.

Kuwahara, H. (1998) 'Industrial Organization of Water Supply Organization: Estimation of Scale Economies and Efficiency (Suido Jigyo no Sangyo Soshiki: Kibo no Keizaisei to Kouritsusei no Keisoku),' *Journal of Public Utility Economics (Koeki Jigyo Kenkyu)*, **50** (1), 45−54 (in Japanese).

Laffont, J-J. and J. Tirole (2000) *Competition in Telecommunications*, Cambridge, MA, USA: MIT Press.

Lawrence, D., J. Houghton and A. George (1997) 'International Comparison of Australia's Infrastructure Performance,' *Journal of Productivity Analysis*, **8** (4), 361−98.

Leibenstein, H. (1966) 'Allocative Efficiency vs. X-Inefficiency,' *American Economic Review*, **56** (3), 392−415.

Liu, Z. (1995) 'The Comparative Performance of Public and Private Enterprises: The Case of British Ports,' *Journal of Transport Economics and Policy*, **29** (3), 263−74.

Maeda, Y. (2003) 'The Transfigulation of the Bus Service after the Deregulation (Kisei Kanwago no Noriai Basu Sabisu no Henyo),' *Annual Report on Transportation Economics (Kotsugaku Kenkyu)*, **47**, 79−88 (in Japanese).

Mann, P. C. (1970) 'Publicly Owned Electric Utility Profits and Resource Allocation,' *Land Economics*, **46** (4), 478−84.

Maskin, E., Y. Qian and C. Xu (2000) 'Incentives, Information, and Organization Form,' *Review of Economic Studies,* **67** (2), 359−78.

McDavid, J. C. (1985) 'The Canadian Experience with Privatizing Residential Solid Waste Collection Services,' *Public Administration Review*, **45** (5), 602−8.

Meyer, R. A. (1975) 'Publicly Owned versus Privately Owned Utilities: A Policy Choice,' *Review of Economics and Statistics*, **57** (4), 391−9.

Millward, R. and R. Ward (1987) 'The Costs of Public and Private Gas Enterprises in Late 19th Century Britain,' *Oxford Economic Paper*,

39 (4), 719—37.

Ministry of Internal Affairs and Communication (2004) *Research Results of the Situations on the Adoption of the Designated Manager System in the Public Facilities (Kou no Shisetsu no Shitei Kanrisya Seido no Donyu Jokyo ni Kansuru Chosa Kekka)*, Tokyo, Japan: Ministry of Internal Affairs and Communication.

Ministry of Internal Affairs and Communications (2005) *Price Regulation in Telecommunication Industry (Denki Tsushin Bunya ni okeru Ryokin Kisei)*, Tokyo, Japan: Ministry of Internal Affairs and Communications, Sogo Tsushi Kibankyoku, Ryokin Sabisuka (in Japanese)

Ministry of Internal Affairs and Communications (2007a) *Materials of Study Meeting on Review of Postal Services and Correspondence System (Yubin Shishobin Seido no Minaoshi ni Kansuru Chosa Kenkyukai Shiryo)*, Tokyo, Japan: Ministry of Internal Affairs and Communications (in Japanese).

Ministry of Internal Affairs and Communications (2007b) *Materials of Study Meeting on Future of the Universal Service System (Yunibasaru Sabisu Seido no Shoraizo ni Kansuru Kenkyukai Shiryo)*, Tokyo, Japan: Ministry of Internal Affairs and Communications (in Japanese).

Ministry of Internal Affairs and Communications (2007c) *Reports of Study Meeting on Future of the Universal Service System (Yunibasaru Sabisu Seido no Shoraizo ni Kansuru Kenkyukai Hokokusho)*, Tokyo, Japan: Ministry of Internal Affairs and Communications (in Japanese).

Ministry of Internal Affairs and Communications (2007d), *2007 White Paper Information and Communications in Japan (Joho Tsushin Hakusyo 2007)*, Tokyo, Japan: Ministry of Internal Affairs and Communications (in Japanese).

Ministry of Internal Affairs and Communications (2008), *2008 White Paper Information and Communications in Japan (Joho Tsushin Hakusyo 2008)*, Tokyo, Japan: Ministry of Internal Affairs and Communications (in Japanese).

Ministry of Land, Infrastructure and Transport (2005) 'Summary of Privatization of Four Highway-related Public Corporations and Report of Preparation for Privatization (Doro Kankei Yonkodan no Mineika no Gaiyo to Mineika ni Muketa Junbijokyo ni Tsuite),' *Expressways and Automobiles (Kosokudoro to Jidosha)*, **48** (4), 29—32 (in Japanese).

Ministry of Land Infrastructure and Transport (2008) *Rail Statistics 2008 (Suji de Miru Tetsudo 2008)*, Tokyo, Japan: Unyu Seisaku Kenkyu

Kiko.

Ministry of Land Infrastructure and Transport (2009) *Automobile Statistics 2009 (Suji de Miru Jidosha 2009)*, Tokyo, Japan: Nihon Jidosha Kaigisho (in Japanese).

Ministry of Transportation (1995), *1995 White Paper Transportation in Japan (Unyu Hakusyo 1995)*, Tokyo, Japan: Ministry of Finance (in Japanese).

Ministry of Transportation (1996), *1996 White Paper Transportation in Japan (Unyu Hakusyo 1996)*, Tokyo, Japan: Ministry of Finance (in Japanese).

Ministry of Transportation (2000), *2000 White Paper Transportation in Japan (Unyu Hakusyo 2000)*, Tokyo, Japan: Ministry of Finance (in Japanese).

Miyajima, M. and S. Lee (1984) 'Research on Efficiency Comparison between Local Public Firms and Private Firms: A Case Study of Rail Industry (Chiho Koei Kigyo to Minkan Kigyo no Koritsusei no Hikaku ni Kansuru Kenkyu: Tetsudogyo wo Rei ni shite),' *Journal of Public Utility Economics (Koeki Jigyo Kenkyu)*, **36** (1), 79–100 (in Japanese).

Mizutani, F. (1994) *Japanese Urban Railways: A Private-Public Comparison*, Aldershot, UK: Avebury.

Mizutani, F. (1997) 'Empirical Analysis of Yardstick Competition in the Japanese Rail Industry,' *International Journal of Transport Economics*, **24** (3), 367–92.

Mizutani, F. (1999a) 'An Assessment of the JR Companies Since Privatization: Performance, Local Rail Service and Debts,' *Transport Reviews*, **19** (2), 117–39.

Mizutani, F. (1999b) 'Changing Trains: Japan,' in Didier M. van de Velde (ed.) *Changing Trains: Railway Reform and the Role of Competition: The Experience of Six Countries*, Aldershot, UK: Ashgate, 254–306.

Mizutani, F. (2000) 'Private Provision and Privatization in the Public Utility Industries (Koeki Jigyo ni okeru Minkan Kyokyu to Mineika),' *Journal of Economics and Business Administration (Kokumin Keizai Zasshi)*, **182** (3), 57–76 (in Japanese).

Mizutani, F. (2004) 'Privately Owned Railway' Cost Function, Organization Size and Ownership,' *Journal of Regulatory Economics*, **25** (3), 297–322.

Mizutani, F. (2005) 'Regulation and Deregulation in the Japanese Rail Industry,' *CESifo DICE Report: Journal for Institutional Comparisons*, **3** (4), 10–15.

Mizutani, F. (2006a) 'The Role of Private Provision in Transport Markets:

Effects of Private Ownership and Business Diversification,' in K. Kobayashi, T. Lakshmanan and W. P. Anderson (eds.) *Structural Change in Transportation and Communications in the Knowledge Society*, Cheltenham, UK: Edward Elgar, 227−47.

Mizutani, F. (2006b) 'Effects of Deregulation in the Local Bus Services (Noriai Basu Jigyo no Kisei Kanwa no Eikyo),' *Public Corporation (Koei Kigyo)*, **38** (9), 2−8 (in Japanese).

Mizutani, F. and K. Nakamura (1996) 'Effects of Japan National Railways' Privatization on Labor Productivity,' *Papers in Regional Science*, **75** (2), 177−99.

Mizutani, F. and K. Nakamura (1997) 'Privatization of the Japan National Railway: Overview of Performance Changes,' *International Journal of Transport Economics*, **24** (1), 75−99.

Mizutani, F. and K. Nakamura (2000) 'Japan Railways Since Privatisation,' in W. Bradshaw and H. Lawton Smith (eds.) *Privatization and Deregulation of Transport*, Basingstoke, UK: Macmillan, 205−35.

Mizutani, F. and K. Nakamura (2004) 'The Japanese Experience with Railway Restructuring,' in T. Ito, and A. O. Krueger (eds.) *Governance, Regulation, and Privatization in the Asia-Pacific Region*, Chicago, USA: The University of Chicago Press, 305−36.

Mizutani, F. and K. Shoji (1997) 'A Comparative Analysis of Financial Performance: U.S. and Japanese Urban Railways,' *International Journal of Transport Economics*, **24** (2), 207−39.

Mizutani, F. and K. Shoji (2004) 'Operation and Infrastructure Separation: The Case of Kobe Rapid Transit Railway,' *Transport Policy*, **11** (3), 251−63.

Mizutani, F. and T. Urakami (2001) 'Identifying Network Density and Scale Economies for Japanese Water Supply Organizations,' *Papers in Regional Science*, **80** (2), 211−30.

Mizutani, F. and T. Urakami (2003) 'A Private-Public Comparison of Bus Service Operators,' *International Journal of Transport Economics*, **30** (2), 167−85.

Mizutani, F. and S. Uranishi (2003) 'The Post Office vs. Parcel Delivery Companies: Competition Effects on Costs and Productivity,' *Journal of Regulatory Economics*, **23** (3), 299−319.

Mizutani, F. and S. Uranishi (2006) 'Special Post Office, Privatization and Universal Service Obligation Costs,' *Discussion Paper Series*, No.2006-5, Graduate School of Business Administration, Kobe University.

Mizutani, F. and S. Uranishi (2007) 'The Effects of Privatization on

Productivity and Capital Adjustment,' *International Journal of Transport Economics*, **34** (2), 197−224.

Mizutani, F. and S. Uranishi (2008) 'Privatization of the Japan Highway Public Corporation: Focusing on Organizational Structure Change,' *Transport Reviews*, **28** (4), 469−93.

Mizutani, F., H. Kozumi and N. Matsushima (2009) 'Does Yardstick Regulation Really Work? Empirical Evidence from Japan's Rail Industry,' *Journal of Regulatory Economics*, **36** (3), 308−23.

Moore, T. G. (1970) 'The Effectiveness of Regulation of Electric Utility Prices,' *Southern Economic Journal*, **36** (4), 365−75.

Morgan, W. (1977) 'Investor-Owned vs. Publicly-Owned Water Agencies,' *Water Resources Bulletin*, **13** (4), 775−81.

Morrison, S. (1981) *Property Rights and Economic Efficiency: A Further Examination of the Australian Airlines,* Unpublished Paper, Canada: University of British Columbia, Faculty of Commerce and Business Administration.

Municipal Transportation Works Association (2006) *Research Report on the Setting-up of the Private Sector Style Management in the Publicly Owned Transportation (Koei Kotsu Jigyo ni Okeru Minkanteki Keiei Syuho no Donyu ni Kansuru Chosa Kenkyu Hokokusho)*, Tokyo, Japan: Municipal Transportation Works Association (in Japanese).

Nakamura, K. (2005) 'Broadcasting Industry (Hoso Jigyo),' in Japan Society of Public Utility Economics (ed.), *Public Utility Industries in Japan (Nihon no Koeki Jigyo)*, Tokyo, Japan: Hakuto Shobo, 97−112 (in Japanese).

Nakano, M. and S. Managi (2008) 'Regulatory Reforms and Productivity: An Empirical Analysis of the Japanese Electricity Industry,' *Energy Policy*, **36** (1), 201−9.

Nakayama, N. (2002) 'Cost Structure of Water Utilities: A Variable Cost Function Approach (Suido Jigyo no Hiyo Kozo: Kahenhiyo Kansu ni yoru Apurohchi),' *Journal of Public Utility Economics (Koeki Jigyo Kenkyu)*, **54** (2), 83−9 (in Japanese).

Nihon Keizai Shinbun (2006) *Post Office: Read Over the Future Figure of Privatization (Yubinkyoku: Mineika no Miraizu wo Yomu)*, Tokyo, Japan: Nihon Keizai Shinbun (in Japanese).

Nihon Minkan Hoso Renmei (2003) *Annual Report on Privately Owned Broadcasting in Japan, 2003 (Nihon Minkan Hoso Nenkan 2003)*, Tokyo, Japan: Koken Syuppan (in Japanese).

Nishimura, K. (2001) 'Will the Innovation of Distributed Generation System Make External Diseconomy to Power Networks of Japan? (Bunsangata Hatsuden Inobesyon ha Gaibu Fukeizai wo Umuka,'

Journal of Public Utility Economics (Koeki Jigyo Kenkyu), **53** (1), 11−19 (in Japanese).

Neuberg, L. (1977) 'Two Issues in the Municipal Ownership of Electric Power Distribution Systems,' *The Bell Journal of Economics*, **8** (1), 303−23.

Niskanen, W. A. (1971) *Bureaucracy and Representative Government*, Chicago, IL, USA: Aldine, Artherton.

NTT West (2006a) 'Explanation Materials on the Universal Service (Yunibasaru Sabisu ni Tsuite no Setsumei Shiryo),' *On Price Setting of the Universal Service (Yunibasaru Sabisuryo no Settei ni Tsuite)*, Osaka, Japan: News Release Material on December 1st, 2006, NTT West (in Japanese).

NTT West (2006b) 'About Grappling of Provision of the Universal Service by NTT West and NTT East (Yunibasaru Sabisu Kakuho ni Okeru NTT Nishinihon, Higashinihon no Torikumi ni Tsuite),' *On Price Setting of the Universal Service (Yunibasaru Sabisuryo no Settei ni Tsuite)*, Osaka, Japan: News Release Material on December 1st, 2006, NTT West (in Japanese).

OECD (1991) *Universal Service and Rate Restructuring in Telecommunications Tariff*, Paris, France: OECD.

OECD (1992) *Regulatory Reform, Privatisation and Competition Policy*, Paris, France: OECD.

OECD (2001) *Restructuring Public Utilities for Competition*, Paris, France: OECD.

Okabe, M. (1997) 'New Passenger Railway Fare System: Outline and Features (Atarashii Ryokyaku Tetsudo Unchin Seido: Gaiyo to Tokushoku),' *Transportation and Economy (Unyu to Keizai)*, **57** (5), 12−27 (in Japanese).

Okabe, M. (2004) 'New Passenger Railway Fares,' *Japan Railway and Transport Review*, **37**, January, 4−15.

Ooi, H. (2008) 'Research on Deregulation Effects on Omnibus Industries from the Viewpoint of Companies' Cost Structure (Noriai Basu Jigyo ni Okeru Kisei Kanwa no Eikyo ni Kansuru Teiryoteki Ichi Kosatsu: Hiyomen no Bunseki kara),' *Annual Report on Transportation Economics (Kotsugaku Kenkyu)*, **52**, 161−70 (in Japanese).

Oshima, K. (1979) *Management of Public Corporation (Kokigyo no Keieigaku)*, Tokyo, Japan: Hakuto Shobou (in Japanese).

Parker, D. (1994) 'Nationalisation, Privatisation, and Agency Status with Government: Testing for the Importance of Ownership,' in P. M. Jackson and C. M. Price (eds.) *Privatisation and Regulation*, London, UK: Longman, 149−69.

Parker, D. (1998) *Privatisation in the European Union: Theory and Policy Perspectives*, London, UK: Routledge.

Perry, J. L. and T. Babitsky (1986) 'Comparative Performance in Urban Bus Transit: Assessing Privatization Strategies,' *Public Administration Review*, **46** (1), 57−66.

Peltzman, S. (1971) 'Pricing in Public and Private Enterprises: Electric Utilities in the United States,' *Journal of Law and Economics*, **14** (1), 109−47.

Pescatrice, D. R. and J. M. Trapani (1980) 'The Performance and Objectives of Public and Private Utilities Operating in the United States,' *Journal of Public Economics*, **13** (2), 259−76.

Pier, W., R. Vernon and J. Wicks (1974) 'An Empirical Comparison of Government and Private Production Efficiency,' *National Tax Journal*, **27** (4), 653−6.

Pommerehne, N. (1976) 'Private versus Offentliche Muellabfuhr,' *Finanzarchiv*, **35** (2), 272−94.

Pommerehne, W. N. and B. S. Frey (1977) 'Public Versus Private Production Efficiency in Switzerland: A Theoretical and Empirical Comparison,' in V. Ostrom and F. P. Bish (eds.) *Comparing Urban Delivery Systems: Structure and Performance*, London, UK: Sage Publications, 221−41.

Potters, J., B. Rockenbach, A. Sadrieh and E van Damme (2004) 'Collusion under Yardstick Competition: An Experimental Study,' *International Journal of Industrial Organization*, **22** (7), 1017−38.

Price, C. W. (2003) 'Yardstick Competition and Comparative Performance Measures in Practice,' in Lester C. Hunt (ed.) *Energy in a Competitive Market: Essays in Honour of Colin Robinson*, Cheltenham, UK and Northampton, MA, USA: Edward Elgar, 17−34.

Ramamurti, R. (1996) *Privatizing Monopolies: Lessons from the Telecommunications and Transport Sectors in Latin America*, Baltimore, ML, USA: The Johns Hopkins University Press.

Robinson, R. and F. Rodriguez (2000) 'Liberalization of the Postal Market and the Cost of the Universal Service Obligation: Some Estimates for the UK,' in M. A. Crew and P. R. Kleindorfer (eds.) *Current Directions in Postal Reforms*, Boston, MA, USA: Kluwer Academic Publishers, 107−32.

Saito, T. (1993) *Private Rail Industry: Development of Japanese Style Railway Management (Shitetsu Sangyo: Nihongata Tetsudo Keiei no Tenkai)*, Kyoto, Japan: Koyo Shobo (in Japanese).

Sasaki, H. （1992）'Public Corporation (Kokigyo),' in Economic Institute of Osaka City University (ed.) *Dictionary of Economics (Keizaigaku Jiten)*, Third edition, Tokyo, Japan: Iwanami Shoten, 376−7 (in Japanese).

Sasaki, H. （1997） 'Distinct Features of Management of Public Corporations (Koeikigyo Keiei no Tokushitsu),' in H. Sasaki and Koeikigyo Kinyu Koko (eds.) *Management of Public Corporations (Koeikigyo no tameno Keieigaku)*, Tokyo, Japan: Chiho Zaimu Kyokai, 1−25 (in Japanese).

Sasaki, H. and F. Mizutani (2000) 'Public Utility Enterprises,' in Y. Toyama, Y. Fujii, H. Sasaki, M. Sugaya, M. Uekusa, and S. Yamaya (eds.) *Public Utility Industries in Japan,* East Lansing, MI, USA: The Institute of Public Utilities and Network Industries, Michigan State University, 1−18.

Satake, M. (2002) 'Future Perspective in the Electric Power Industry (Denki Jigyo ni Okeru Kisei Kanwa to Kongo no Tenbo),' *Journal of Public Utility Economics (Koeki Jigyo Kenkyu)*, **54** (1), 49−56 (in Japanese).

Sato, H. (2002) 'Movement of Setting-up of the Private Sector Style Management and Its Examples (Chiho Koei Kigyo ni Okeru Minkanteki Keiei Syuho Donyu no Doko to Sono Jirei),' *Public Corporation (Koei Kigyo)*, **34** (4), 24−32 (in Japanese).

Savas, E. S. (1977) 'Policy Analysis for Local Government: Public vs. Private Refuse Collection,' *Policy Analysis*, **3** (1), 49−74.

Savas, E. S. (1987） *Privatization: The Key to Better Government,* Chatham, NJ, USA: Chatham House Publishers.

Scitovsky, T. (1954) 'Two Concepts of External Economies,' *Journal of Political Economy*, **62** (2), 143−51.

Segawa, K. (2005) *Postal Services: What is Asked (Yusei: Naniga Tomarete Iruka)*, Tokyo, Japan: Gendai Shokan (in Japanese).

Shepherd, W. G. (1966) 'Utility Growth and Profits under Regulation,' in W. G. Shepherd and T. G. Gies (eds.) *Utility Regulation: New Directions in Theory and Practice*, New York, NY, USA: Random House, 3−57.

Shleifer, A. (1985) 'A Theory of Yardstick Competition,' *Rand Journal of Economics*, **16** (3), 319−27.

Sioshansi, F. P. (2006) 'Electricity Market Reform: What Have We Learned? What Have We Gained?' *The Electricity Journal*, **19** (9), 70−83.

Sobel, J. (1999) 'A Reexamination of Yardstick Competition,' *Journal of Economics and Management Strategy*, **8** (1), 33−60.

Spann, R. (1977) 'Public versus Private Provision of Government

Services,' in T. Borcherding (ed.) *Budgets and Bureaucrats*, Durham, NC, USA: Duke University Press, 71 — 89.

Spulber, D. F. (1989) *Regulation and Markets*, Cambridge, MA, USA: MIT Press.

Stevens, B. (1977) 'Scale, Market Structure, and the Cost of Refuse Collection,' *Review of Economics and Statistics*, **60** (3), 438 — 48.

Stevens, B. and E. S. Savas (1977) 'The Cost of Residential Refuse Collection and the Effect Service Arrangements,' *Municipal Year Book*, **44**, 200 — 205.

Suga, T. (1997) 'The Separation of Operations from Infrastructure in the Provision of Railway Services: Examples in Japan,' in The European Conference of Ministers of Transport (ECMT), *The Separation of Operations from Infrastructure in the Provision of Railway Services*, Paris, France: OECD, 153 — 76.

Sumitomo Seimei Sogo Kenkyusho (1999) *Economic Effects of Deregulation (Kisei Kanwa no Keizai Koka)*, Tokyo, Japan: Toyo Keizai Shinposha (in Japanese).

Takada, S. and R. Shigeno (1998) 'Economies of Scale and Density in the Water Supply Industry (Suido Jigyo ni Okeru Kibo no Keizaisei to Mitsudo no Keizaisei),' *Journal of Public Utility Economics (Koeki Jigyo Kenkyu)*, **50** (1), 37 — 44 (in Japanese).

Takigawa, Y (2004) *Objection To Privatization of Postal Services (Aete Yusei Mineika ni Hantai Suru)*, Tokyo, Japan: Nihon Hyoron-sha (in Japanese).

Tamamura, H. (1993) *Privatization and International Comparison (Mineika to Kokusai Hikaku)*, Tokyo, Japan: Yachiyo Shuppan (in Japanese).

Tanabe, K. (2002) 'The Effects of Three Kinds of Subsidies on the Structure of Production in Japanese Public Bus Industries (Koteki Hojokin ga Kisei Kigyo ni Ataeru Eikyo no Jissho Bunseki),' *Annual Report on Transportation Economics (Kotsugaku Kenkyu)*, **46**, 111 — 20 (in Japanese).

Tanaka, H (2004) *Why is National Government's Provision Wrong? (Kokuei deha Naze Ikenainodesuka: Kokyo Sabisu no Arikata wo Tou)*, Tokyo, Japan: Manejimento sya (in Japanese).

Tangerås, T. (2002) 'Collusion-Proof Yardstick Competition,' *Journal of Public Economics*, **83** (2), 231 — 54.

Teeples, R., S. Feigenbaum and D. Glyer (1986) 'Public versus Private Water Delivery: Cost Comparisons,' *Public Finance Quarterly*, **14** (3), 351 — 66.

Teeples, R. and D. Glyer (1987) 'Cost of Water Delivery Systems:

Specification and Ownership Effects,' *Review of Economics and Statisticsy*, **69** (3), 399 – 408.

Telecommunication Carrier Association (2007) *Calculation Method of the Unit Cost of Registered Telephone in the Universal Service System (Yunibasaru Sabisu Seido ni Okeru Bango Tanka no Santei Hoho ni Tsuite)*, Tokyo, Japan: Telecommunication Carrier Association, October 9th, 2007 (in Japanese).

Terada, K. (2005) 'Road Passenger Transportation (Doro Ryokyaku Unyu),' in Japan Society of Public Utility Economics (Koeki Jigyo Gakkai) (ed.), *Public Utility Industry in Japan (Nippon no Koeki Jigyo)*, Tokyo, Japan: Hakuto Shobo, 171 – 84 (in Japanese).

Thiemeyer, T. and G. Quaden (1986) *The Privatization of Public Enterprises*, Liège, Belgium, CIRIEC.

Tilton, J. E. (1973) 'The Nature of Firm Ownership and the Adoption of Innovations in the Electric Power Industry,' *Paper Presented at the Public Choice Society*, Washington, D.C., USA: the Public Choice Society.

Tittenbrun, J. (1996) *Private Versus Public Enterprise: In Search for the Economic Rationale for Privatisation*, London, UK: Janus Publishing.

Toyama, Y. (1987) *Theory of Modern Public Corporation (Gendai Kokigyo Soron)*, Tokyo, Japan: Toyo Keizai Shinposha (in Japanese).

Tsuru, K. (2002) 'The Trapp of The Managed Deregulation: A Study of Personal Correspondence Mail Service Law (Kanri Sareta Kisei Kanwa no Wana: Shishobin Hoan wo Meguru Kosatsu),' *Economic Review*, **8**, Research Institute of Economy, Trade and Industry, 1 – 15 (in Japanese).

Tullock, G. (1970) *Private Wants, Public Means*, New York, NY, USA: Basic Books.

Uekusa, M. (1991) *Economics of Public Regulation (Koteki Kisei no Keizaigaku)*, Tokyo, Japan: Chikuma Shobo (in Japanese).

Uekusa, M. (1996) 'Theory and Policy of Incentive Regulation (Insenthibu Kisei no Riron to Seisaku),' *Journal of Public Utility Economics (Koeki Jigyo Kenkyu)*, **48** (1), 1 – 8 (in Japanese).

Uekusa, M. (2000) *Economic of Public Regulation (Koteki Kisei no Keizaigaku)*, Tokyo, Japan: NTT Shuppan (in Japanese).

Urakami, T. (2007) 'Economies of Vertical Integration in the Japanese Water Supply Industry,' *Jahrbuch für Regionalwissenschaft*, **27** (2), 129 – 41.

Urakami, T. (2008) 'The Effect of Wide-Area Consolidations of Water Supply Systems in Japan (Shichoson Gappei ga Suido Jigyo ni Ataeru Eikyo no Bunseki),' *Journal of Public Utility Economics*

(Koeki Jigyo Kenkyu), **60** (2), 63 − 71 (in Japanese).

Urakami, T. and D. Parker (2009) 'The Effects of Consolidation Amongst Japanese Water Utilities: A Hedonic Cost Analysis,' *Paper Presented at the 36th Annual Conference of the European Association for Research in Industrial Economics (EARIE),* Ljubljana, Slovenia: September 3 − 5, 2009, Ljubljana University.

Uranishi, S. (2007) 'Simulation Regarding Universal Service Obligation for Post Service (Yubin Jigyo ni Okeru Yunibasaru Sabisu Iji ni Kansuru Shimyureshon),' *Journal of Public Utility Economics (Koeki Jigyo Kenkyu),* **59** (2), 55 − 68 (in Japanese).

Vickers, J. and G. Yarrow (1988) *Privatization: An Economic Analysis,* Cambridge, MA, USA: MIT Press.

Viscusi, W. K., J. M. Vernon and J. E. Harrington, Jr. (1995) *Economics of Regulation and Antitrust,* Second Edition, Cambridge, MA, USA: MIT Press.

Viscusi, W. K., J. E. Harrington, Jr. and J. M. Vernon (2005) *Economics of Regulation and Antitrust,* Fourth Edition, Cambridge, MA, USA: MIT Press.

Wallace, R. and P. E. Junk (1970) 'Economic Inefficiency of Small Municipal Electric Generating Systems,' *Land Economics,* **46** (1), 98 − 104.

Watanabe, T. (2005) 'The Function and Role of Electric Power System Council of Japan (Denryoku Keito Riyo Kyogikai no Kinou to Yakuwari),' *Journal of Public Utility Economics (Koeki Jigyo Kenkyu),* **57** (1), 1 − 6 (in Japanese).

Waterson, M. (1988) *Regulation of the Firm and Natural Monopoly,* Cambridge, MA, USA: Basil Blackwel.

Waterworks Association (2007) *Waterworks Statistics: Facilities and Services (Suido Tokei: Shisetsu, Gyomu Hen),* Tokyo, Japan: Waterworks Association (in Japanese).

Weyman-Jones, T. (2003) 'Yardstick Competition and Efficiency Benchmarking in Electricity Distribution,' in Lester C. Hunt (ed.) *Energy in a Competitive Market: Essays in Honour of Colin Robinson,* Cheltenham, UK and Northampton, MA, USA: Edward Elgar, 35 − 60.

Yajima, M. (2001) 'Liberalization of the Electricity Markets and Energy Security (Denryoku Shijo Jiyuka to Enerugi Sekyuriti),' *Journal of Public Utility Economics (Koeki Jigyo Kenkyu),* **53** (1), 49 − 55 (in Japanese).

Yajima, M. (2002) 'Liberalization of Electricity Markets and Nuclear Development (Denryoku Shijo Jiyuka to Genshiryoku Hatsuden),' *Journal of Public Utility Economics (Koeki Jigyo Kenkyu),* **54** (2),

43 − 7 (in Japanese).

Yajima, M. (2005) 'Electric Power Supply Industry (Denki Jigyo),' in Japan Public Utility Economics Society (ed.) *Public Utility Industries in Japan (Nihon no Koeki Jigyo)*, Tokyo, Japan: Hakuto Shobo, 35 − 48 (in Japanese).

Yamamoto, T. (1994) *Market or Government (Shijo ka Seifu ka)*, Tokyo, Japan: Nihon Keizai Hyoronsha (in Japanese).

Yamashige S. (2004) 'Universal Service (Yunibasaru Sabisu),' *DIR Management Strategy Research (DIR Keiei Senryaku Kenkyu)*, Daiwa Soken, **2**, Autumn, 58 − 71 (in Japanese).

Yamaya, S. (1996) 'Characteristics and Issues of Yardstick Regulation in Electricity Supply and Gas Industries (Denki, Gasu Yado Suthikku Kisei no Tokucho to Kadai),' *Journal of Public Utility Economics (Koeki Jigyo Kenkyu)*, **48** (1), 31 − 42 (in Japanese).

Ylvinger, S. (1998) 'The Operation of Swedish Motor-Vehicle Inspections: Efficiency and Some Problems Concerning Regulation,' *Transportation*, **25** (1), 23 − 36.

Yunker, J. A. (1975) 'Economic Performance of Public and Private Enterprise: The Case of U.S. Electric Industries,' *Journal of Economics and Business*, **28** (1), 60 − 67.

Yokokura, T. (1994) 'Regulatory Policy (Kisei Seisaku),' in M. Uekusa and T. Yokokura (eds.) *Public Regulation and Industries: Gas Utility Industry (Koteki Kisei to Sangyo: Toshi Gasu)*, Tokyo, Japan: NTT Syuppan, 136 − 81 (in Japanese).

Yokokura, T. (1996) 'Theory and Policy of Yardstick Regulation (Yado Suthikku Kisei no Riron to Seisaku),' *Journal of Public Utility Economics (Koeki Jigyo Kenkyu)*, **48** (1), 21 − 9 (in Japanese).

Subject Index

Accountability, 23
Accounting separation, 43, 61
Advance-reporting system, 109
Affordability, 194
Agency for Natural Resources
    and Energy, 53
Allocative efficiency. *See*
    Efficiency,
Automatic adjustment scheme, 54
    −5, 69, 71−2
Availability, 33, 38, 115, 117, 194
Average cost pricing, 11, 26
Averch-Johnson effect, 17
Avoidable cost principle, 98

Basic Standard of Establishment
    of Broadcasting
    Stations, 159, 241
Basic water volume system, 83
    −4, 241
Beneficiary-pays principle, 41
Broadcasting industry, 151−3,
    155−9, 161, 163
Broadcast Law, 151, 157−8, 161,
    241
Broadcasting license, 161
Broadcasting Satellite, 152, 155
Broadcasting System by Use of
    Telecommunications
    Services, 161−2
BS. *See* Broadcasting Satellite,
Bureau, 29−30, 79, 91, 105, 107,
    121

Bureaucracy, 28
Bus industry. *See* Local bus
    industry,
Business diversification, 7, 104

Cabinet Office, 223−4, 226
Cable Television Broadcast Law,
    151, 157−8, 241
Ceiling price, 20, 95−6, 99−100,
    102, 111−13, 116−17,
    241
Civil minimum, 4, 14,
Collusion, 18−19, 169−170,
    183−4
  explicit collusion, 19
  tacit collusion, 19
Communication Satellite, 155
Community gas supply company.
    See Gas supply
    company,
Community water supply
    organization. *See*
    Waterworks
    organization,
Competitive market, 4
Competitive tendering, 17−18
Comprehensive Outsourcing, 221
    −2, 226−8, 241
Contracting out, 40, 84, 123, 162,
    217−18
Corporatization, 64
Cost plus type regulation, 17, 24
Council for Regulatory Reform,

228, 241
Cream skimming, 116−17, 201
Cross-subsidization, 99, 210
CS. *See* Communication Satellite,

Daily living necessities, 23
Data Envelopment Analysis, 182
DEA. *See* Data Envelopment
　　Analysis,
Demerit goods, 6
Deregulation, 5−6, 23, 62−4, 68,
　　73, 92, 94, 99, 102, 107,
　　109−11, 116−18, 124,
　　131−3, 137, 160, 172
Designated Manager System, 85,
　　221−2, 228−31, 241
Destructive competition, 6, 23
Division separation, 61

Economic efficiency. *See*
　　Efficiency,
Economic regulation, 5−6, 8
Economic stability, 4, 14
Economies of scale, 49, 79, 128
Efficiency, 5, 14, 16−22, 25, 27,
　　31−8, 41, 45, 55, 72,
　　79, 101, 103, 117, 135,
　　167−8, 170−72, 174
　　−83, 185, 187−8, 206,
　　219, 229
　　allocative efficiency, 34
　　economic efficiency, 35
　　inefficiency as
　　　　monopoly-induced
　　　　waste, 34
　　internal efficiency, 19, 34−5,
　　　　38, 45, 168
　　Pareto efficiency, 34−5
　　productive efficiency, 34−5,
　　　　37, 182−3
　　technical efficiency, 34−5,

182
　　X-inefficiency, 34−5, 37
Electric Power Development
　　Company, 51−2, 57,
　　59
Electric power industry, 6, 49−50,
　　54−5, 57, 60, 62−3,
　　65, 69, 71, 137, 171−2,
　　174−6, 180, 184−5
Electric Power System Council of
　　Japan, 51, 53, 61, 64,
　　241
Electricity company, 50−53, 55,
　　57−63, 171−5, 180−
　　81, 242, 244−5
　　general electricity company,
　　　　50−53, 55, 57−61, 63,
　　　　171−3, 180−81, 242
　　power producer and
　　　　supplier company, 50−
　　　　52, 58−9, 61, 244
　　special electricity company,
　　　　50−53, 58−9, 61, 245
　　wholesale electricity
　　　　company, 50−53, 58,
　　　　61, 245
Electricity Enterprise Law, 51−2,
　　242
Electricity rate, 53−7, 62
EMS. *See* Express Mail Service,
Enforcement Regulation of the
　　Railway Business Law,
　　98, 242
Enforcement Regulation of the
　　Telecommunications
　　Business Law, 194, 242
Entry regulation, 6−8, 10, 14, 71,
　　81, 92−3, 101−2, 105,
　　109, 116, 121, 128, 141,
　　145−7, 150−51, 158

Environmental regulation, 6 — 8
Essentiality, 194
Essentials for daily living, 23
Excess facilities, 17
Exit regulation, 6 — 8, 81, 92 — 4,
    102, 105, 109, 116, 141,
    145 — 6
Explicit collusion. *See* Collusion.
Express Mail Service, 189
Externalities, 3 — 4, 7, 13, 23, 99,
    188
External diseconomies, 6, 13, 63
External effects, 23
    pecuniary external effects, 23
    technical external effects, 23

Failure in regulation, 21, 22
Fairness of redistribution, 4
Fair rate of return, 15 — 17, 24
Fair rate of return regulation. *See*
    Rate of return
    regulation,
Fair return, 15 — 16
Fare based on block-km. *See* Fare
    system,
Fare based on km. *See* Fare
    system,
Fare regulation, 95 — 6, 105, 111,
    116
Fare revision, 19, 22, 112, 168,
    178, 210, 228
Fare system, 97 — 8
    fare based on block-km, 97
    fare based on km, 97
    flat fare, 97 — 8
    zone fare, 97
Flat fare. *See* Fare system,
Franchise, 4, 17 — 19, 35, 126,
    208
    franchise bidding, 4, 17 —
    18

franchising system, 18
Franchise bidding. *See* Franchise,
Franchising system. *See*
    Franchise,
Free rider problem, 13, 26
Full cost principle, 4, 11, 15 — 16,
    55, 69, 95 — 6, 111
Full privatization. *See*
    Privatization,
Functional separation, 43, 45, 206,
    208, 216, 219 — 20

Gas supply company, 66 — 8, 71 —
    3, 237, 241 — 3
    community gas supply
    company, 66 — 7, 241
    gas transmission and
    distribution company,
    66 — 7, 73, 242
    general gas supply company,
    66 — 7, 71 — 2, 242
    large-scale gas supply
    company, 66 — 7, 71,
    237
Gas transmission and distribution
    company. *See* Gas
    supply company
Gas Utility Enterprise Law, 66, 71
    — 3, 242
Gas utility industry, 65, 68 — 9, 71,
    73 — 4, 171, 175 — 8,
    185
Gas utility rate, 68, 74
General electricity company. *See*
    Electricity company
General gas supply company. *See*
    Gas supply company
General water supply organization.
    See Waterworks
    organization
Government failure, 23

Government intervention, 22
Government involvement, 3 — 5,
    26 — 7

Highway Company Law, 214, 242
Horizontal separation, 43, 45, 183,
    206, 208, 212 — 13

Imperfect competition, 23
Imperfect information, 3 — 4, 6,
    13 — 14
Incentive regulation, 4, 17, 19,
    167
Income redistribution, 14, 22
Increasing return to scale, 8
Incumbent, 14, 18, 59, 102 — 3,
    146, 187
Independent Power Producer, 51
    — 2, 59, 61, 242
Inefficiency. *See* Efficiency
Infrastructure organization, 93
Integrated rail organization, 93
Internal efficiency. *See* Efficiency
Investment regulation, 6 — 7
IPP. *See* Independent Power
    Produce

Japan Electric Power Exchange,
    51, 53, 60 — 61, 242
Japan Expressway Holding and
    Debt Repayment Agency,
    212, 220, 242
Japan National Railways, 8, 14,
    18, 22, 32 — 3, 40, 43, 89, 91
    — 2, 100, 104, 178, 183, 203,
    206 — 7, 209, 211, 219, 242
Japan National Railway Law, 92,
    100, 242
Japan National Railway
    Settlement Corporation, 206,
    209, 243

Japan Post, 45, 121 — 2, 124 — 8,
    131 — 5, 201, 204, 214
    — 6, 243
Japan Post Bank. *See* Japan Post
    companies
Japan Post companies, 122 — 3,
    126, 128 — 9, 132, 191,
    193, 216 — 9, 243
Japan Post Bank, 122 — 3,
    132, 216 — 8, 243
Japan Post Holding
    Company, 122 — 3, 132,
    193, 216 — 8, 243
Japan Post Network, 122 — 3,
    126, 132, 191, 216 — 9,
    243
Japan Post Service, 122 — 3,
    126, 128 — 9, 132, 191,
    216 — 9, 243
Japan Post Holding Company. *See*
    Japan Post companies
Japan Post Network. *See* Japan
    Post companies
Japan Post Public Corporation, 30,
    121, 126, 131, 134, 187,
    189, 203, 205, 214 — 17,
    220, 243
Japan Post Service. *See* Japan
    Post companies
JR Central. *See* JR companies
JR companies, 18, 43, 59, 91 — 3,
    98, 100, 103, 170, 183,
    206 — 10, 219 — 20
JR Central, 91 — 2, 206 — 8,
    219
JR East, 59, 91 — 3, 206 — 8,
    219
JR Freight, 93, 98, 100, 206
    — 9, 219
JR Hokkaido, 91, 206 — 9,

219
JR Kyushu, 91, 206−9, 219
JR Shikoku, 91, 206−9, 219
JR West, 91−3, 103, 206−8, 219
JR East. *See* JR companies
JR Freight. *See* JR companies
JR Hokkaido. *See* JR companies
JR Kyushu. *See* JR companies
JR Shikoku. *See* JR companies
JR West. *See* JR companies

KDDI, 137, 139, 140, 143−4

Labor unions, 33, 205
Large private railways, 8, 91, 93, 96, 98, 100−101, 168, 170, 178, 181, 243
Large-scale gas supply company. *See* Gas supply company
Legal separation, 61
Liberalization, 5, 8, 40, 49−50, 52−5, 57−60, 63, 65, 68, 71−4, 101, 121, 130−32, 137
Liberalized rate, 55
License, *see* License system
License system, 13−4, 92, 100−102, 109, 116, 128, 157−8, 161, 243
Light parcel mail, 130−31
Local Autonomy Law, 85, 228, 243
Local bus industry, 105, 117
Local Independent Administrative Institution, *see* Local Independent Administrative Institution Scheme
Local Independent Administrative Institution Scheme, 221−2, 233−4, 243
Local Independent Administrative Law, 233, 243
Local Public Corporation Law, 81−2, 99, 113, 243
Local Railway Law, 92, 100, 243

Management Stability Fund, 207, 209, 219−20, 243
Managerial efficiency. *See* Efficiency
Marginal cost pricing, 10, 26, 45
Market failure, 3−4, 6, 14, 21, 23, 26, 31
Market mechanism, 4, 29
Marketability, 28−9, 42
Merit goods, 4, 14, 45, 188
M-form, 186
Monitoring, 17, 18, 23, 30, 38
Monopoly, 8−10, 18, 21, 26, 34−5, 38, 66, 81, 102, 128, 132, 146, 168, 202, 237−8
Monopoly price, 181
Moral hazard, 185

Natural monopoly, 4, 6, 8, 26, 237−8
Net avoidable cost approach, 201
Network externalities, 188
NHK, 13, 152−3, 155, 157, 204
Non-excludability, 11−12, 26−7
Non-rivalry in consumption, 11−12, 26−7
NTT, 40, 137−42, 146−7, 150, 187, 194−5, 197, 203−4
NTT Communications. *See* NTT group

NTT Data. *See* NTT group
NTT Docomo. *See* NTT group
NTT East Japan. *See* NTT group
NTT group, 139−44, 147, 149−
    50, 194−5, 197−8,
    200
    NTT Communications, 139
        −40, 147, 195
    NTT Data, 139−40, 147
    NTT Docomo, 139−40, 143
        −4, 147
    NTT East Japan, 139, 141,
        143−4, 147, 149−50,
        194−5, 197−8, 200
    NTT Stockholding Company,
        139−40, 147
    NTT West Japan, 139−44,
        147, 149−50, 194−5,
        197−8, 200
NTT Stockholding Company. *See*
    NTT group
NTT West Japan. *See* NTT group

Operation-infrastructure
    separation, 93
Ordinal post office, 125−6, 133
    −4, 244

Pareto efficiency. *See* Efficiency
Pareto optimal, 4, 34−5
Partial privatization. *See*
    Privatization
Pecuniary external effects. *See*
    External Effects
Permission, *see* Permission
    system
Permission system, 6, 22, 59−60,
    66, 81, 92−4, 101−2,
    109, 111, 116, 128, 132,
    145−6, 158, 225, 229,

    244
Personal Correspondence Mail
    Service Law, 128, 132,
    244
PFI. *See* Private Finance Initiative
Postal Law, 189−90, 193, 244
Postal Network Enforcement
    Regulation, 130, 244
Postal Network Law, 190, 244
Postal Service Bureau, 121
Postal Service Enforcement
    Regulation, 130, 189−
    90, 244
Postal service industry, 121, 131
    −2, 189, 191, 201
Post office, 121−2, 124−8, 130,
    132−5, 190, 192−3,
    215−16, 220, 241, 244
    −5
Power producer and supplier, 50
    −52, 58−9, 61, 171,
    244
Power producer and supplier
    company. *See*
    Electricity company
PPS. *See* Power Producer and
    Supplier
Price-cap, 20, 143, 148
Price-cap regulation, 4, 20, 100,
    141−2, 147
Price ceiling, *see* Ceiling price
Price regulation, 6−8, 11, 14, 49,
    54, 65, 68, 72, 81, 121,
    128−9, 141−2, 145,
    150−51, 158
Price revision, 16
Principle of de-concentration of
    the mass media, 155
Private Finance Initiative, 221−6,
    234−5
Private sector styple management,

40, 221−2, 234, 244
Private water supply organization.
  See Waterworks
  organization
Privatization, 5, 14, 25, 39−43,
  45, 64, 89, 91−92, 100,
  104, 121−2, 125−7,
  130−33, 135, 137, 140,
  146, 150, 178, 183−4,
  189, 193, 195, 201, 203
  −20, 222
  full privatization, 39, 40, 42
    −3, 214, 216−18
  partial privatization, 39
Productive efficiency. *See*
  Efficiency
Productivity, 20, 62, 104, 115,
  143, 178, 180, 219
Profit sharing, 4, 21
Property rights theory, 25−6, 33
  −4, 38
Public choice theory, 25, 33-34
Public corporation, 3, 5, 25, 27−
  34, 37−8, 40−42, 45,
  81−3, 91, 99, 113, 121
  −2, 126, 131−2, 134,
  137, 139, 145, 152, 157,
  187, 189, 191, 195, 203
  −5, 210−17, 219−22,
  227−8, 233−4, 243
Public enterprise. *See* Public
  corporation
Public goods, 3−4, 11−2, 26−7,
  157
  pure public goods, 12
Public independent agency, 29−
  31
Public interest, 26−9, 33, 42, 102,
  158
Public utility industries, 3−9, 11

−12, 14−16, 19−20,
  22, 25−6, 28, 32, 36−
  7, 43, 45, 55, 84, 105,
  121, 130, 133, 137, 167,
  170, 180, 183, 185−8,
  204
Publicness, 28−9
Pure public goods. *See* Public
  goods

Qualitative regulation, 6, 23
Quantitative regulation, 6, 23

Radio Law, 151, 157−8, 161,
  244
Rail fare, 41, 95−9, 102, 170,
  205, 219
Rail operation organization, 93
Rail track fee, 89, 98
Railway Accounting Regulations,
  99, 244
Railway Business Law, 92, 94−5,
  98−102, 242, 244
Railway industry, 15, 20, 84, 89,
  92, 95, 99, 100, 105,
  172, 181, 209, 213
Rate base, 15−7
Rate of return regulation, 4, 15−
  17, 21, 24
Regional balance, 4, 14
Regional council, 94−5, 109−11,
  113, 116, 244
Regional separation. *See* Regional
  subdivision
Regional subdivision, 43, 183,
  206, 208, 210−11, 213,
  220
Register system, 6, 141, 150
Regulated rate, 55
Regulation for non-utility service,
  6

Rent-seeking costs, 22−3
Report in advance, 93, 109, 244
Report system, 6, 53−5, 60, 68−
    9, 72, 82, 93, 96, 100,
    109, 111, 115−17, 128
    −9, 141−5, 147−8,
    150, 158, 198, 244
Resource allocation, 4−5, 8, 13
    −14, 20, 34−5
Restructuring method, 45
Risk, 23, 32, 63, 170, 223−4
Road Transportation Law, 109,
    115−16, 244

Safety regulation, 6−8
Scale economies. *See* Economies
    of scale
Scarcity of resources, 8
Search costs, 13
Second best solution, 10
Service quality regulation, 6
Sliding scale, 21
Social and Regional Maintenance
    Fund, 132, 218, 245
Social regulation, 5−6, 13, 23
Soft-budget hypothesis, 33, 38
Special electricity company. *See*
    Electricity company
Special Law on the Merger of
    Municipalities, 79, 245
Special post office, 125−6, 133
    −5, 215, 245
Standard cost, 96, 99, 104, 111−
    13, 170, 179−80, 185,
    199
Stochastic frontier model, 182
Subadditivity in costs, 8
Subdivision of government, 29−
    31
Summary post office, 125−7,

134, 245
Sunk costs, 18
Supply-demand adjustment
    regulation, 115, 245

Tacit collusion. *See* Collusion
Technical external effects. *See*
    External effects
Telecommunications Business
    Dispute Settlement
    Commission, 144, 149
Telecommunications Business
    Law, 141, 145, 147, 149,
    194, 242
Telecommunications industry, 5,
    137, 139, 141−2, 145
    −6, 149, 151, 170, 187
    −8, 194, 196−7
Telephone rate, 143, 147
TFP. *See* Total factor productivity
Third sector, 30−31, 41, 91
Total factor productivity, 62, 219
Transaction costs, 19−20, 163
Transportation Council, 112
Transport industry, 87
Trust-Entrust Broadcasting
    System, 161−2, 245
Two-part tariffs, 56, 70, 82

U-form, 186
Unbundling, 43
Uncertainty, 19, 23
Unfair treatment, 5, 8, 60, 68
Universal service, 128, 129, 158,
    187−90, 193−5, 197
    −8, 201,215
Universal service cost. 187, 194,
    197−201
Universal service obligation, 121,
    129, 149, 187−91, 193
    −4, 196−7, 200−201

Universal service obligation cost.
See Universal service
cost
Universal service obligation fund,
214
USO. *See* Universal service
obligation
Utility industries. *See* Public
utility industries

Vertical integration, 79, 93, 203,
206, 209, 220
Vertical separation, 43, 163, 203,
209, 211 – 13, 220

Water rate, 81 – 2
Water supply industry, 75 – 7, 79
– 82, 84 – 5, 168, 171,
227, 234
Water supply organization. *See*
Waterworks
organization
Waterworks Law, 77, 81, 84, 222,
227, 245
Waterworks organization, 76 – 85,
227, 241 – 2, 244 – 5
community water supply
organization, 77 – 8,
241
general water supply
organization, 77 – 80,
242
private water supply
organization, 77 – 8,
244
water supply organization,
76 – 7, 79 – 85, 227,
245
wholesale water supply
organization, 78, 245
Welfare, 4, 27 – 8, 32, 35, 84, 128,

169, 189, 224, 230 – 1,
237 – 8
Wholesale electricity company.
See Electricity company
Wholesale water supply
organization. *See*
Waterworks
organization

X-inefficiency. *See* Efficiency

Yardstick competition, 18, 45, 103,
170 – 71, 179 – 80, 182
– 3, 186, 210, 220
Yardstick regulation, 4, 18 – 20,
54 – 5, 69, 71, 89, 96,
99, 100 – 101, 104, 111
– 13, 167 – 72, 174 –
81, 183 – 6, 206 – 7,
210, 220, 245

Zone fare. *See* Fare system